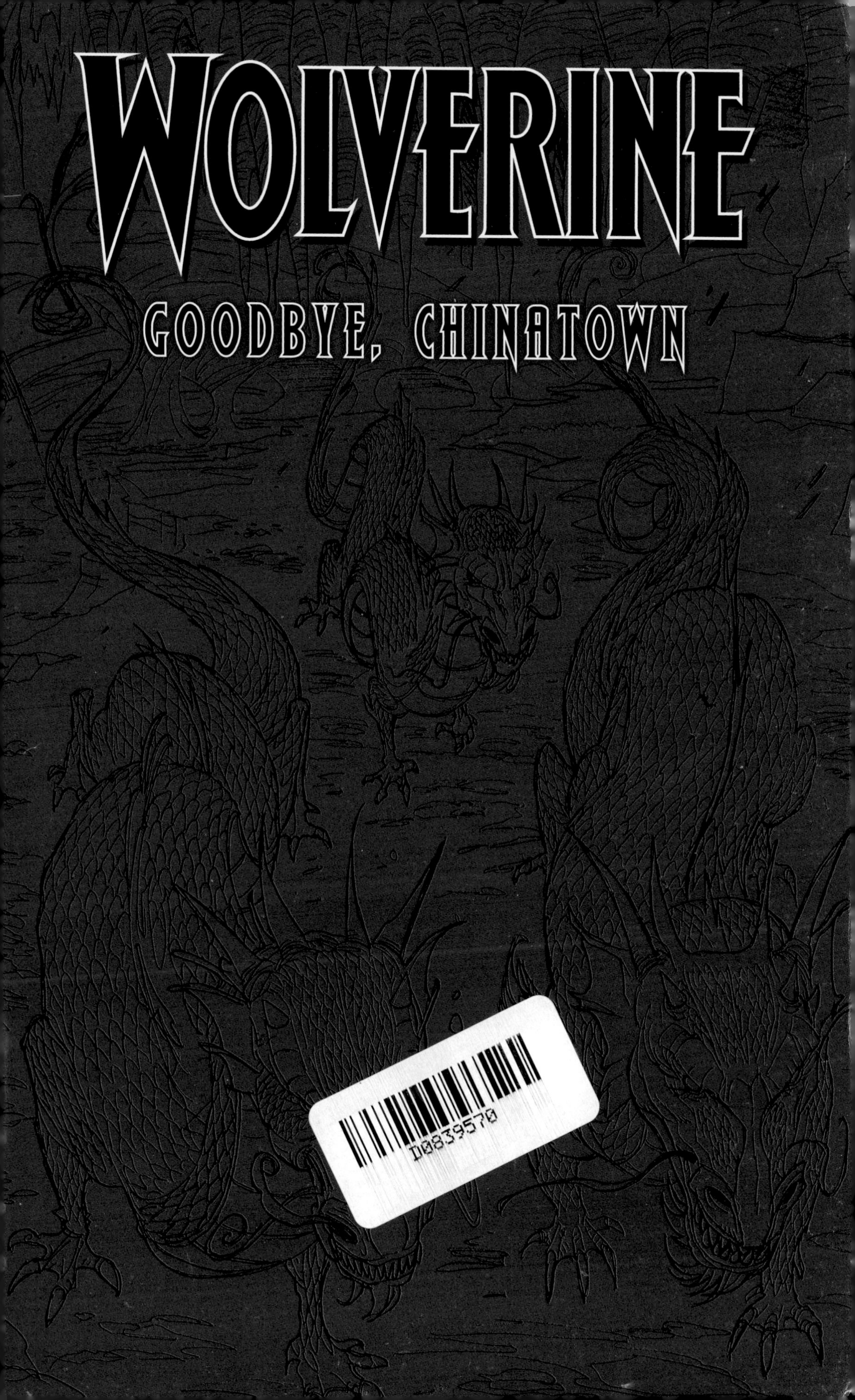
WOLVERINE
GOODBYE, CHINATOWN

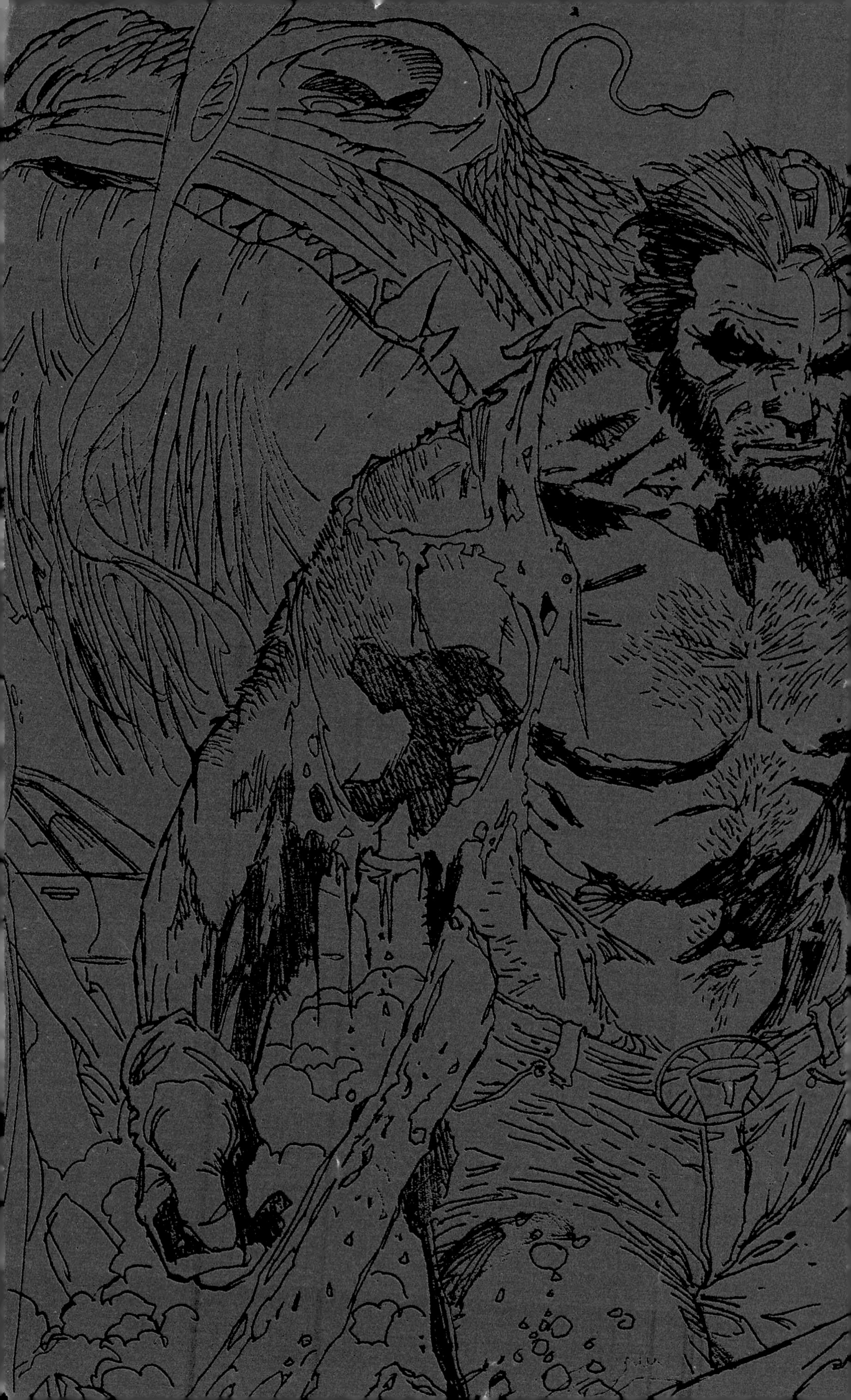

GOODBYE, CHINATOWN

WRITER **JASON AARON**

ISSUES #17-19
PENCILER **RON GARNEY**
COLOR ART **JASON KEITH**

ISSUE #20
PENCILER **RENATO GUEDES**
INKER **JOSE WILSON MAGALHAES**
COLOR ART **MATTHEW WILSON**

LETTERS **VC'S CORY PETIT**
COVER ART
RON GARNEY & JASON KEITH (#17-19)
AND **RENATO GUEDES** (#20)
ASSISTANT EDITORS **JODY LeHEUP &**
SEBASTIAN GIRNER
EDITOR **JEANINE SCHAEFER**
GROUP EDITOR **NICK LOWE**

Collection Editor JENNIFER GRÜNWALD
Assistant Editors ALEX STARBUCK & NELSON RIBEIRO
Editor, Special Projects MARK D. BEAZLEY
Senior Editor, Special Projects JEFF YOUNGQUIST
Senior Vice President of Sales DAVID GABRIEL
SVP of Brand Planning & Communications
MICHAEL PASCIULLO

Editor in Chief AXEL ALONSO
Chief Creative Officer JOE QUESADA
Publisher DAN BUCKLEY
Executive Producer ALAN FINE

WOLVERINE: GOODBYE, CHINATOWN. Contains material originally published in magazine form as WOLVERINE #17-20. First printing 2012. Hardcover ISBN# 978-0-7851-6141-7. Softcover ISBN# 978-0-7851-6142-4. Published by MARVEL WORLDWIDE, INC., a subsidiary of MARVEL ENTERTAINMENT, LLC. OFFICE OF PUBLICATION: 135 West 50th Street, New York, NY 10020. Copyright © 2011 and 2012 Marvel Characters, Inc. All rights reserved. Hardcover: $19.99 per copy in the U.S. and $21.99 in Canada (GST #R127032852). Softcover: $16.99 per copy in the U.S. and $18.99 in Canada (GST #R127032852). Canadian Agreement #40668537. All characters featured in this issue and the distinctive names and likenesses thereof, and all related indicia are trademarks of Marvel Characters, Inc. No similarity between any of the names, characters, persons, and/or institutions in this magazine with those of any living or dead person or institution is intended, and any such similarity which may exist is purely coincidental. **Printed in the U.S.A.** ALAN FINE, EVP - Office of the President, Marvel Worldwide, Inc. and EVP & CMO Marvel Characters B.V.; DAN BUCKLEY, Publisher & President - Print, Animation & Digital Divisions; JOE QUESADA, Chief Creative Officer; DAVID BOGART, SVP of Business Affairs & Talent Management; TOM BREVOORT, SVP of Publishing; C.B. CEBULSKI, SVP of Creator & Content Development; DAVID GABRIEL, SVP of Publishing Sales & Circulation; MICHAEL PASCIULLO, SVP of Brand Planning & Communications; JIM O'KEEFE, VP of Operations & Logistics; DAN CARR, Executive Director of Publishing Technology; SUSAN CRESPI, Editorial Operations Manager; ALEX MORALES, Publishing Operations Manager; STAN LEE, Chairman Emeritus. For information regarding advertising in Marvel Comics or on Marvel.com, please contact John Dokes, SVP Integrated Sales and Marketing, at jdokes@marvel.com. For Marvel subscription inquiries, please call 800-217-9158. **Manufactured between 2/6/2012 and 3/5/2012 (hardcover), and 2/6/2012 and 9/3/2012 (softcover), by R.R. DONNELLEY, INC., SALEM, VA, USA.**

10 9 8 7 6 5 4 3 2 1

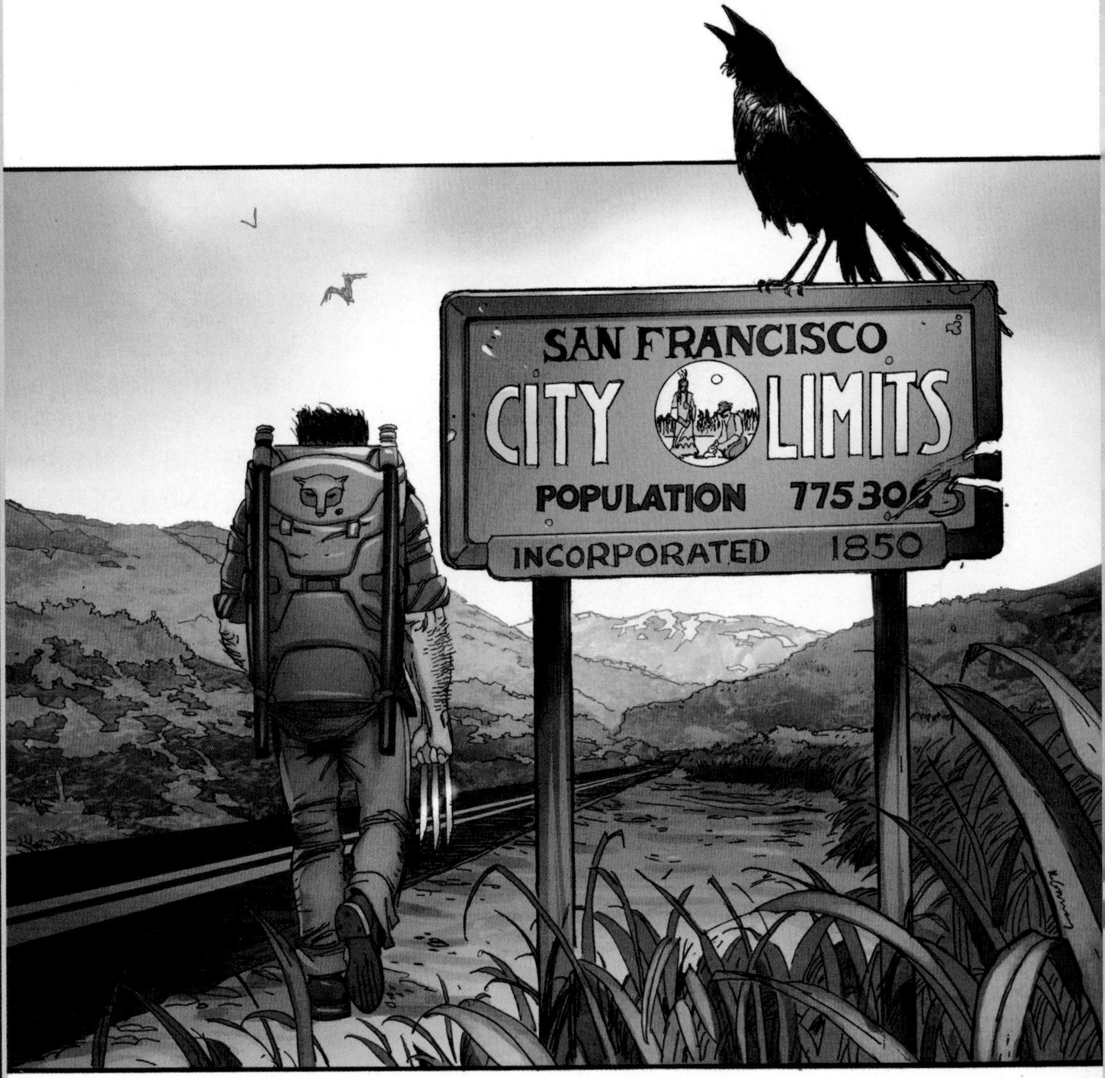
SAN FRANCISCO
CITY LIMITS
POPULATION 77530
INCORPORATED 1850

claws and the ability to heal from any wound. In their attempt to create the perfect living weapon, the organization bonded the unbreakable metal Adamantium to his skeleton. The process was excruciating and by the end, there was little left of the man known as Logan. He had become...

WOLVERINE

PREVIOUSLY...

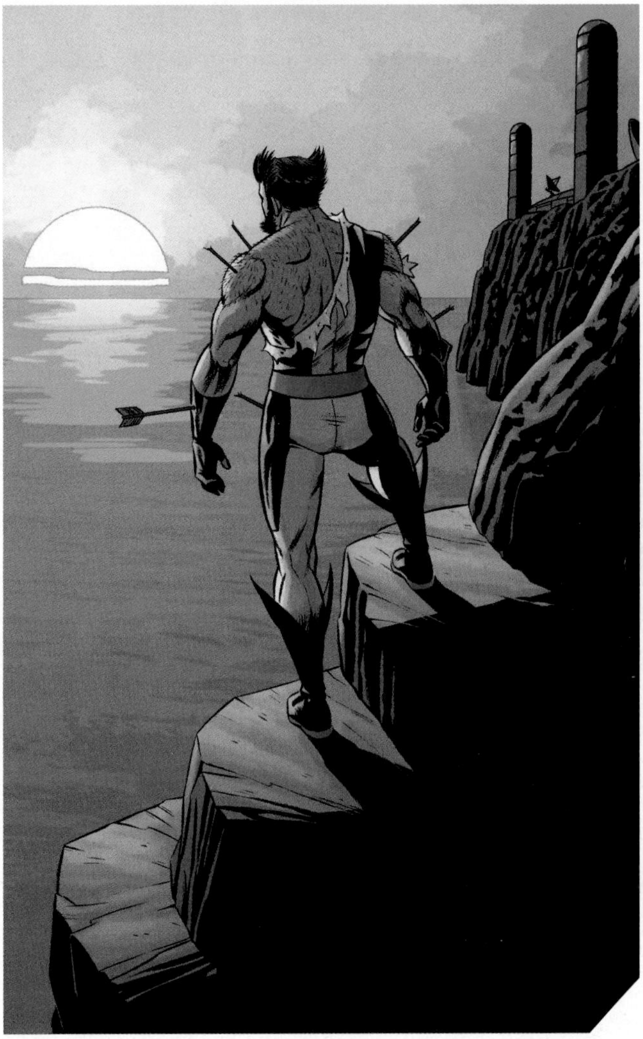

Since the X-Men moved to San Francisco, Wolverine has been put through the wringer. He's fought Adamantium Men, gotten locked up in an insane asylum, defended innocents from assassination at the hands of cyborg soldiers from the future, witnessed the death of his friend Nightcrawler, fallen in love with reporter Melita Garner, been to hell and back, battled his fellow X-Men and most recently fought against the revenge seeking group called the Red Right Hand that resulted in the deaths of the illegitimate children he didn't even know he had. He even cleaned up Chinatown with the help of his old Kung Fu mentor Master Po by defeating the evil Triad gangs that tormented the locals and assuming the mantle of the Black Dragon, the leader of Chinatown organized crime.

All of these events affected Logan deeply and he's just returned from a journey of self-discovery and affirmation of his purpose in life. Now it's time to make some changes...

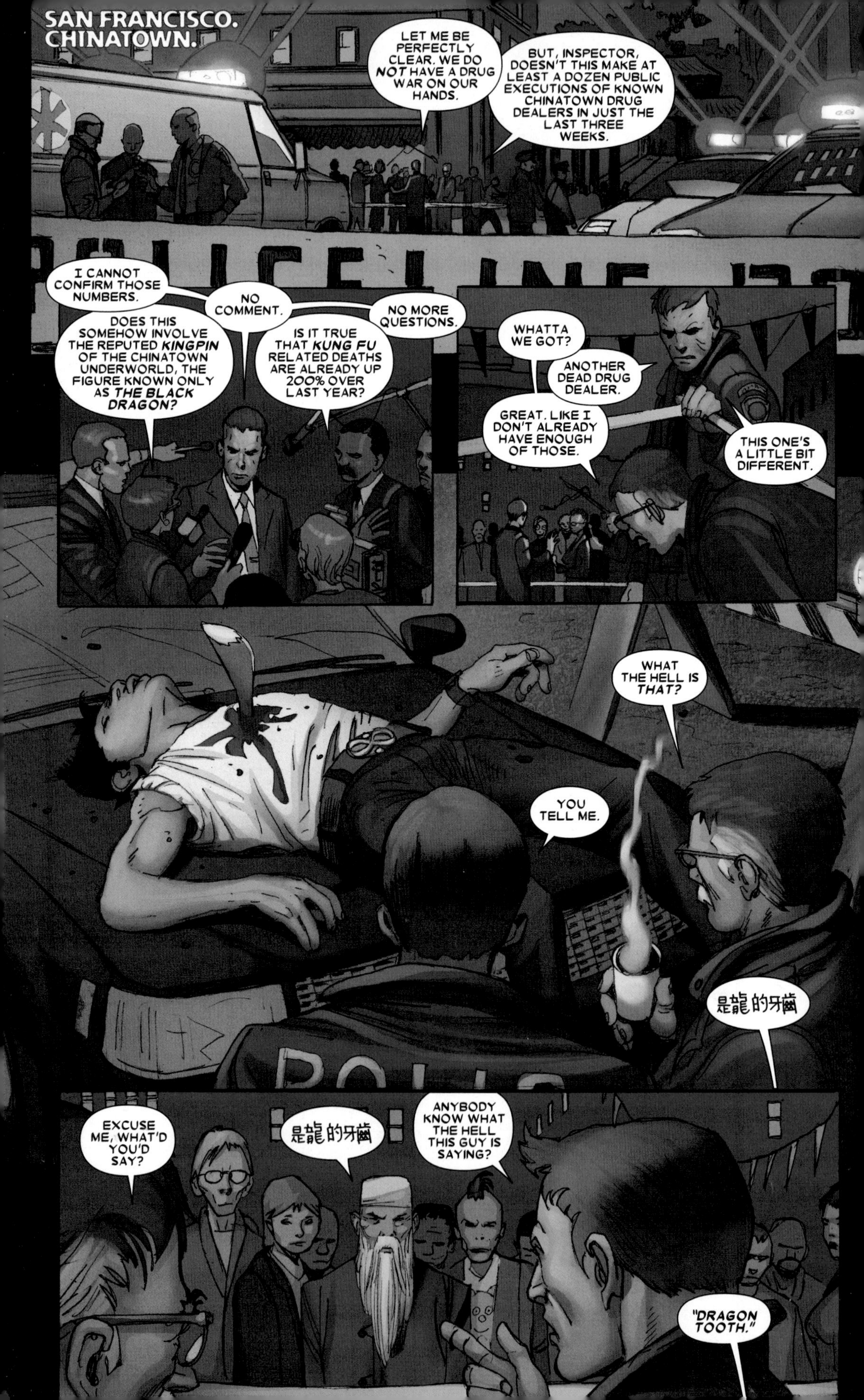

SAN FRANCISCO. CHINATOWN.
LET ME BE PERFECTLY CLEAR. WE DO NOT HAVE A DRUG WAR ON OUR HANDS.
BUT, INSPECTOR, DOESN'T THIS MAKE AT LEAST A DOZEN PUBLIC EXECUTIONS OF KNOWN CHINATOWN DRUG DEALERS IN JUST THE LAST THREE WEEKS.
I CANNOT CONFIRM THOSE NUMBERS.
DOES THIS SOMEHOW INVOLVE THE REPUTED KINGPIN OF THE CHINATOWN UNDERWORLD, THE FIGURE KNOWN ONLY AS THE BLACK DRAGON?
NO COMMENT.
IS IT TRUE THAT KUNG FU RELATED DEATHS ARE ALREADY UP 200% OVER LAST YEAR?
NO MORE QUESTIONS.
WHATTA WE GOT?
ANOTHER DEAD DRUG DEALER.
GREAT. LIKE I DON'T ALREADY HAVE ENOUGH OF THOSE.
THIS ONE'S A LITTLE BIT DIFFERENT.
WHAT THE HELL IS THAT?
YOU TELL ME.
是龍的牙齒
EXCUSE ME, WHAT'D YOU'D SAY?
是龍的牙齒
ANYBODY KNOW WHAT THE HELL THIS GUY IS SAYING?
"DRAGON TOOTH."

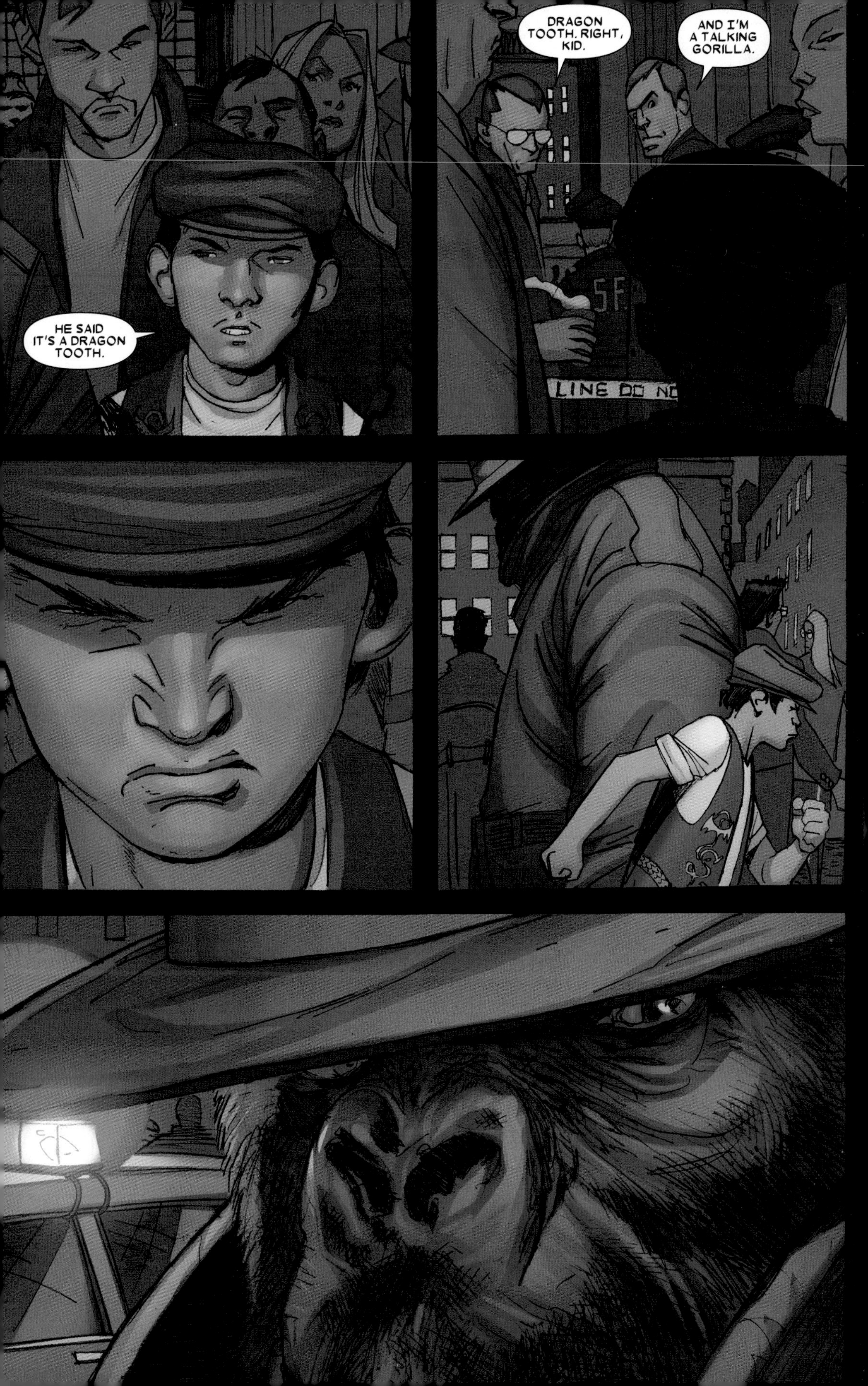

HE SAID IT'S A DRAGON TOOTH.
DRAGON TOOTH. RIGHT, KID.
AND I'M A TALKING GORILLA.
LINE DO NO

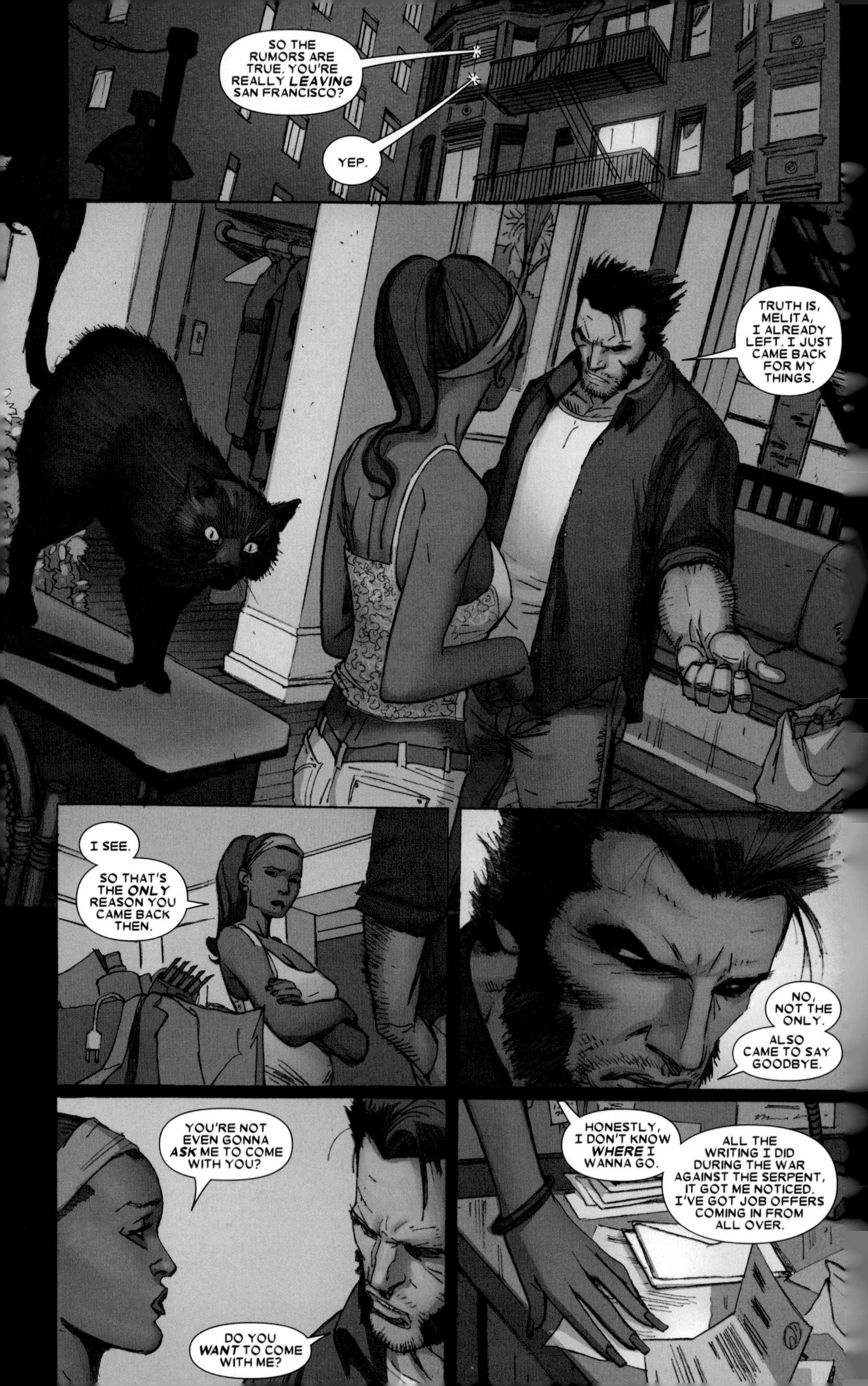
SO THE RUMORS ARE TRUE. YOU'RE REALLY *LEAVING* SAN FRANCISCO?
YEP.
TRUTH IS, MELITA, I ALREADY LEFT. I JUST CAME BACK FOR MY THINGS.
I SEE.
SO THAT'S THE *ONLY* REASON YOU CAME BACK THEN.
NO, NOT THE ONLY.
ALSO CAME TO SAY GOODBYE.
YOU'RE NOT EVEN GONNA *ASK* ME TO COME WITH YOU?
DO YOU *WANT* TO COME WITH ME?
HONESTLY, I DON'T KNOW *WHERE* I WANNA GO.
ALL THE WRITING I DID DURING THE WAR AGAINST THE SERPENT, IT GOT ME NOTICED. I'VE GOT JOB OFFERS COMING IN FROM ALL OVER.

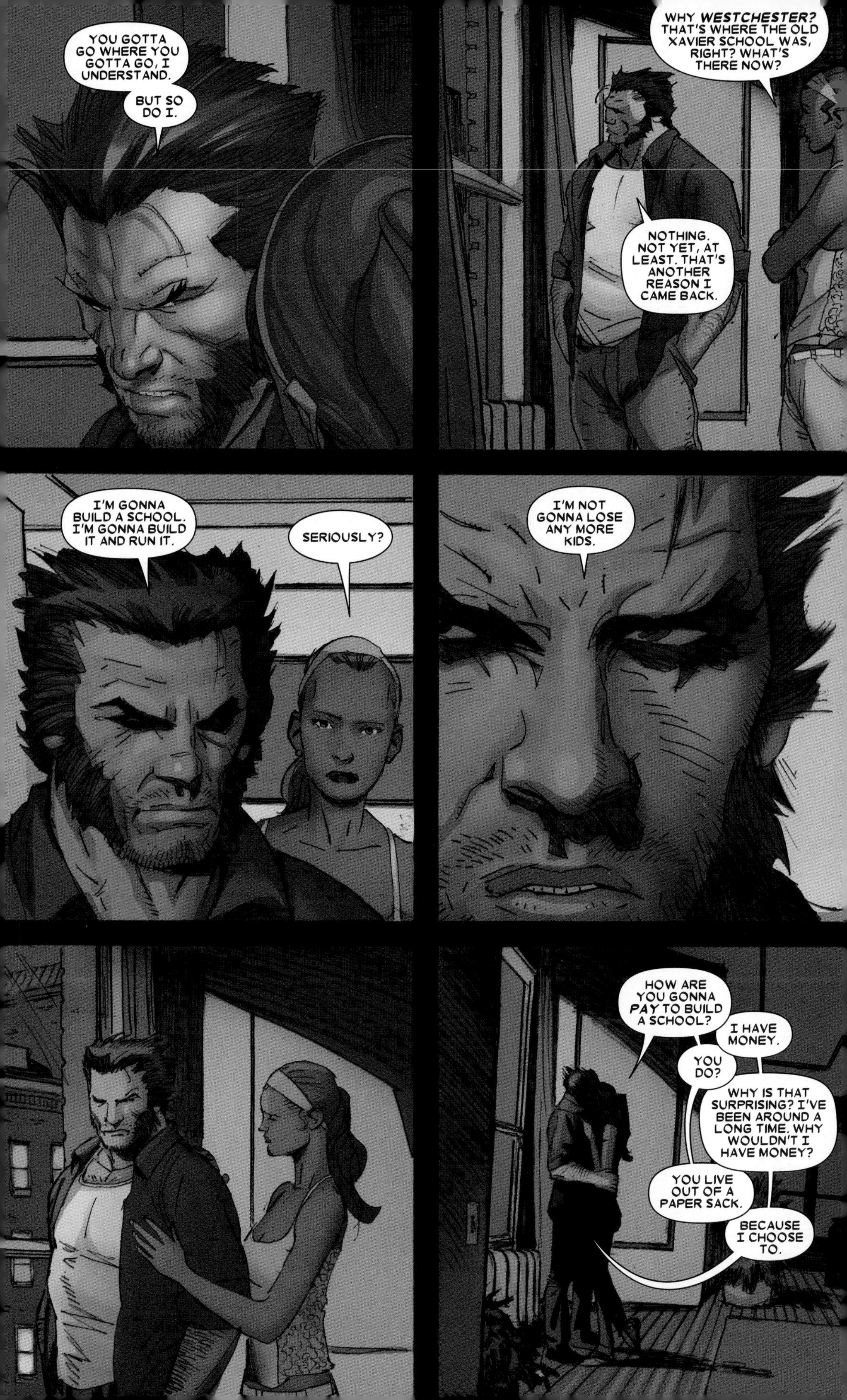

YOU GOTTA GO WHERE YOU GOTTA GO, I UNDERSTAND.
BUT SO DO I.
WHY WESTCHESTER? THAT'S WHERE THE OLD XAVIER SCHOOL WAS, RIGHT? WHAT'S THERE NOW?
NOTHING. NOT YET, AT LEAST. THAT'S ANOTHER REASON I CAME BACK.
I'M GONNA BUILD A SCHOOL. I'M GONNA BUILD IT AND RUN IT.
SERIOUSLY?
I'M NOT GONNA LOSE ANY MORE KIDS.
HOW ARE YOU GONNA PAY TO BUILD A SCHOOL?
I HAVE MONEY.
YOU DO?
WHY IS THAT SURPRISING? I'VE BEEN AROUND A LONG TIME. WHY WOULDN'T I HAVE MONEY?
YOU LIVE OUT OF A PAPER SACK.
BECAUSE I CHOOSE TO.

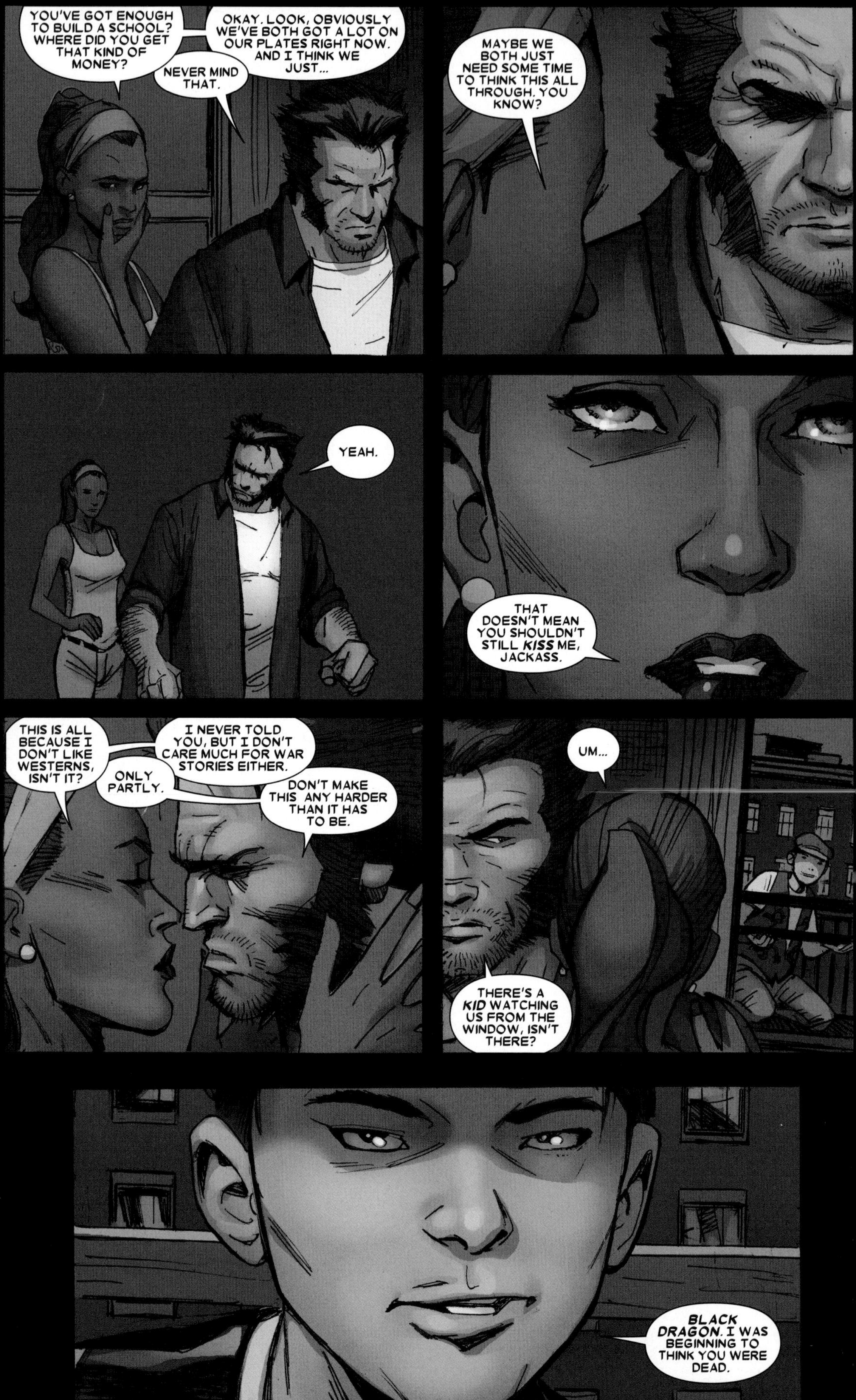
YOU'VE GOT ENOUGH TO BUILD A SCHOOL? WHERE DID YOU GET THAT KIND OF MONEY?
OKAY. LOOK, OBVIOUSLY WE'VE BOTH GOT A LOT ON OUR PLATES RIGHT NOW. AND I THINK WE JUST...
NEVER MIND THAT.
MAYBE WE BOTH JUST NEED SOME TIME TO THINK THIS ALL THROUGH. YOU KNOW?
YEAH.
THAT DOESN'T MEAN YOU SHOULDN'T STILL KISS ME, JACKASS.
THIS IS ALL BECAUSE I DON'T LIKE WESTERNS, ISN'T IT?
I NEVER TOLD YOU, BUT I DON'T CARE MUCH FOR WAR STORIES EITHER.
ONLY PARTLY.
DON'T MAKE THIS ANY HARDER THAN IT HAS TO BE.
UM...
THERE'S A KID WATCHING US FROM THE WINDOW, ISN'T THERE?
BLACK DRAGON. I WAS BEGINNING TO THINK YOU WERE DEAD.

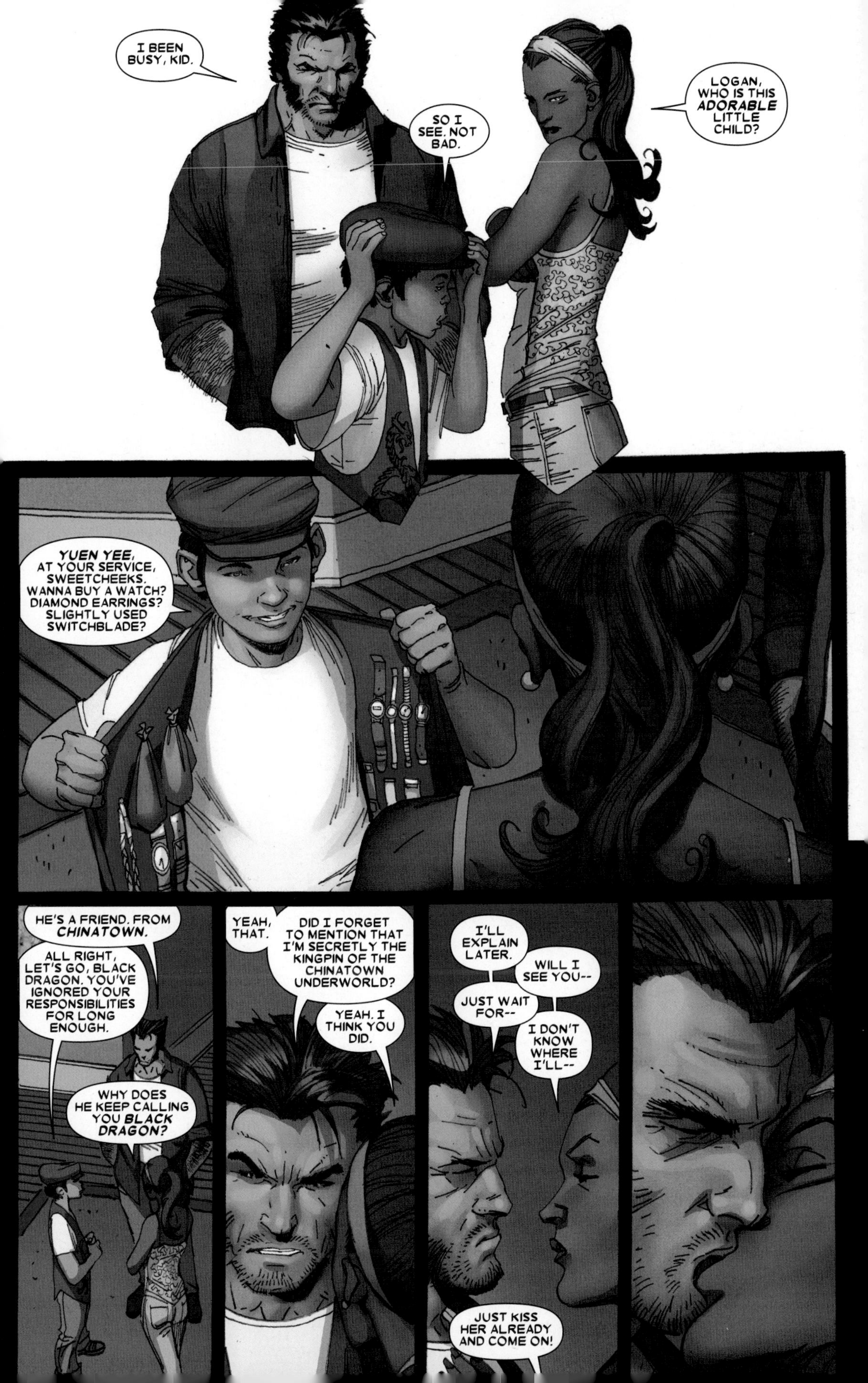
I BEEN BUSY, KID.
SO I SEE. NOT BAD.
LOGAN, WHO IS THIS *ADORABLE* LITTLE CHILD?
YUEN YEE, AT YOUR SERVICE, SWEETCHEEKS. WANNA BUY A WATCH? DIAMOND EARRINGS? SLIGHTLY USED SWITCHBLADE?
HE'S A FRIEND. FROM *CHINATOWN.*
ALL RIGHT, LET'S GO, BLACK DRAGON. YOU'VE IGNORED YOUR RESPONSIBILITIES FOR LONG ENOUGH.
WHY DOES HE KEEP CALLING YOU *BLACK DRAGON?*
YEAH, THAT.
DID I FORGET TO MENTION THAT I'M SECRETLY THE KINGPIN OF THE CHINATOWN UNDERWORLD?
YEAH. I THINK YOU DID.
I'LL EXPLAIN LATER.
WILL I SEE YOU--
JUST WAIT FOR--
I DON'T KNOW WHERE I'LL--
JUST KISS HER ALREADY AND COME ON!

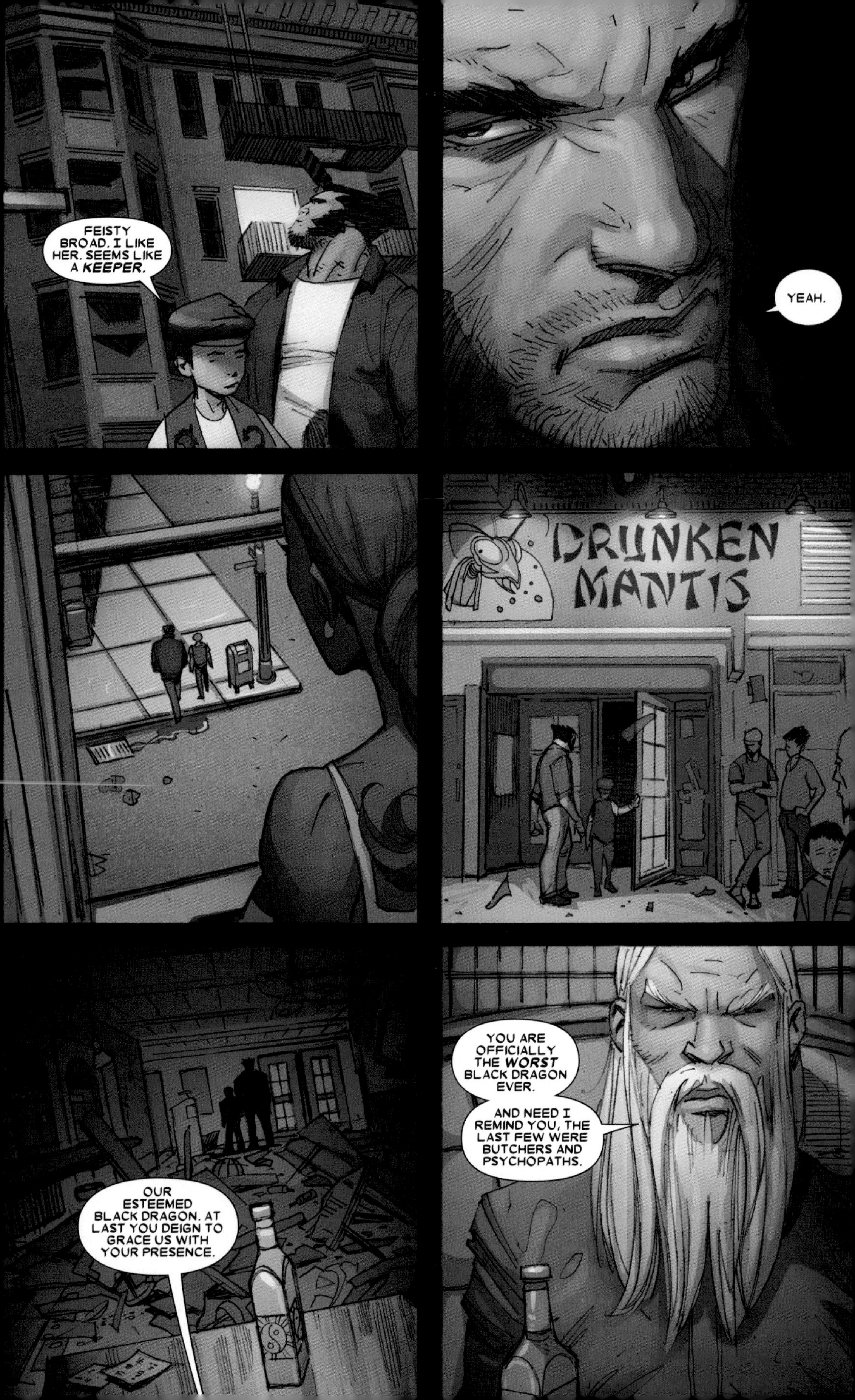

FEISTY BROAD. I LIKE HER. SEEMS LIKE A *KEEPER.*
YEAH.
DRUNKEN MANTIS
OUR ESTEEMED BLACK DRAGON. AT LAST YOU DEIGN TO GRACE US WITH YOUR PRESENCE.
YOU ARE OFFICIALLY THE *WORST* BLACK DRAGON EVER.
AND NEED I REMIND YOU, THE LAST FEW WERE BUTCHERS AND PSYCHOPATHS.

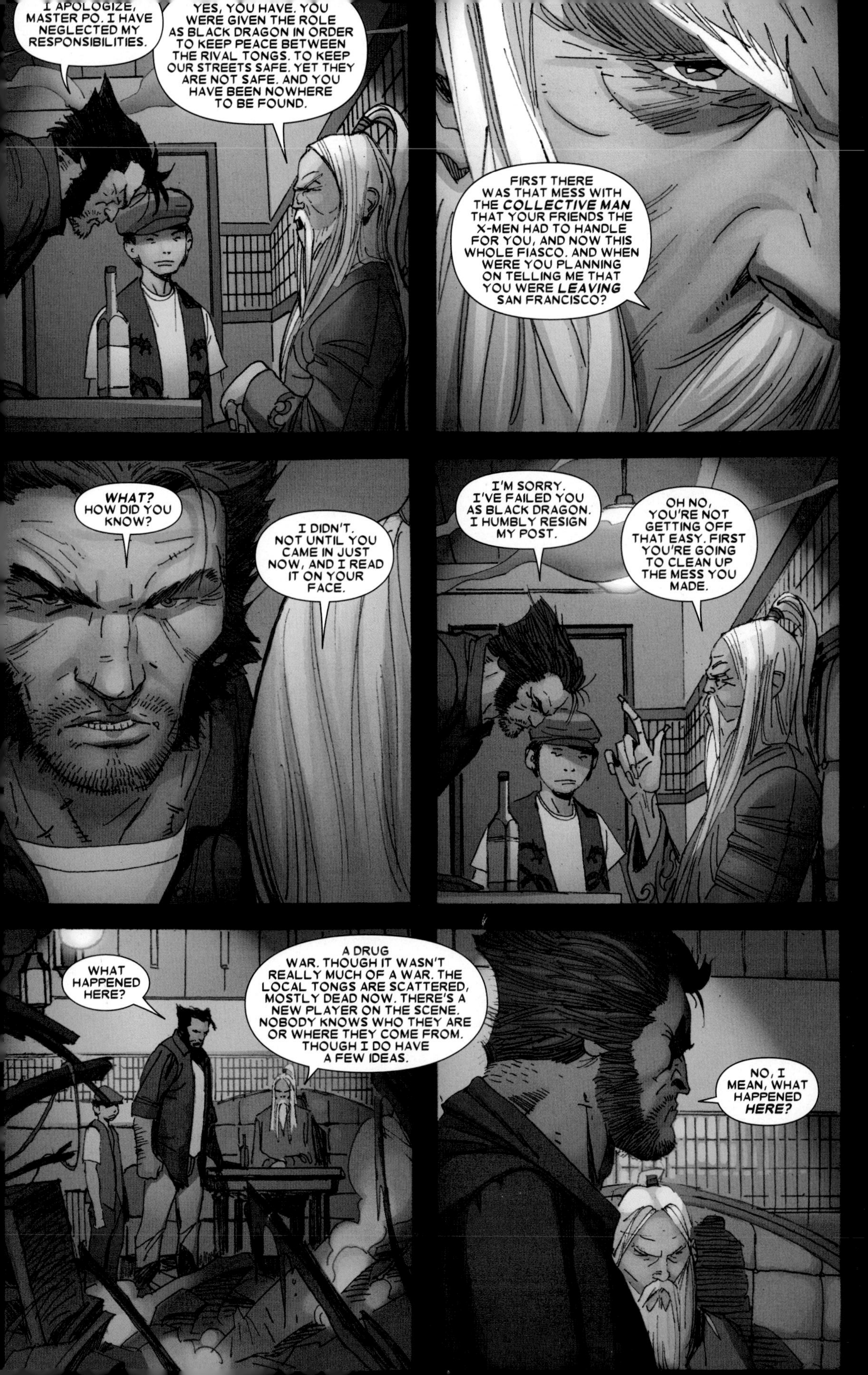
I APOLOGIZE, MASTER PO. I HAVE NEGLECTED MY RESPONSIBILITIES.
YES, YOU HAVE. YOU WERE GIVEN THE ROLE AS BLACK DRAGON IN ORDER TO KEEP PEACE BETWEEN THE RIVAL TONGS. TO KEEP OUR STREETS SAFE. YET THEY ARE NOT SAFE. AND YOU HAVE BEEN NOWHERE TO BE FOUND.
FIRST THERE WAS THAT MESS WITH THE COLLECTIVE MAN THAT YOUR FRIENDS THE X-MEN HAD TO HANDLE FOR YOU, AND NOW THIS WHOLE FIASCO. AND WHEN WERE YOU PLANNING ON TELLING ME THAT YOU WERE LEAVING SAN FRANCISCO?
WHAT? HOW DID YOU KNOW?
I DIDN'T. NOT UNTIL YOU CAME IN JUST NOW, AND I READ IT ON YOUR FACE.
I'M SORRY. I'VE FAILED YOU AS BLACK DRAGON. I HUMBLY RESIGN MY POST.
OH NO, YOU'RE NOT GETTING OFF THAT EASY. FIRST YOU'RE GOING TO CLEAN UP THE MESS YOU MADE.
WHAT HAPPENED HERE?
A DRUG WAR. THOUGH IT WASN'T REALLY MUCH OF A WAR. THE LOCAL TONGS ARE SCATTERED, MOSTLY DEAD NOW. THERE'S A NEW PLAYER ON THE SCENE. NOBODY KNOWS WHO THEY ARE OR WHERE THEY COME FROM. THOUGH I DO HAVE A FEW IDEAS.
NO, I MEAN, WHAT HAPPENED HERE?

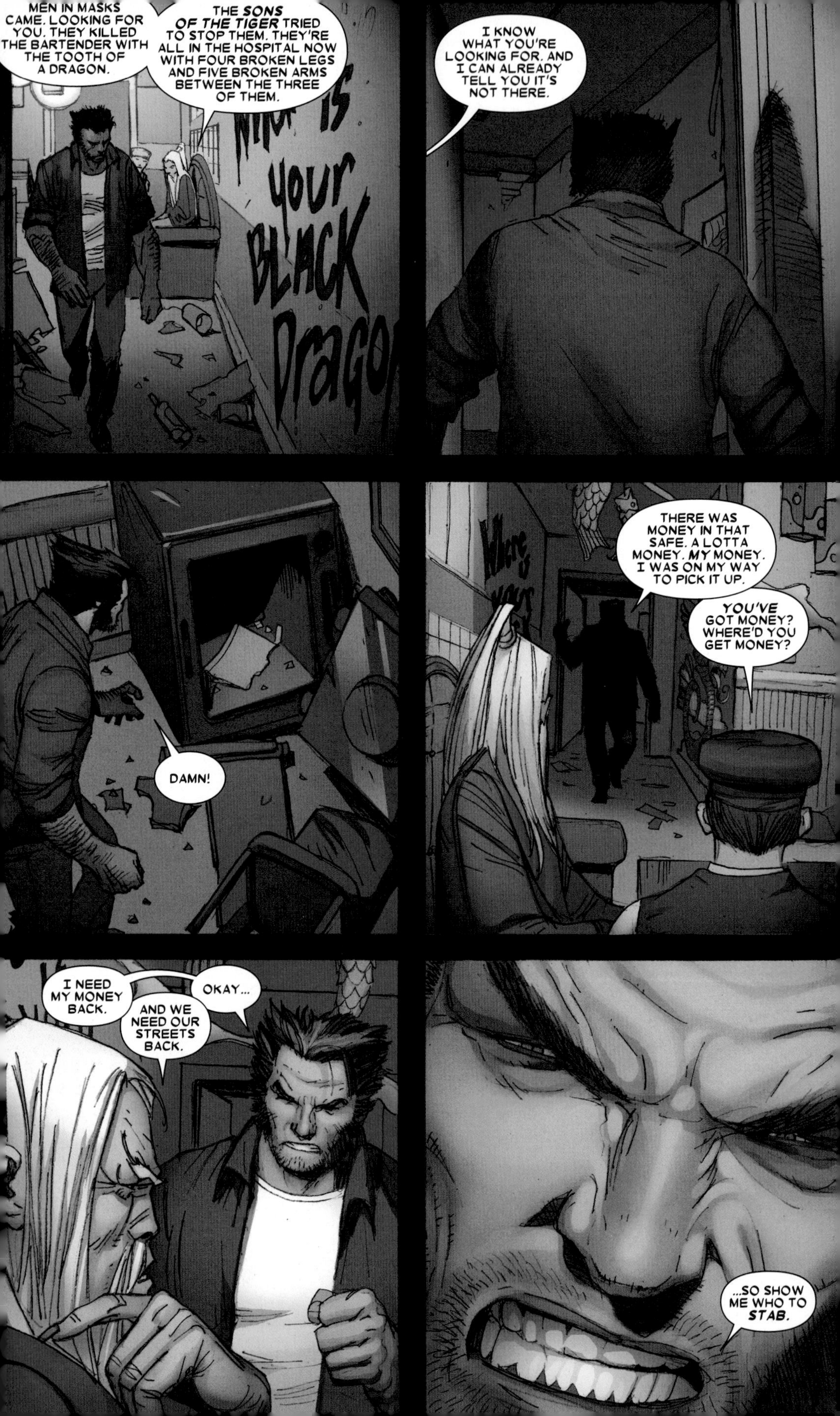
MEN IN MASKS CAME. LOOKING FOR YOU. THEY KILLED THE BARTENDER WITH THE TOOTH OF A DRAGON.
THE SONS OF THE TIGER TRIED TO STOP THEM. THEY'RE ALL IN THE HOSPITAL NOW WITH FOUR BROKEN LEGS AND FIVE BROKEN ARMS BETWEEN THE THREE OF THEM.
I KNOW WHAT YOU'RE LOOKING FOR. AND I CAN ALREADY TELL YOU IT'S NOT THERE.
DAMN!
THERE WAS MONEY IN THAT SAFE. A LOTTA MONEY. MY MONEY. I WAS ON MY WAY TO PICK IT UP.
YOU'VE GOT MONEY? WHERE'D YOU GET MONEY?
I NEED MY MONEY BACK.
AND WE NEED OUR STREETS BACK.
OKAY...
...SO SHOW ME WHO TO STAB.

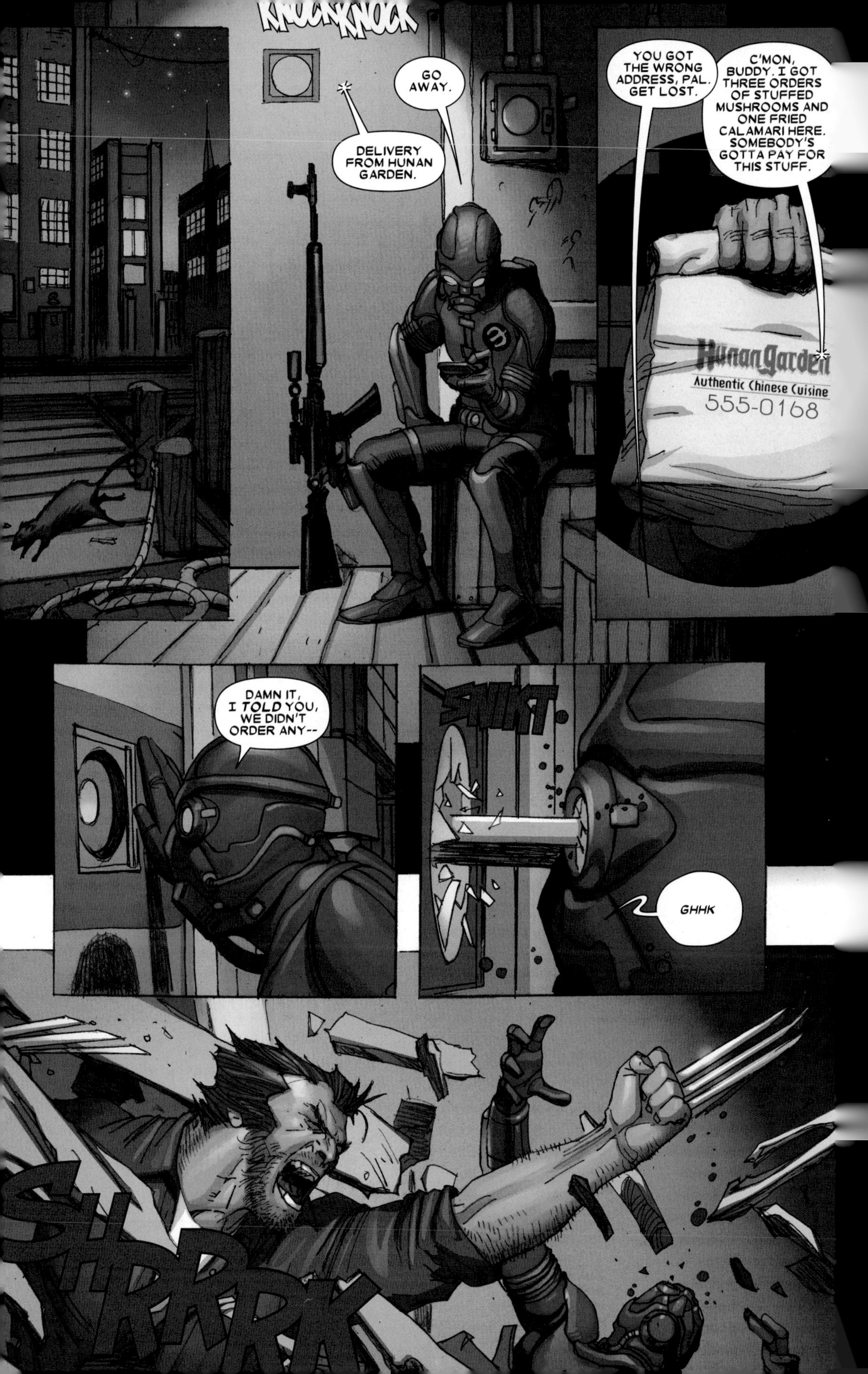

KNOCK KNOCK
DELIVERY FROM HUNAN GARDEN.
GO AWAY.
YOU GOT THE WRONG ADDRESS, PAL. GET LOST.
C'MON, BUDDY. I GOT THREE ORDERS OF STUFFED MUSHROOMS AND ONE FRIED CALAMARI HERE. SOMEBODY'S GOTTA PAY FOR THIS STUFF.
Hunan Garden
Authentic Chinese Cuisine
555-0168
DAMN IT, I *TOLD* YOU, WE DIDN'T ORDER ANY--
SNIKT
GHHK
SHRRRK

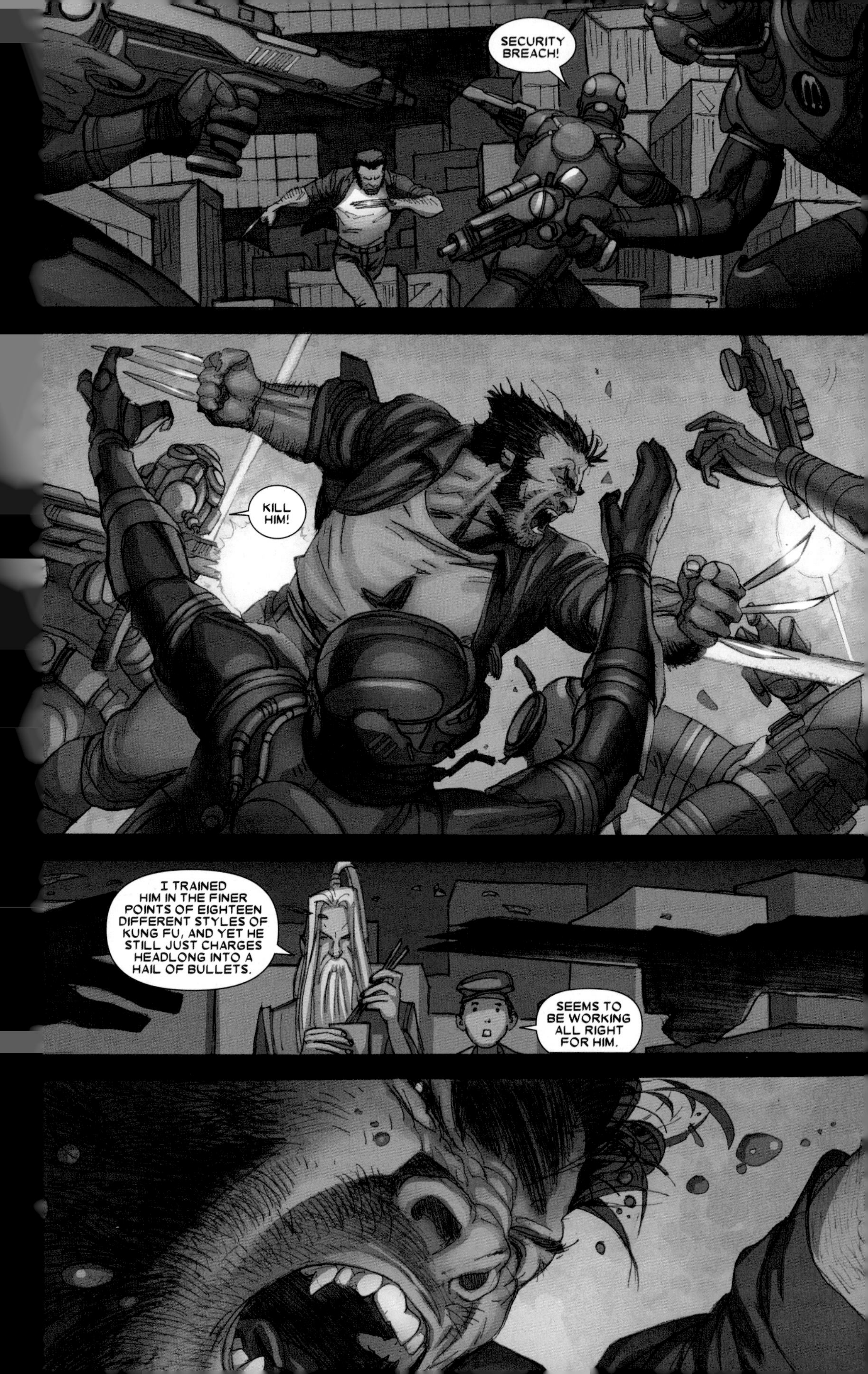
SECURITY BREACH!
KILL HIM!
I TRAINED HIM IN THE FINER POINTS OF EIGHTEEN DIFFERENT STYLES OF KUNG FU, AND YET HE STILL JUST CHARGES HEADLONG INTO A HAIL OF BULLETS.
SEEMS TO BE WORKING ALL RIGHT FOR HIM.

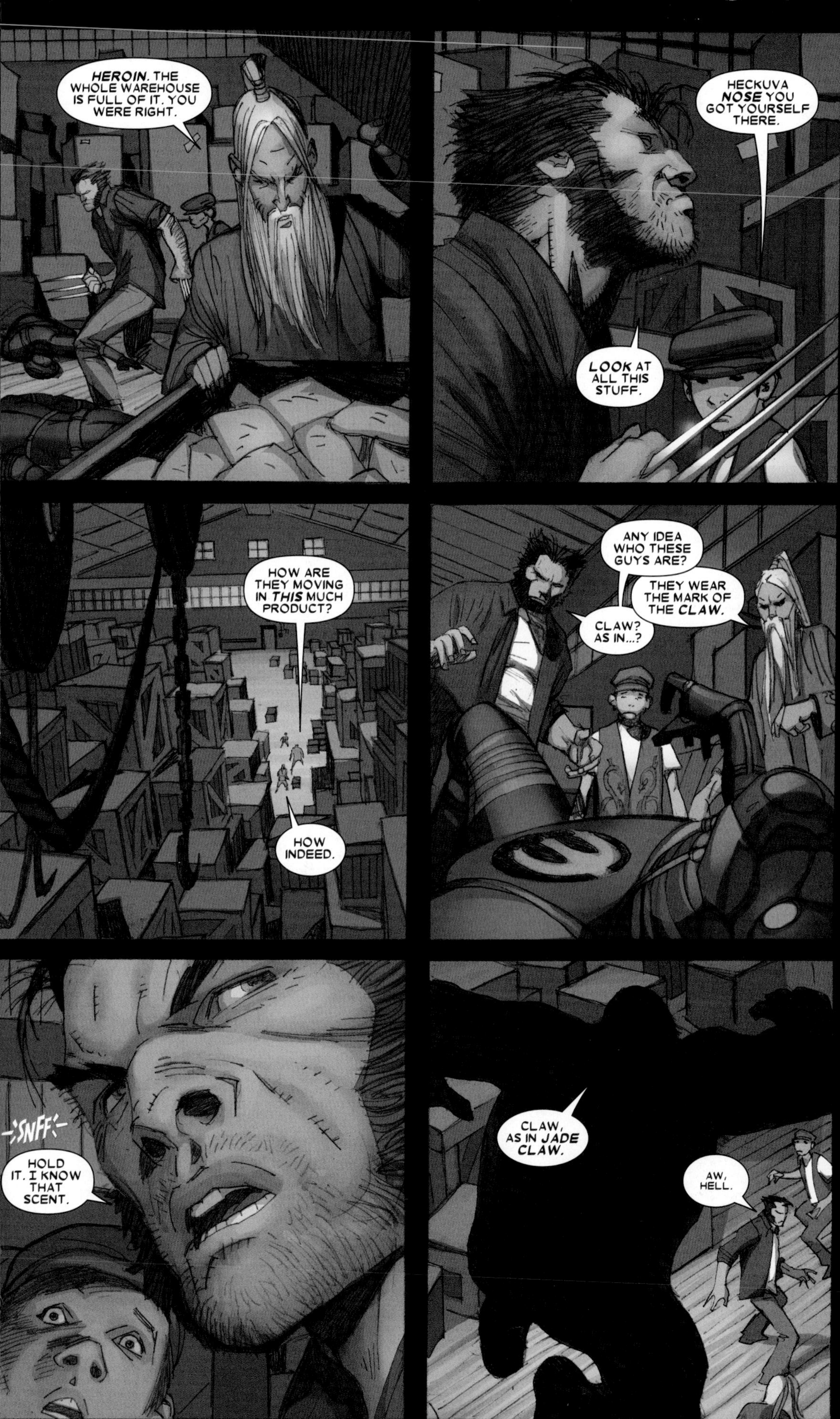
HEROIN. THE WHOLE WAREHOUSE IS FULL OF IT. YOU WERE RIGHT.
HECKUVA NOSE YOU GOT YOURSELF THERE.
LOOK AT ALL THIS STUFF.
HOW ARE THEY MOVING IN THIS MUCH PRODUCT?
HOW INDEED.
ANY IDEA WHO THESE GUYS ARE?
THEY WEAR THE MARK OF THE CLAW.
CLAW? AS IN...?
SNFF
HOLD IT. I KNOW THAT SCENT.
CLAW, AS IN JADE CLAW.
AW, HELL.

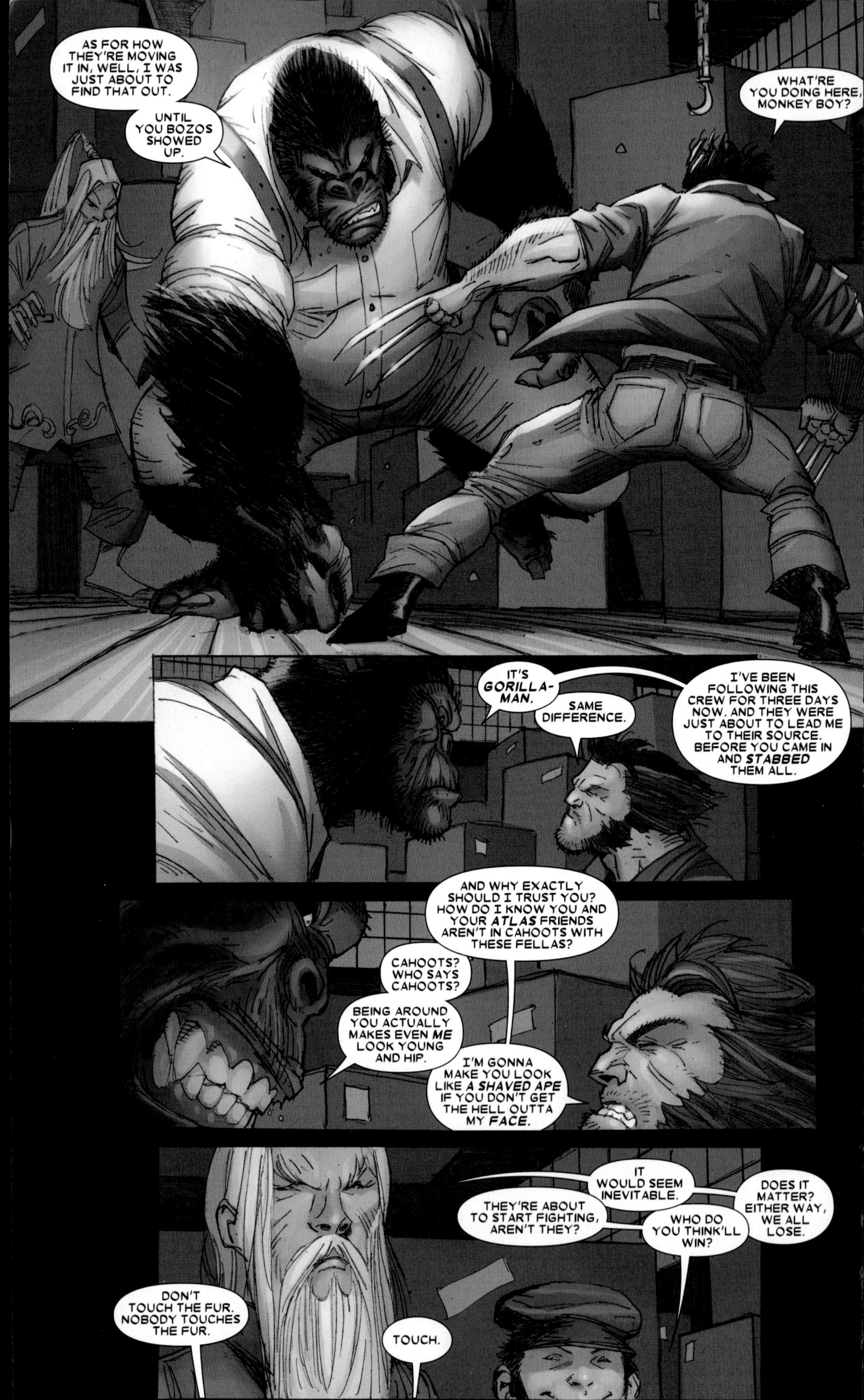
AS FOR HOW THEY'RE MOVING IT IN, WELL, I WAS JUST ABOUT TO FIND THAT OUT.
UNTIL YOU BOZOS SHOWED UP.
WHAT'RE YOU DOING HERE, MONKEY BOY?
IT'S GORILLA-MAN.
SAME DIFFERENCE.
I'VE BEEN FOLLOWING THIS CREW FOR THREE DAYS NOW. AND THEY WERE JUST ABOUT TO LEAD ME TO THEIR SOURCE. BEFORE YOU CAME IN AND STABBED THEM ALL.
AND WHY EXACTLY SHOULD I TRUST YOU? HOW DO I KNOW YOU AND YOUR ATLAS FRIENDS AREN'T IN CAHOOTS WITH THESE FELLAS?
CAHOOTS? WHO SAYS CAHOOTS?
BEING AROUND YOU ACTUALLY MAKES EVEN ME LOOK YOUNG AND HIP.
I'M GONNA MAKE YOU LOOK LIKE A SHAVED APE IF YOU DON'T GET THE HELL OUTTA MY FACE.
THEY'RE ABOUT TO START FIGHTING, AREN'T THEY?
IT WOULD SEEM INEVITABLE.
WHO DO YOU THINK'LL WIN?
DOES IT MATTER? EITHER WAY, WE ALL LOSE.
DON'T TOUCH THE FUR. NOBODY TOUCHES THE FUR.
TOUCH.

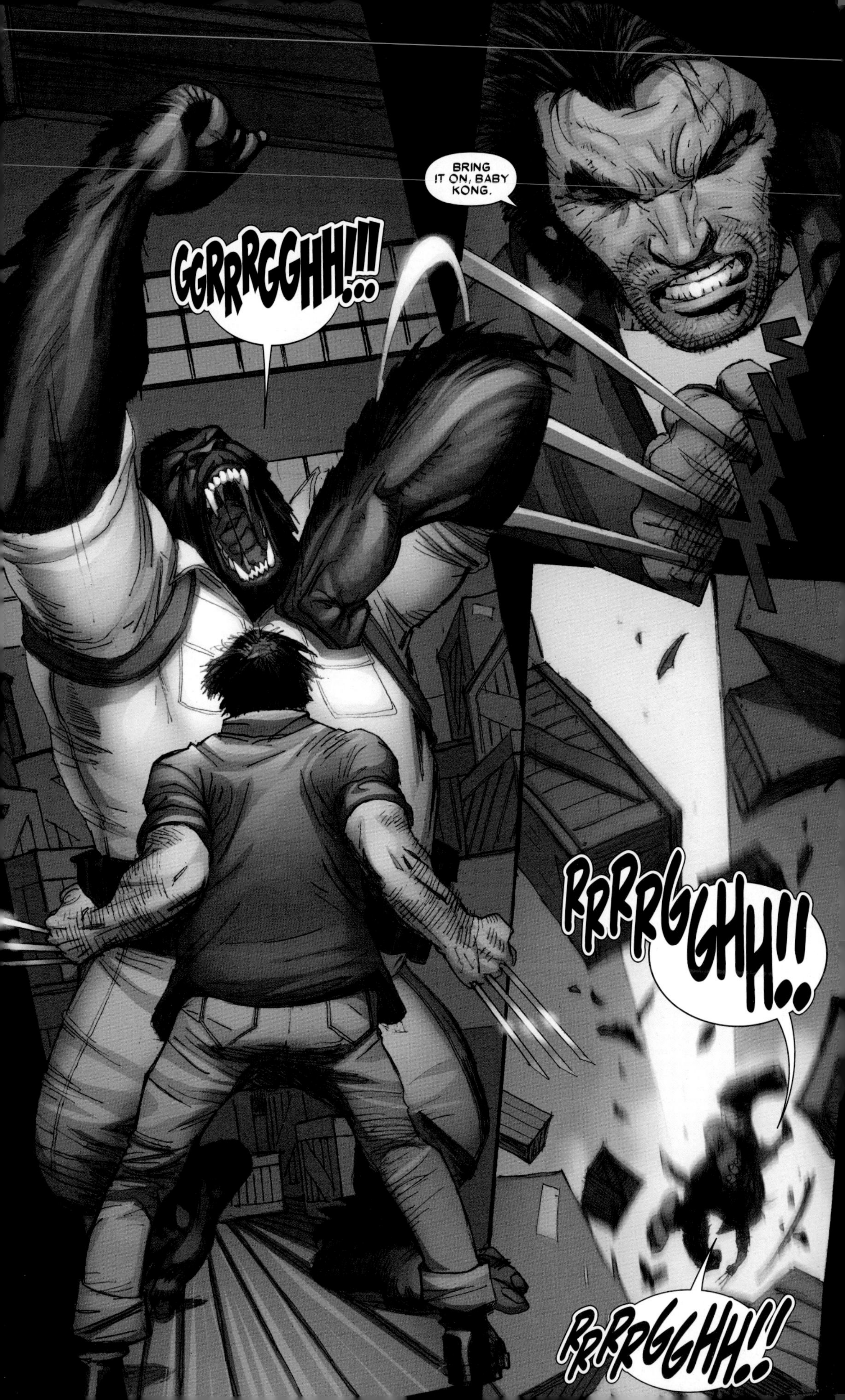
GGRRRGGHH!!!..
BRING IT ON, BABY KONG.
RRRRGGHH!!..
RRRRGGHH!!!..

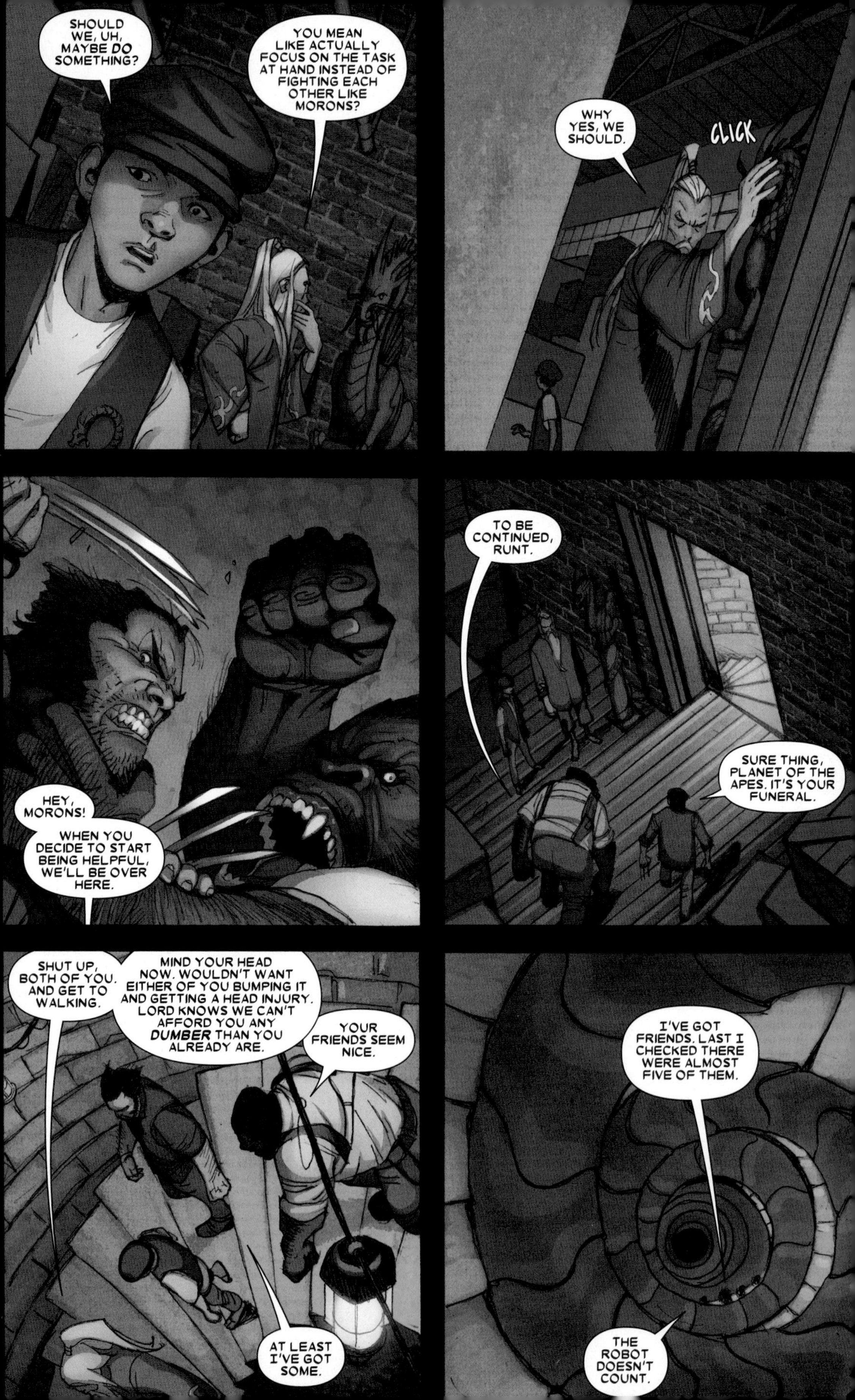
SHOULD WE, UH, MAYBE DO SOMETHING?
YOU MEAN LIKE ACTUALLY FOCUS ON THE TASK AT HAND INSTEAD OF FIGHTING EACH OTHER LIKE MORONS?
WHY YES, WE SHOULD.
CLICK
HEY, MORONS!
WHEN YOU DECIDE TO START BEING HELPFUL, WE'LL BE OVER HERE.
TO BE CONTINUED, RUNT.
SURE THING, PLANET OF THE APES. IT'S YOUR FUNERAL.
SHUT UP, BOTH OF YOU. AND GET TO WALKING.
MIND YOUR HEAD NOW. WOULDN'T WANT EITHER OF YOU BUMPING IT AND GETTING A HEAD INJURY. LORD KNOWS WE CAN'T AFFORD YOU ANY DUMBER THAN YOU ALREADY ARE.
YOUR FRIENDS SEEM NICE.
AT LEAST I'VE GOT SOME.
I'VE GOT FRIENDS. LAST I CHECKED THERE WERE ALMOST FIVE OF THEM.
THE ROBOT DOESN'T COUNT.

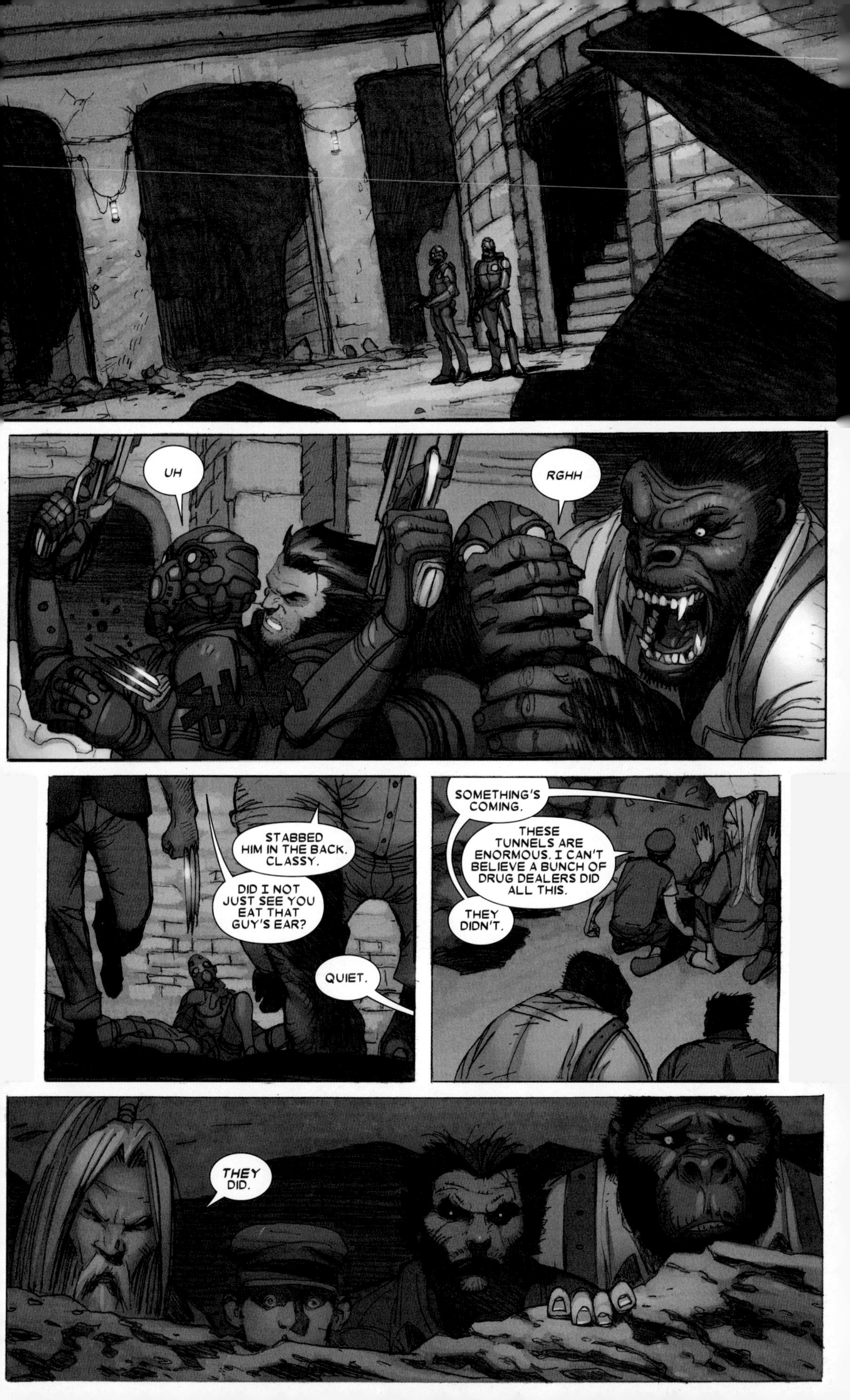
UH
RGHH
STABBED HIM IN THE BACK. CLASSY.
DID I NOT JUST SEE YOU EAT THAT GUY'S EAR?
QUIET.
SOMETHING'S COMING.
THESE TUNNELS ARE ENORMOUS. I CAN'T BELIEVE A BUNCH OF DRUG DEALERS DID ALL THIS.
THEY DIDN'T.
THEY DID.

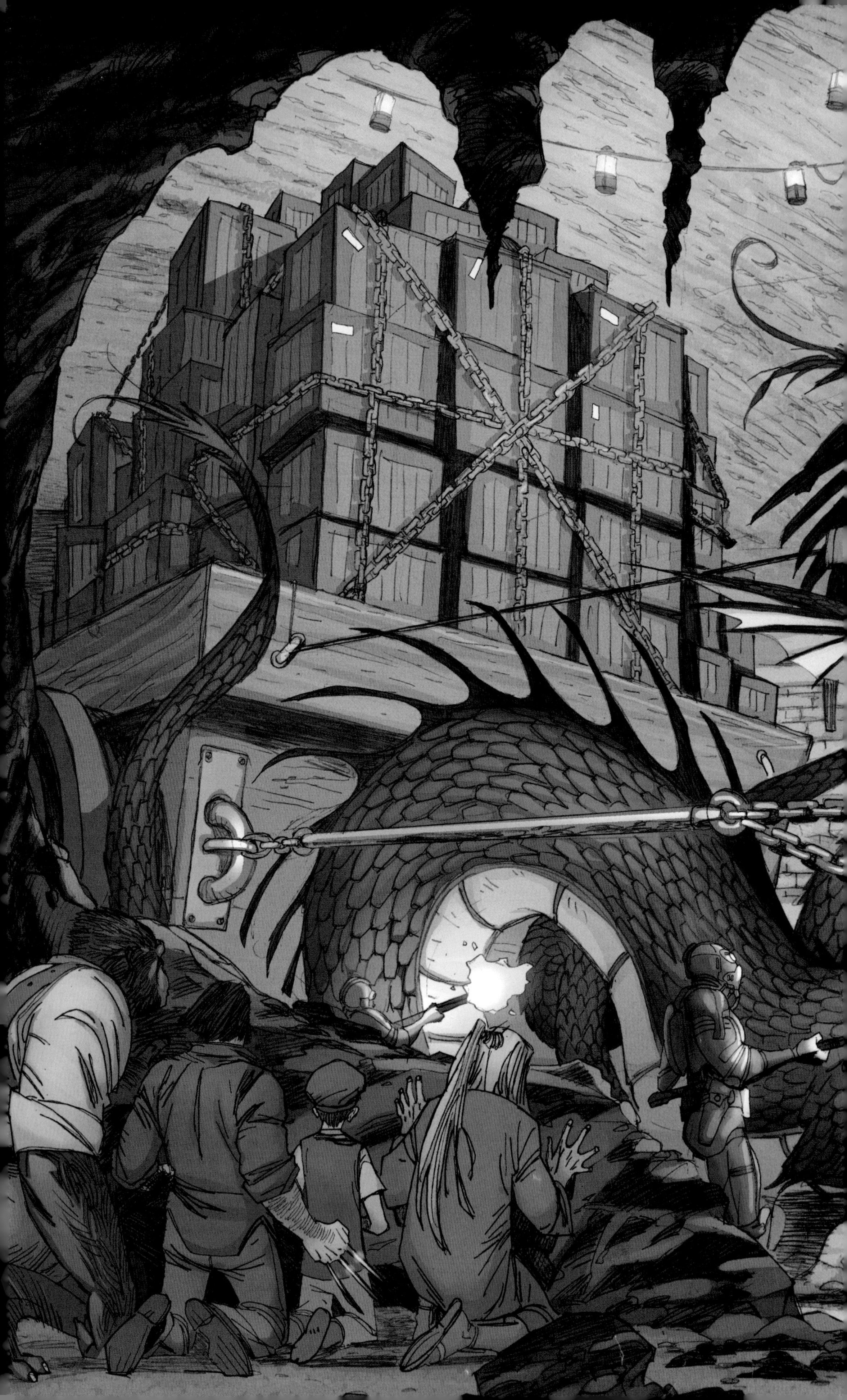

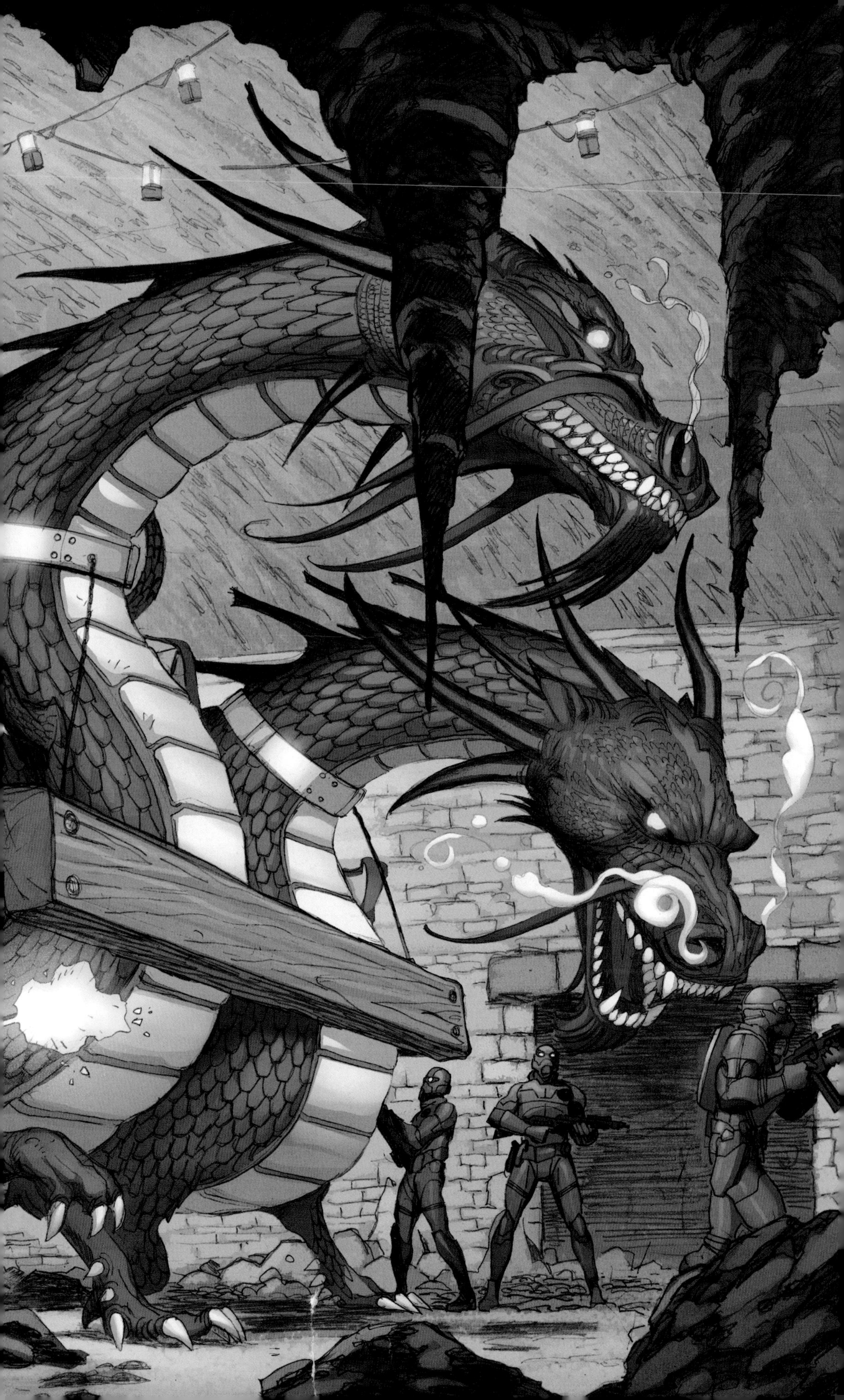

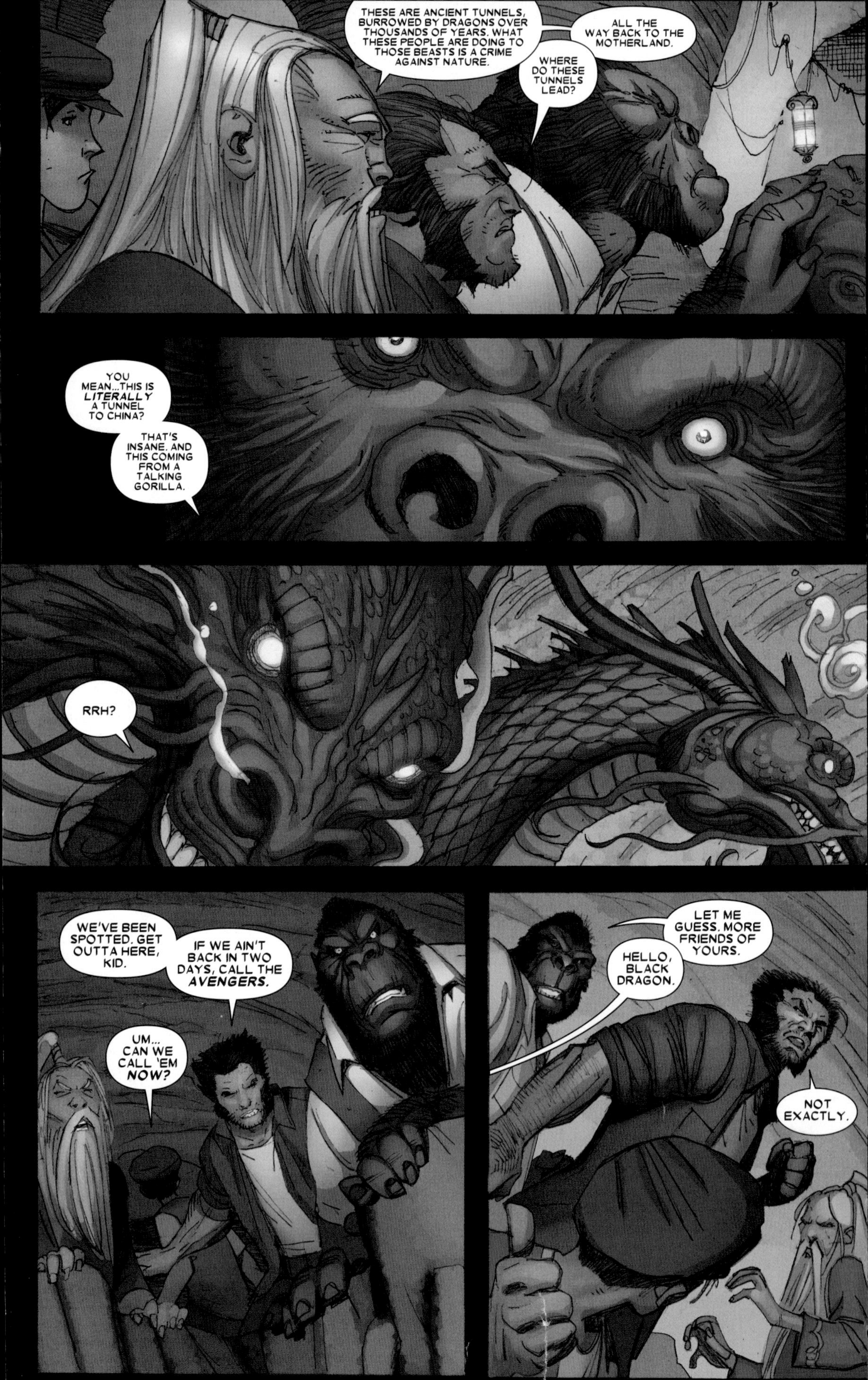
THESE ARE ANCIENT TUNNELS, BURROWED BY DRAGONS OVER THOUSANDS OF YEARS. WHAT THESE PEOPLE ARE DOING TO THOSE BEASTS IS A CRIME AGAINST NATURE.
WHERE DO THESE TUNNELS LEAD?
ALL THE WAY BACK TO THE MOTHERLAND.
YOU MEAN...THIS IS *LITERALLY* A TUNNEL TO CHINA?
THAT'S INSANE. AND THIS COMING FROM A TALKING GORILLA.
RRH?
WE'VE BEEN SPOTTED. GET OUTTA HERE, KID.
IF WE AIN'T BACK IN TWO DAYS, CALL THE ***AVENGERS.***
UM... CAN WE CALL 'EM ***NOW?***
LET ME GUESS. MORE FRIENDS OF YOURS.
HELLO, BLACK DRAGON.
NOT EXACTLY.

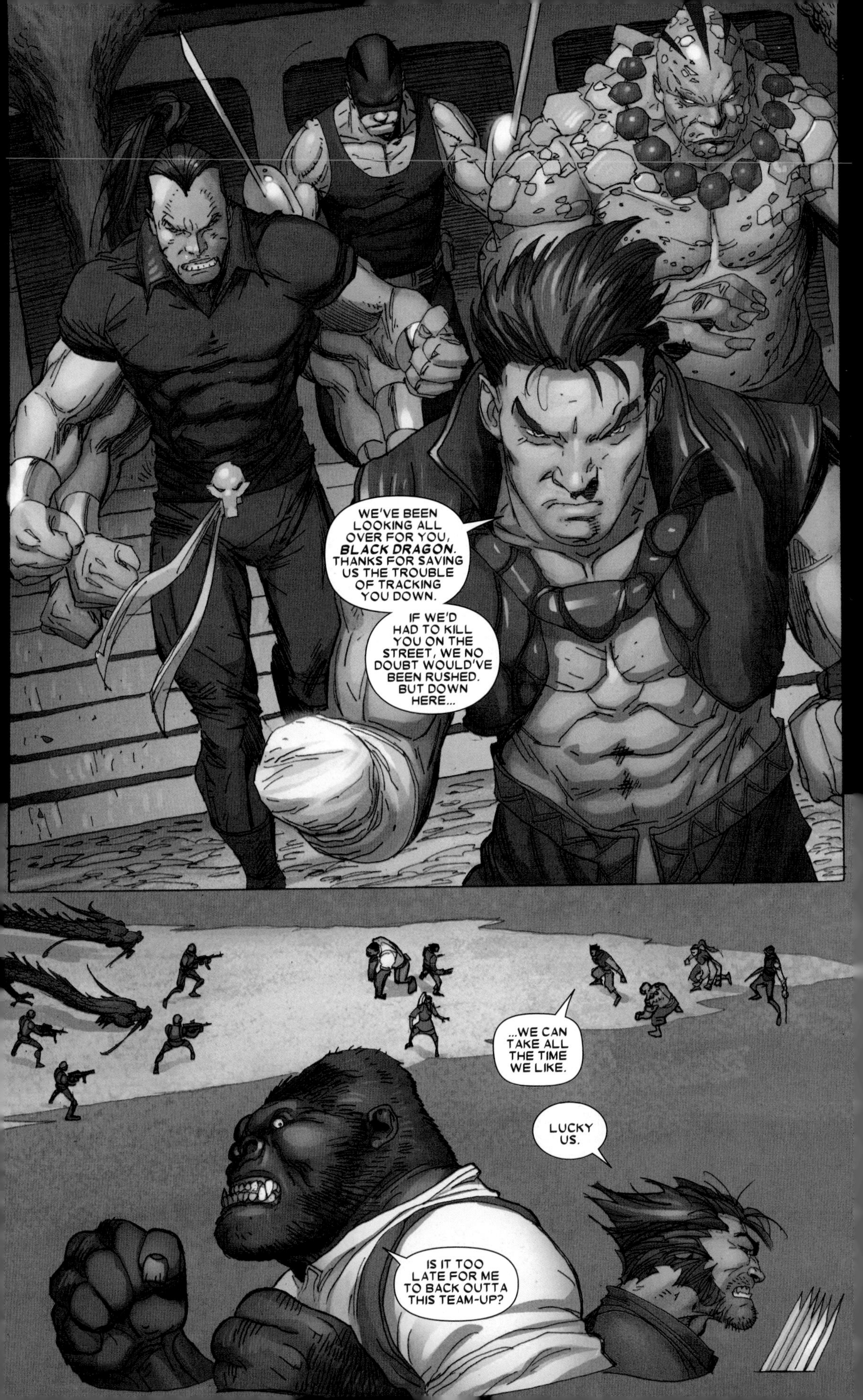
WE'VE BEEN LOOKING ALL OVER FOR YOU, BLACK DRAGON. THANKS FOR SAVING US THE TROUBLE OF TRACKING YOU DOWN.
IF WE'D HAD TO KILL YOU ON THE STREET, WE NO DOUBT WOULD'VE BEEN RUSHED. BUT DOWN HERE...
...WE CAN TAKE ALL THE TIME WE LIKE.
LUCKY US.
IS IT TOO LATE FOR ME TO BACK OUTTA THIS TEAM-UP?

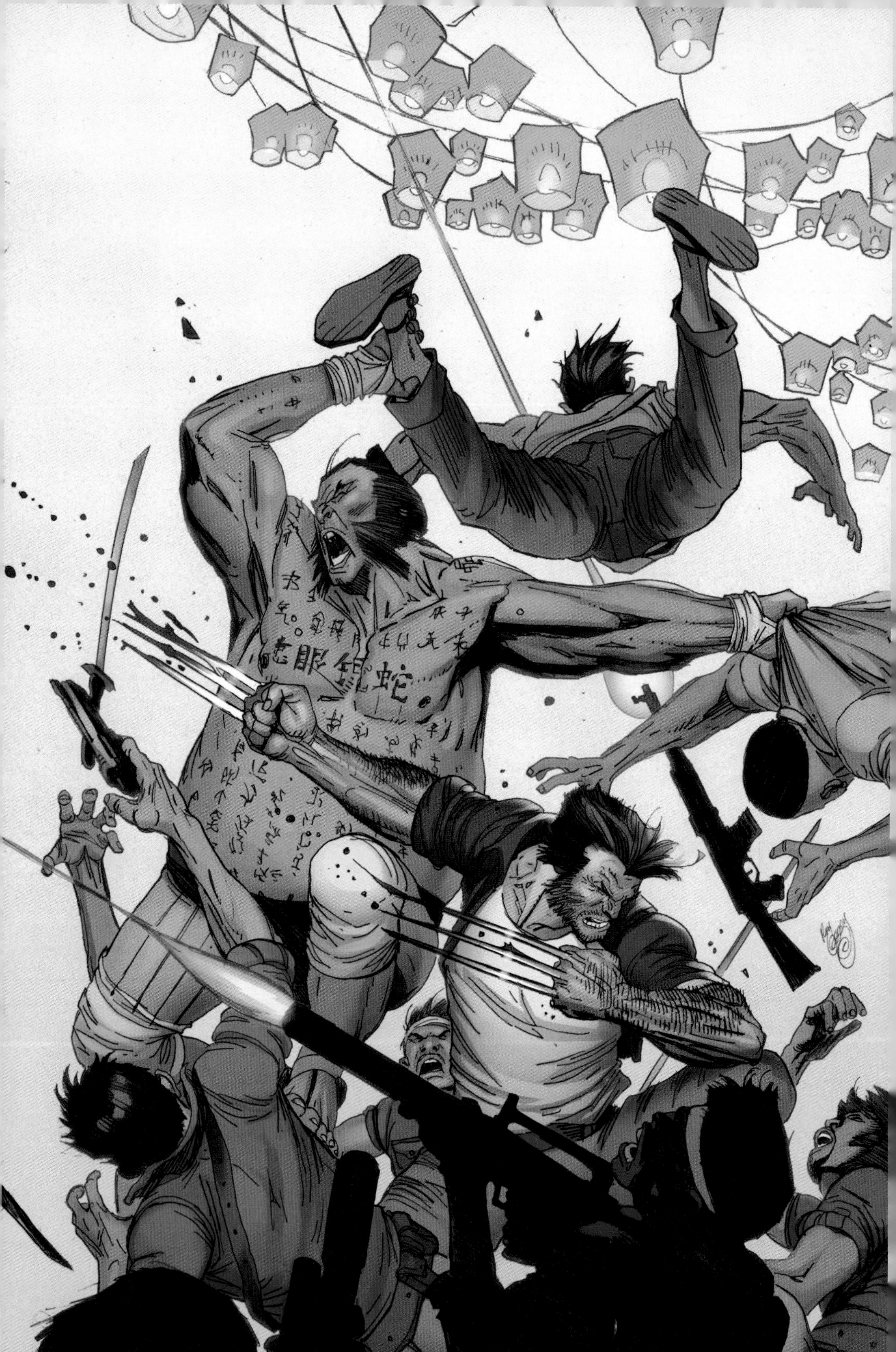

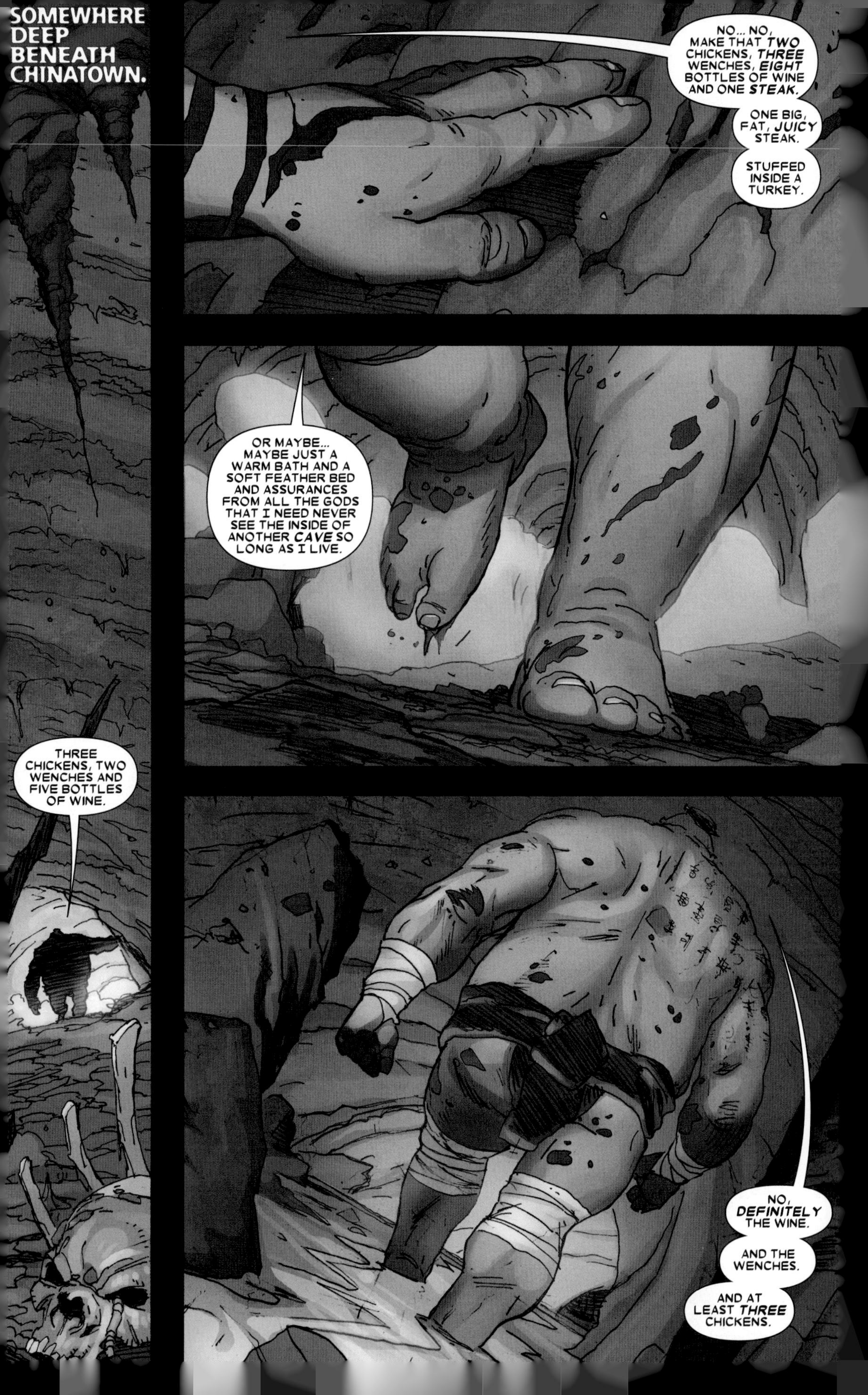
SOMEWHERE DEEP BENEATH CHINATOWN.
NO... NO, MAKE THAT TWO CHICKENS, THREE WENCHES, EIGHT BOTTLES OF WINE AND ONE STEAK.
ONE BIG, FAT, JUICY STEAK.
STUFFED INSIDE A TURKEY.
OR MAYBE... MAYBE JUST A WARM BATH AND A SOFT FEATHER BED AND ASSURANCES FROM ALL THE GODS THAT I NEED NEVER SEE THE INSIDE OF ANOTHER CAVE SO LONG AS I LIVE.
THREE CHICKENS, TWO WENCHES AND FIVE BOTTLES OF WINE.
NO, DEFINITELY THE WINE.
AND THE WENCHES.
AND AT LEAST THREE CHICKENS.

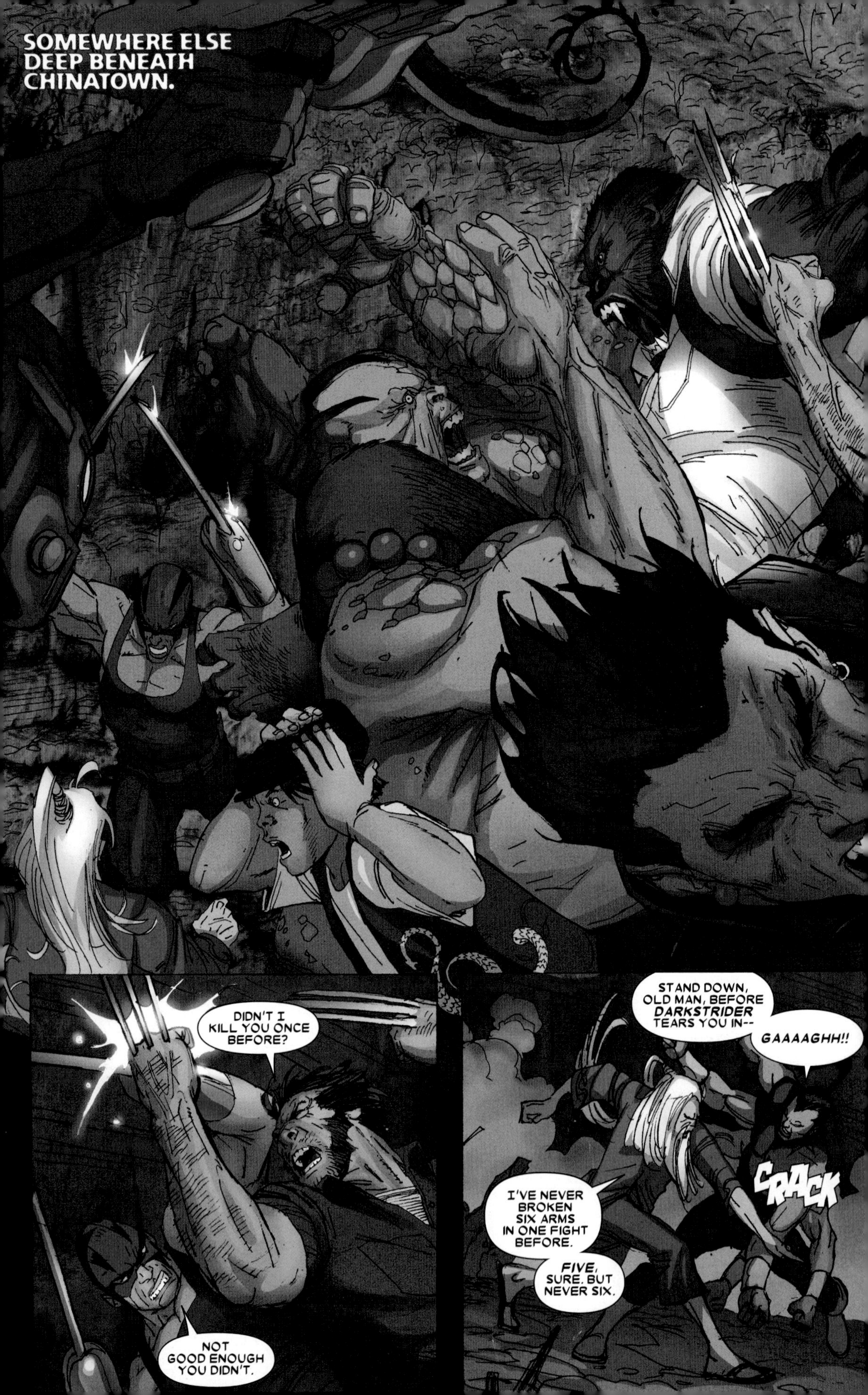
SOMEWHERE ELSE DEEP BENEATH CHINATOWN.
DIDN'T I KILL YOU ONCE BEFORE?
NOT GOOD ENOUGH YOU DIDN'T.
STAND DOWN, OLD MAN, BEFORE DARKSTRIDER TEARS YOU IN--
GAAAAGHH!!
CRACK
I'VE NEVER BROKEN SIX ARMS IN ONE FIGHT BEFORE.
FIVE, SURE. BUT NEVER SIX.

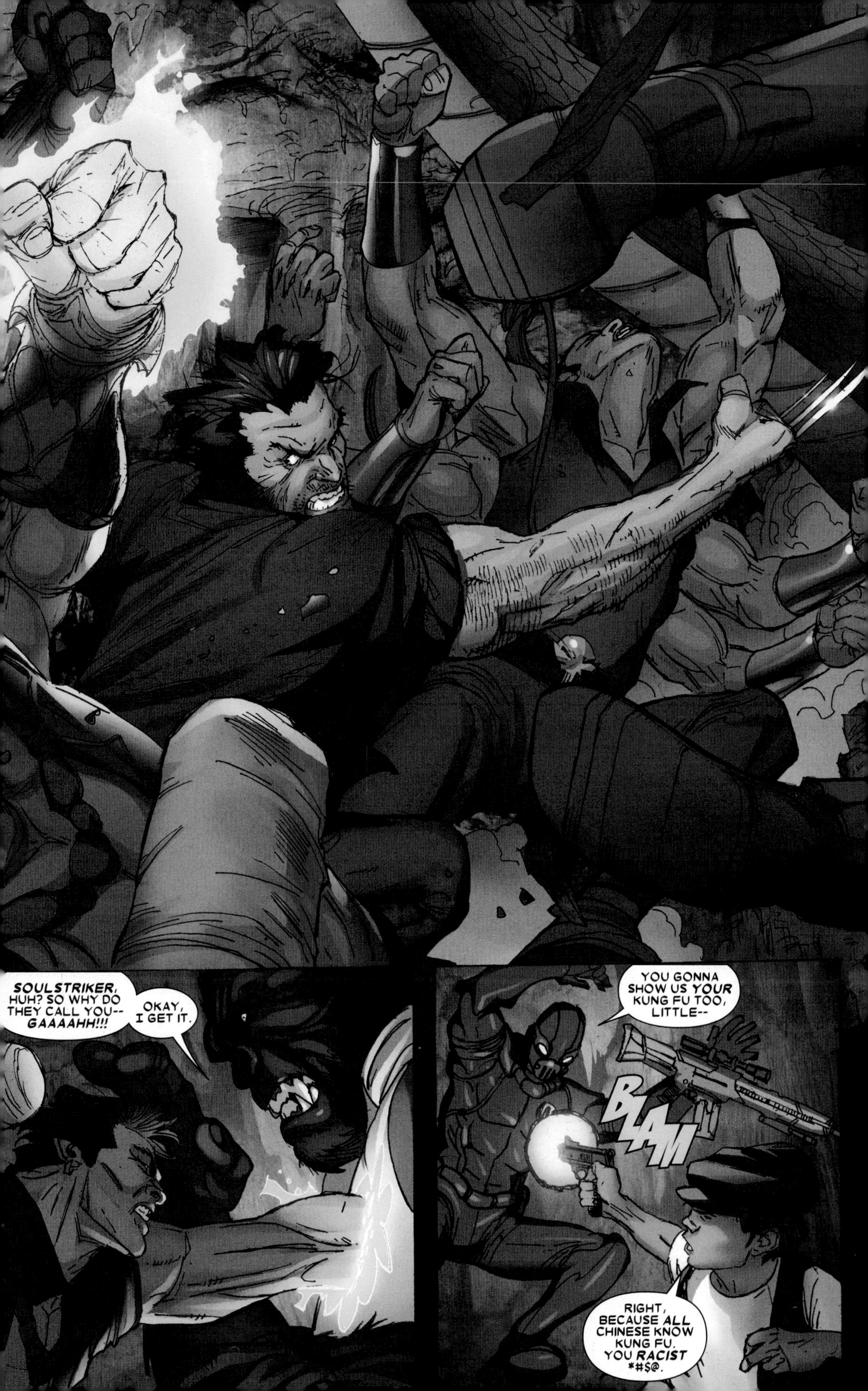
SOULSTRIKER, HUH? SO WHY DO THEY CALL YOU-- GAAAAHH!!!
OKAY, I GET IT.
YOU GONNA SHOW US YOUR KUNG FU TOO, LITTLE--
BLAM
RIGHT, BECAUSE ALL CHINESE KNOW KUNG FU. YOU RACIST *#$@.

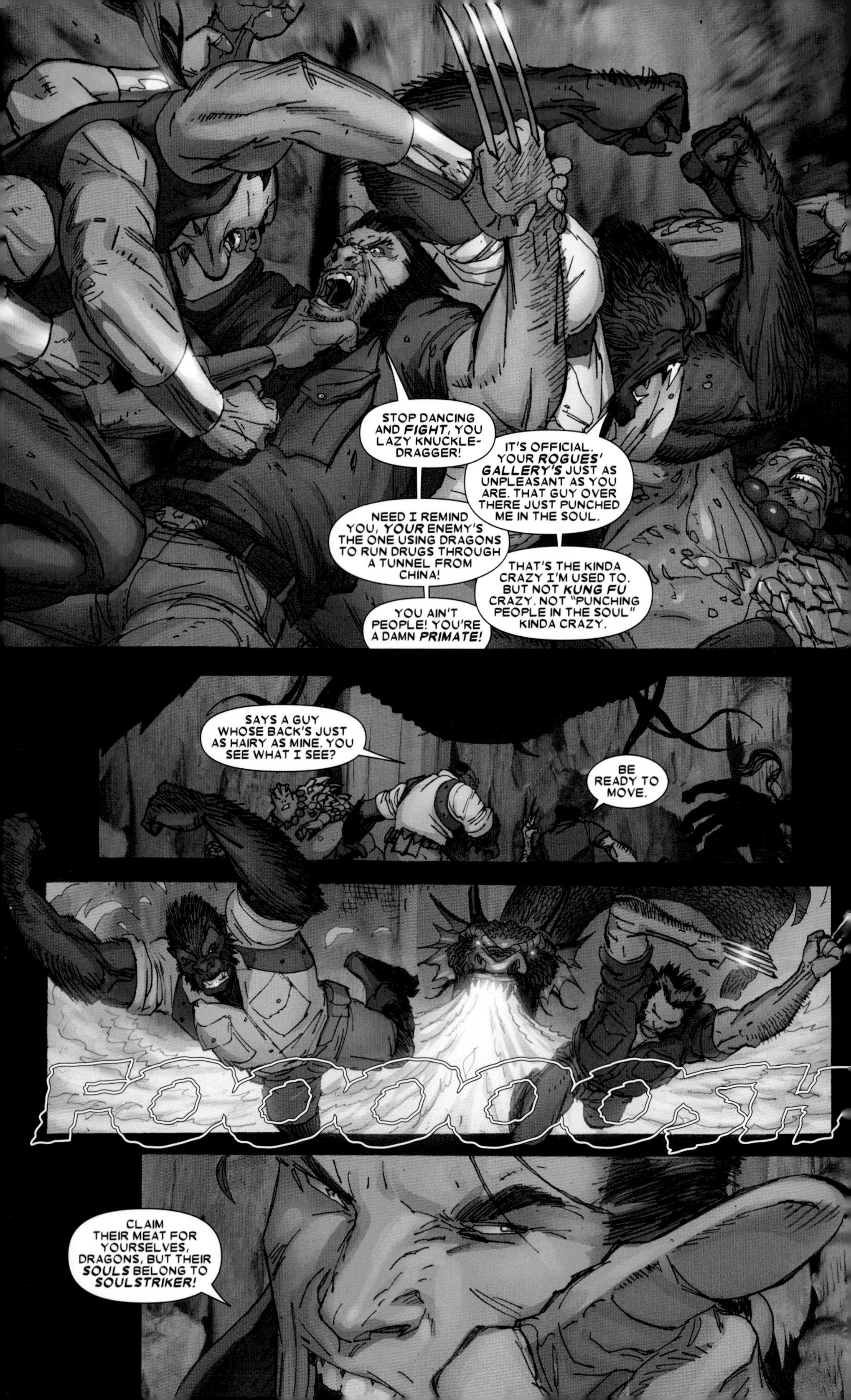
STOP DANCING AND FIGHT, YOU LAZY KNUCKLE-DRAGGER!
IT'S OFFICIAL. YOUR ROGUES' GALLERY'S JUST AS UNPLEASANT AS YOU ARE. THAT GUY OVER THERE JUST PUNCHED ME IN THE SOUL.
NEED I REMIND YOU, YOUR ENEMY'S THE ONE USING DRAGONS TO RUN DRUGS THROUGH A TUNNEL FROM CHINA!
THAT'S THE KINDA CRAZY I'M USED TO. BUT NOT KUNG FU CRAZY. NOT "PUNCHING PEOPLE IN THE SOUL" KINDA CRAZY.
YOU AIN'T PEOPLE! YOU'RE A DAMN PRIMATE!
SAYS A GUY WHOSE BACK'S JUST AS HAIRY AS MINE. YOU SEE WHAT I SEE?
BE READY TO MOVE.
FOOOOOOOSH
CLAIM THEIR MEAT FOR YOURSELVES, DRAGONS, BUT THEIR SOULS BELONG TO SOULSTRIKER!

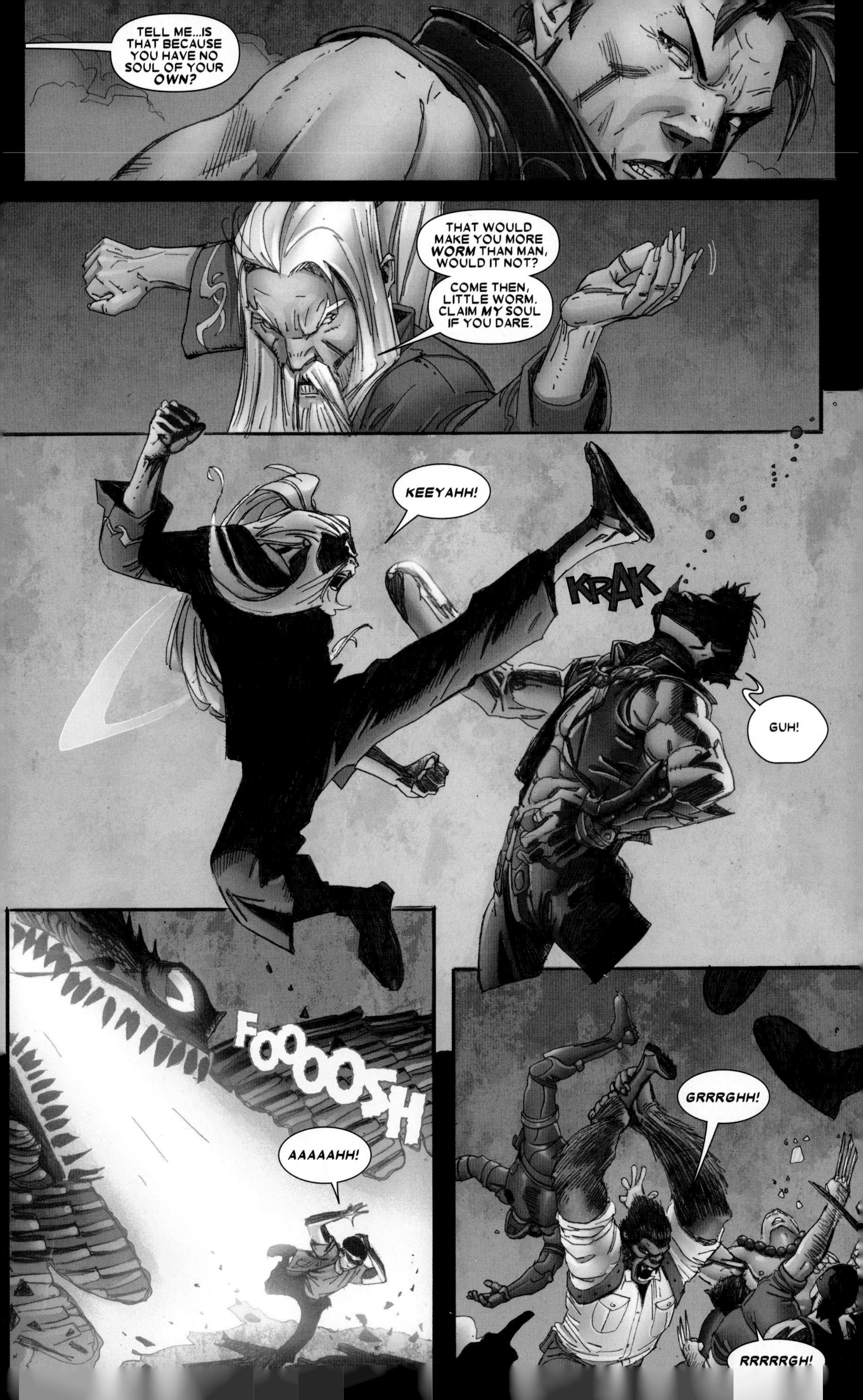
TELL ME...IS THAT BECAUSE YOU HAVE NO SOUL OF YOUR OWN?
THAT WOULD MAKE YOU MORE WORM THAN MAN, WOULD IT NOT?
COME THEN, LITTLE WORM. CLAIM MY SOUL IF YOU DARE.
KEEYAHH!
KRAK
GUH!
FOOOOSH
AAAAAHH!
GRRRGHH!
RRRRRGH!

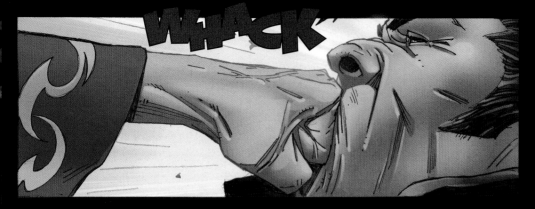

WHACK

YOU HAVE DISHONORED YOURSELF AND YOUR FAMILY HERE TODAY. WHAT YOU HAVE DONE TO THESE *NOBLE DRAGONS*, FORCING THEM TO SERVE AS YOUR DRUG-FERRYING BEASTS OF BURDEN, WILL FOREVER BE YOUR SHAME.

NOBLE, YOU SAY?

YOU DON'T KNOW MUCH ABOUT DRAGONS, OLD MAN.

SNORT

ENOUGH!

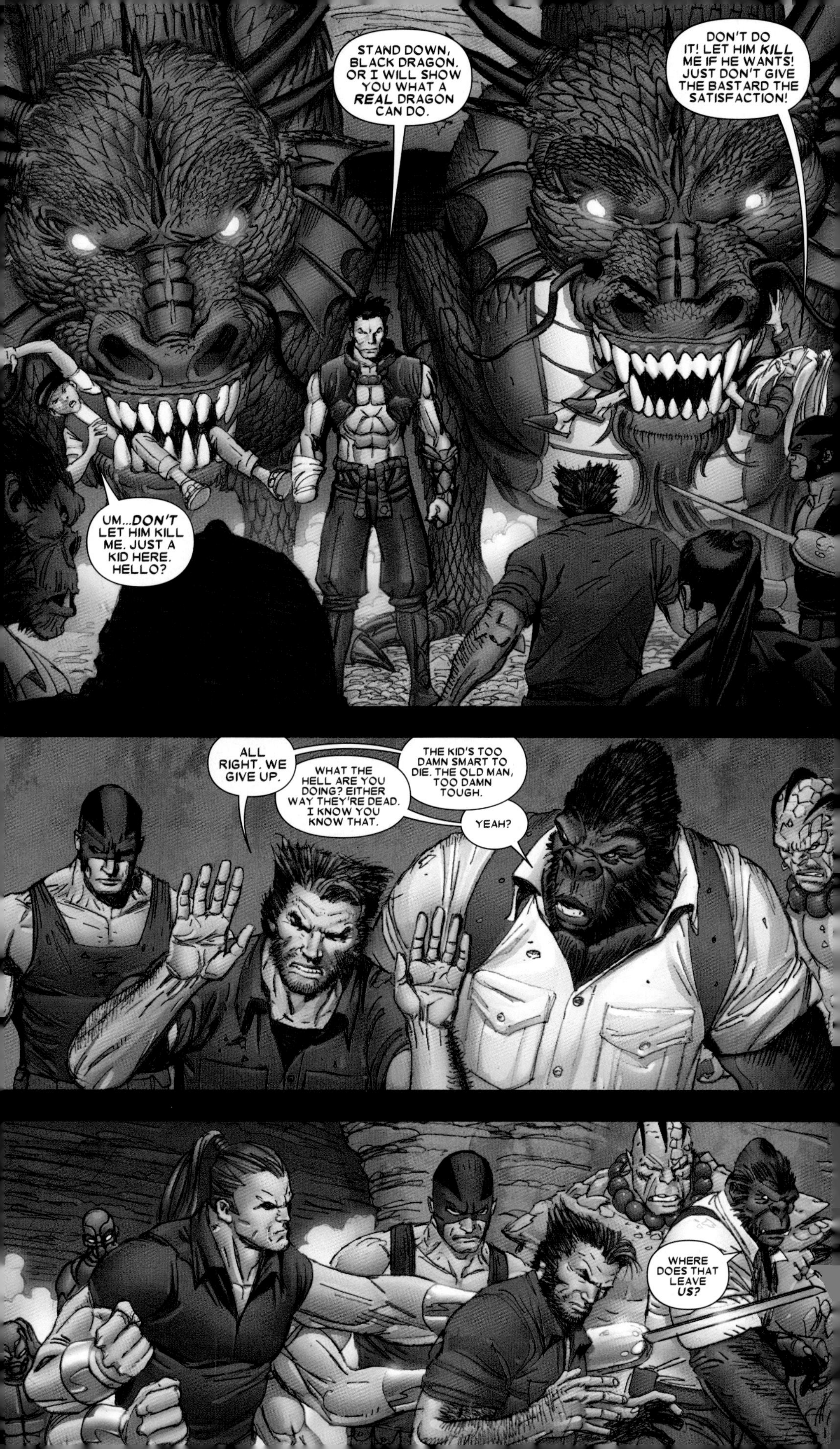
STAND DOWN, BLACK DRAGON. OR I WILL SHOW YOU WHAT A REAL DRAGON CAN DO.
DON'T DO IT! LET HIM KILL ME IF HE WANTS! JUST DON'T GIVE THE BASTARD THE SATISFACTION!
UM...DON'T LET HIM KILL ME. JUST A KID HERE. HELLO?
ALL RIGHT. WE GIVE UP.
WHAT THE HELL ARE YOU DOING? EITHER WAY THEY'RE DEAD. I KNOW YOU KNOW THAT.
THE KID'S TOO DAMN SMART TO DIE. THE OLD MAN, TOO DAMN TOUGH.
YEAH?
WHERE DOES THAT LEAVE US?

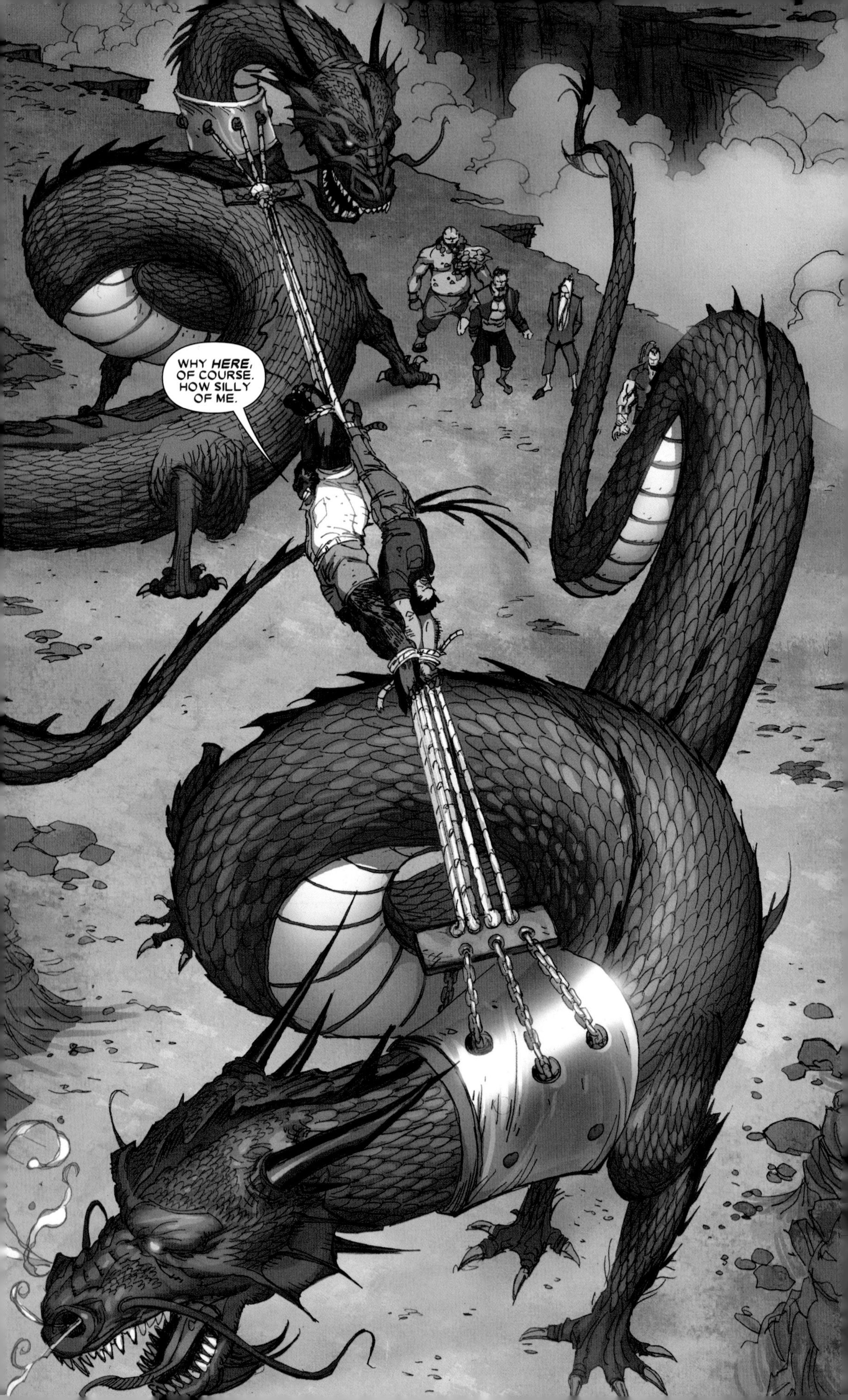
WHY *HERE*, OF COURSE. HOW SILLY OF ME.

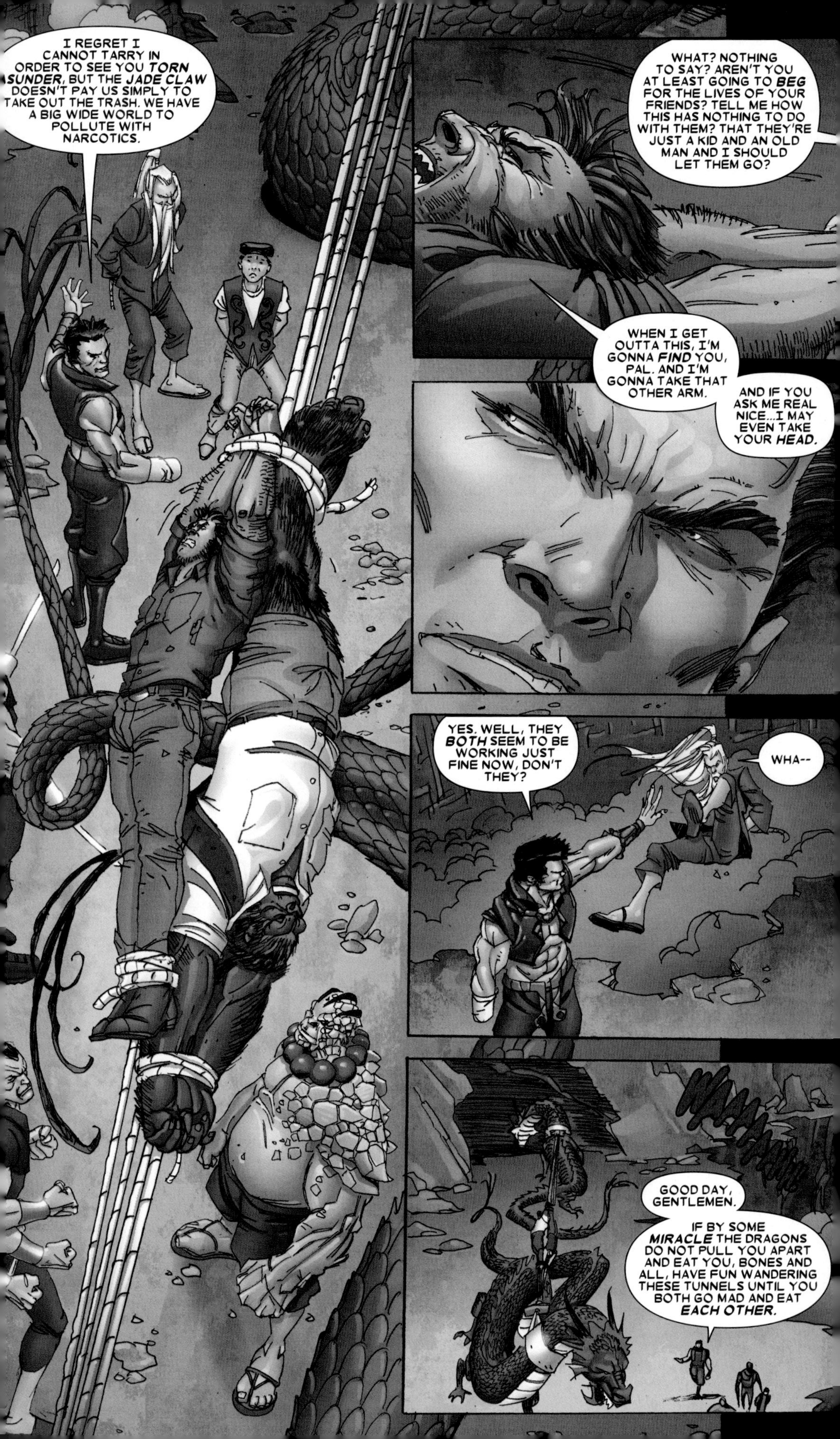

I REGRET I CANNOT TARRY IN ORDER TO SEE YOU TORN ASUNDER, BUT THE JADE CLAW DOESN'T PAY US SIMPLY TO TAKE OUT THE TRASH. WE HAVE A BIG WIDE WORLD TO POLLUTE WITH NARCOTICS.
WHAT? NOTHING TO SAY? AREN'T YOU AT LEAST GOING TO BEG FOR THE LIVES OF YOUR FRIENDS? TELL ME HOW THIS HAS NOTHING TO DO WITH THEM? THAT THEY'RE JUST A KID AND AN OLD MAN AND I SHOULD LET THEM GO?
WHEN I GET OUTTA THIS, I'M GONNA FIND YOU, PAL. AND I'M GONNA TAKE THAT OTHER ARM.
AND IF YOU ASK ME REAL NICE...I MAY EVEN TAKE YOUR HEAD.
YES. WELL, THEY BOTH SEEM TO BE WORKING JUST FINE NOW, DON'T THEY?
WHA--
GOOD DAY, GENTLEMEN.
IF BY SOME MIRACLE THE DRAGONS DO NOT PULL YOU APART AND EAT YOU, BONES AND ALL, HAVE FUN WANDERING THESE TUNNELS UNTIL YOU BOTH GO MAD AND EAT EACH OTHER.

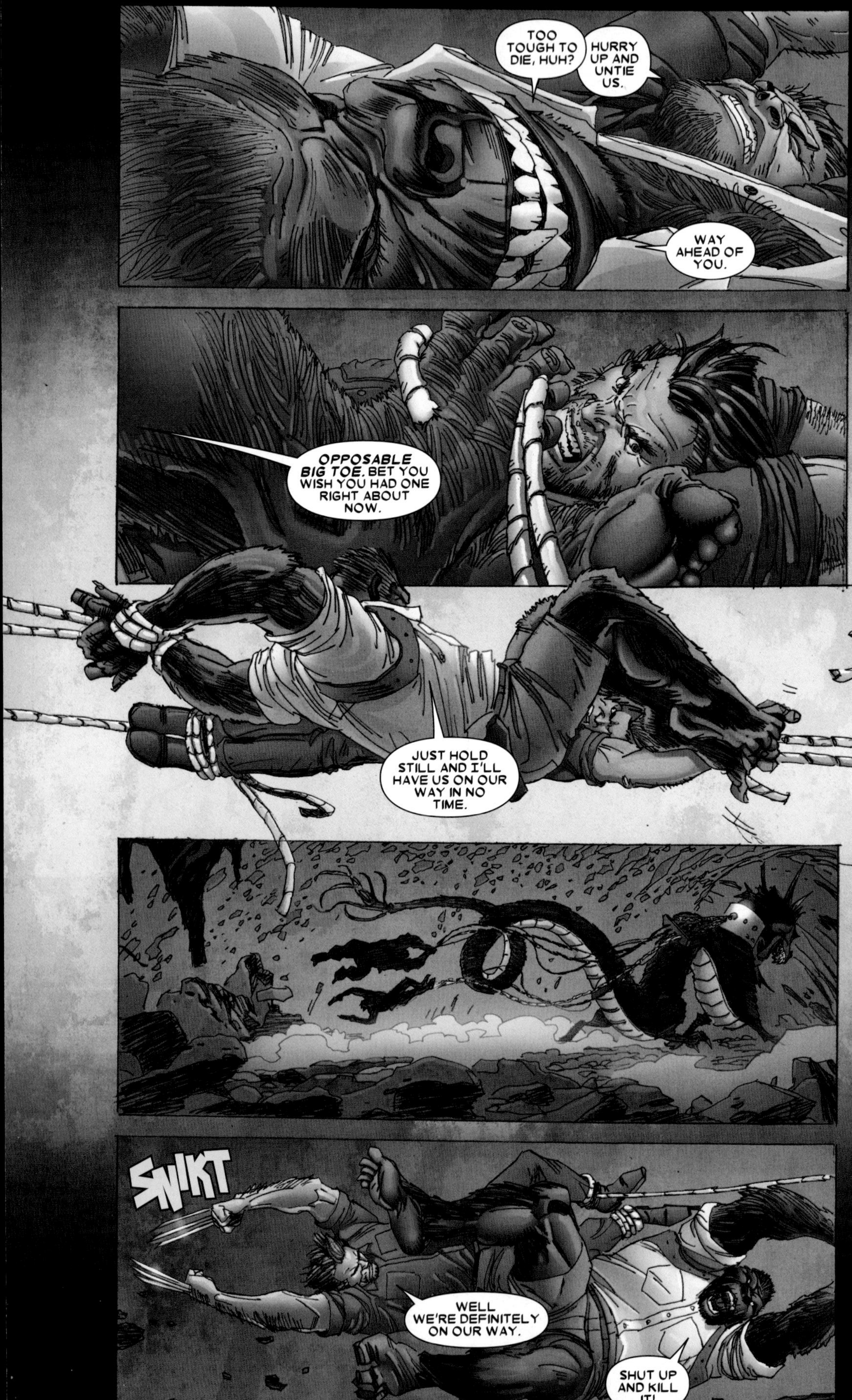
TOO TOUGH TO DIE, HUH?
HURRY UP AND UNTIE US.
WAY AHEAD OF YOU.
OPPOSABLE BIG TOE. BET YOU WISH YOU HAD ONE RIGHT ABOUT NOW.
JUST HOLD STILL AND I'LL HAVE US ON OUR WAY IN NO TIME.
SNIKT
WELL WE'RE DEFINITELY ON OUR WAY.
SHUT UP AND KILL IT!

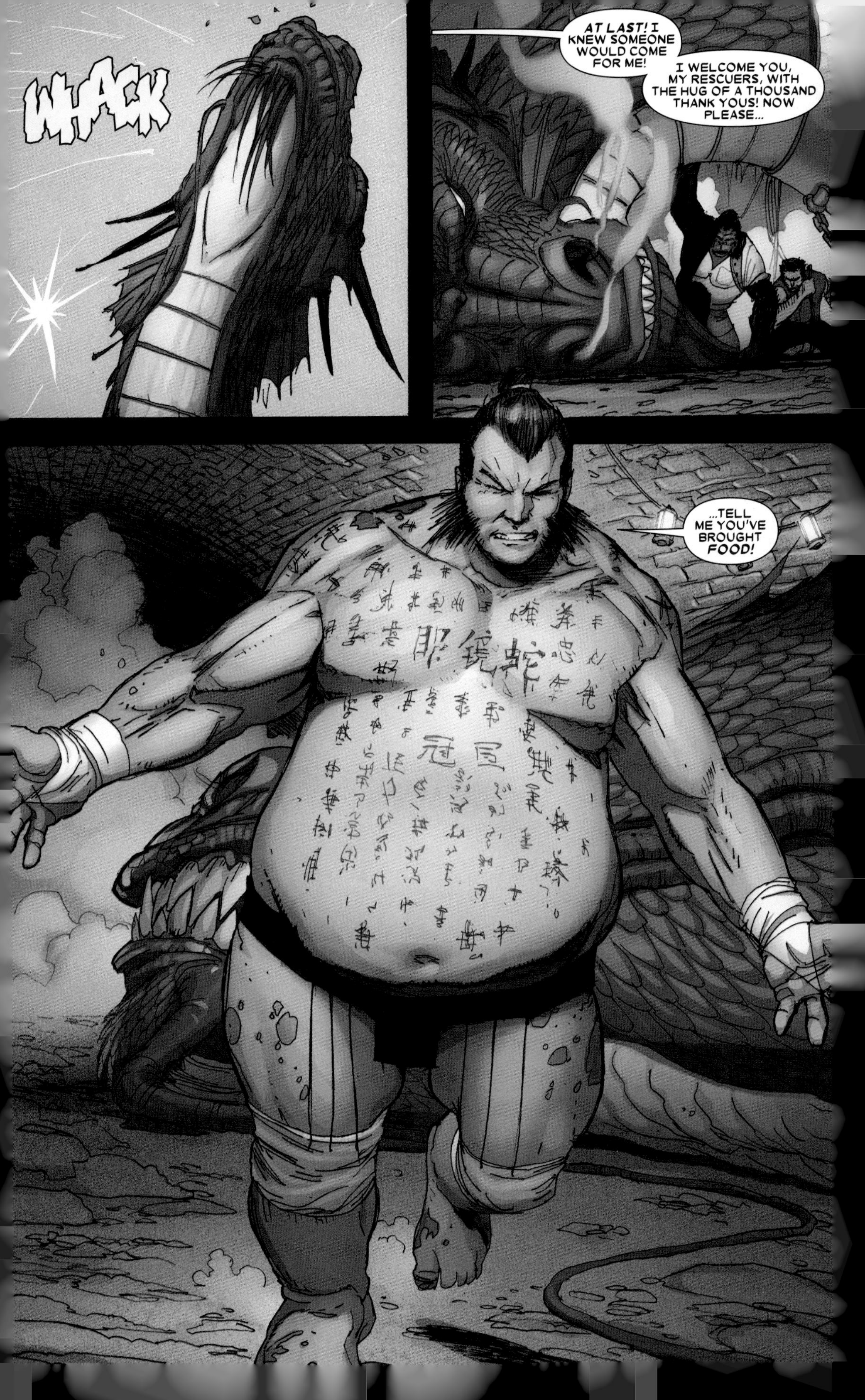
WHACK
AT LAST! I KNEW SOMEONE WOULD COME FOR ME!
I WELCOME YOU, MY RESCUERS, WITH THE HUG OF A THOUSAND THANK YOUS! NOW PLEASE...
...TELL ME YOU'VE BROUGHT FOOD!

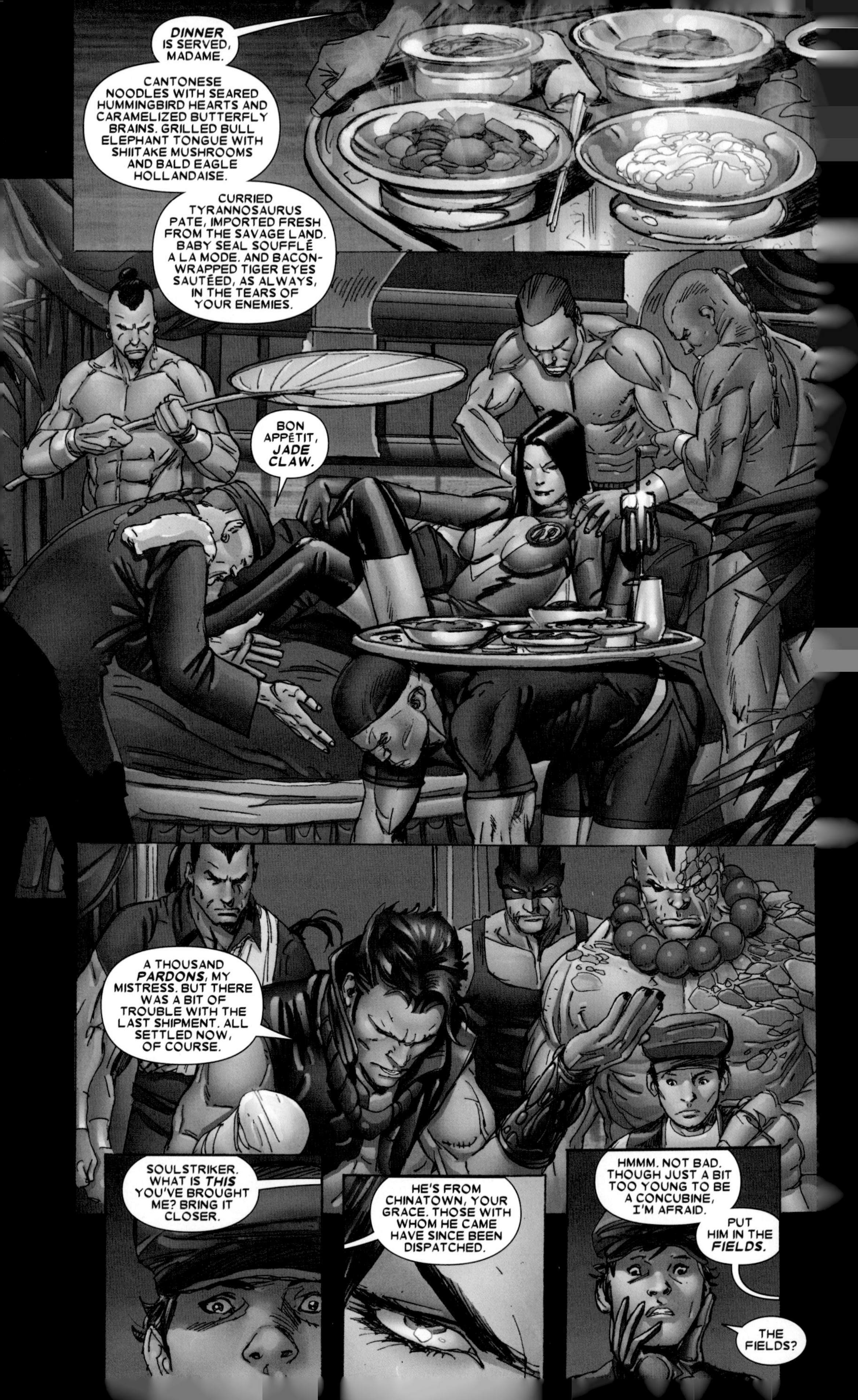
DINNER IS SERVED, MADAME.
CANTONESE NOODLES WITH SEARED HUMMINGBIRD HEARTS AND CARAMELIZED BUTTERFLY BRAINS. GRILLED BULL ELEPHANT TONGUE WITH SHIITAKE MUSHROOMS AND BALD EAGLE HOLLANDAISE.
CURRIED TYRANNOSAURUS PATE, IMPORTED FRESH FROM THE SAVAGE LAND. BABY SEAL SOUFFLÉ A LA MODE. AND BACON-WRAPPED TIGER EYES SAUTÉED, AS ALWAYS, IN THE TEARS OF YOUR ENEMIES.
BON APPÉTIT, JADE CLAW.
A THOUSAND PARDONS, MY MISTRESS. BUT THERE WAS A BIT OF TROUBLE WITH THE LAST SHIPMENT. ALL SETTLED NOW, OF COURSE.
SOULSTRIKER. WHAT IS THIS YOU'VE BROUGHT ME? BRING IT CLOSER.
HE'S FROM CHINATOWN, YOUR GRACE. THOSE WITH WHOM HE CAME HAVE SINCE BEEN DISPATCHED.
HMMM. NOT BAD. THOUGH JUST A BIT TOO YOUNG TO BE A CONCUBINE, I'M AFRAID.
PUT HIM IN THE FIELDS.
THE FIELDS?

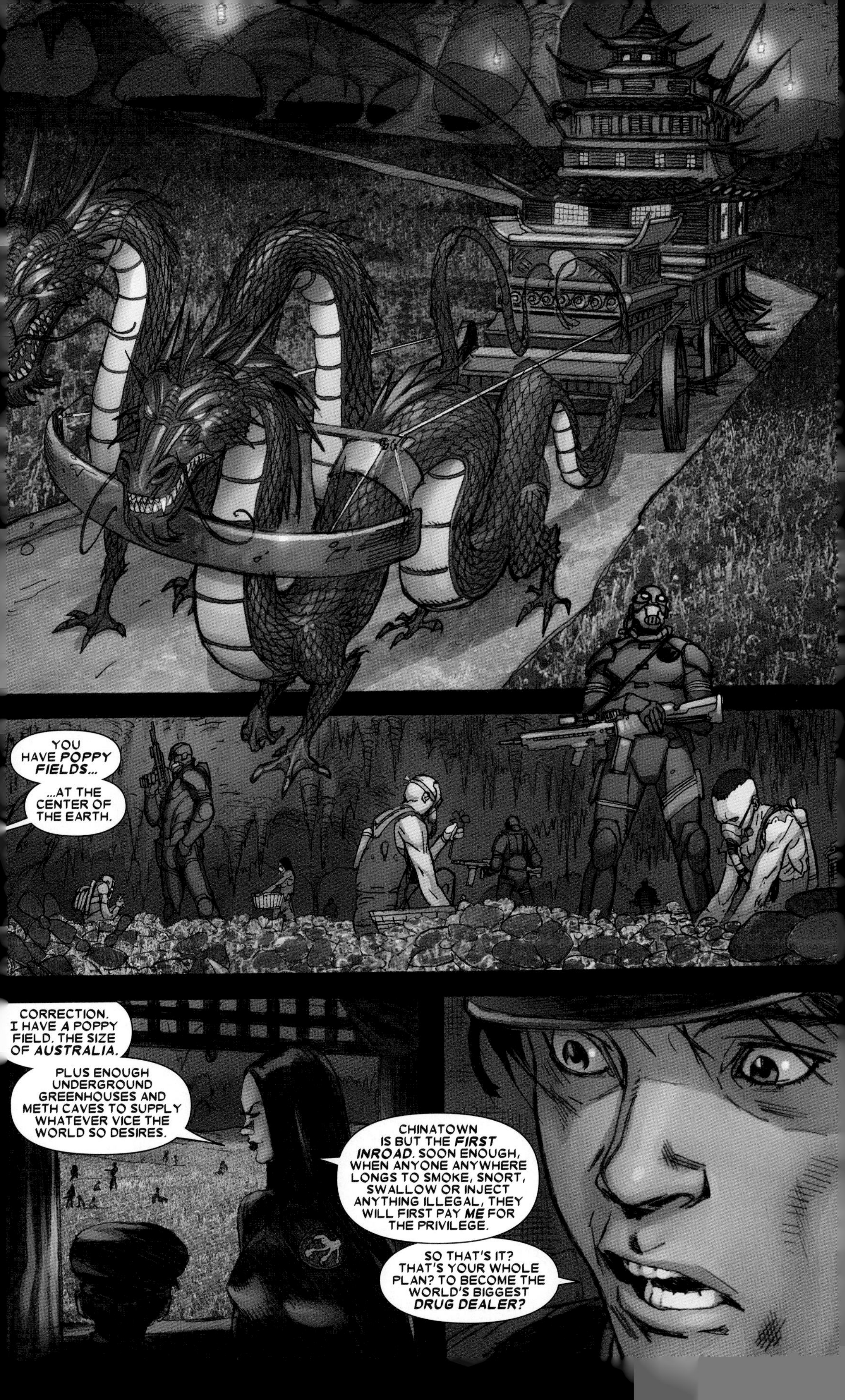
YOU HAVE POPPY FIELDS...
...AT THE CENTER OF THE EARTH.
CORRECTION. I HAVE A POPPY FIELD. THE SIZE OF AUSTRALIA.
PLUS ENOUGH UNDERGROUND GREENHOUSES AND METH CAVES TO SUPPLY WHATEVER VICE THE WORLD SO DESIRES.
CHINATOWN IS BUT THE FIRST INROAD. SOON ENOUGH, WHEN ANYONE ANYWHERE LONGS TO SMOKE, SNORT, SWALLOW OR INJECT ANYTHING ILLEGAL, THEY WILL FIRST PAY ME FOR THE PRIVILEGE.
SO THAT'S IT? THAT'S YOUR WHOLE PLAN? TO BECOME THE WORLD'S BIGGEST DRUG DEALER?

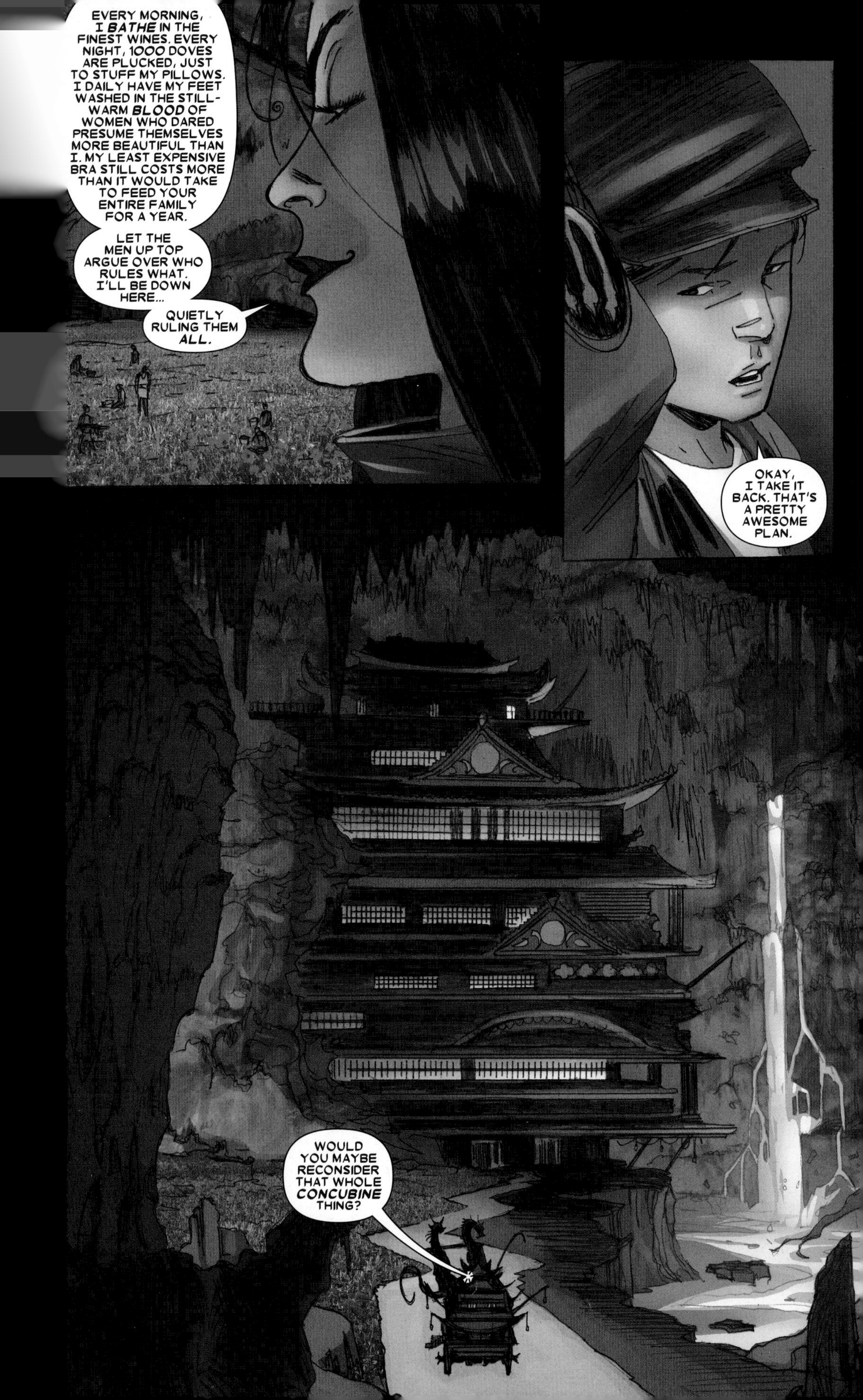
EVERY MORNING, I BATHE IN THE FINEST WINES. EVERY NIGHT, 1000 DOVES ARE PLUCKED, JUST TO STUFF MY PILLOWS. I DAILY HAVE MY FEET WASHED IN THE STILL-WARM BLOOD OF WOMEN WHO DARED PRESUME THEMSELVES MORE BEAUTIFUL THAN I. MY LEAST EXPENSIVE BRA STILL COSTS MORE THAN IT WOULD TAKE TO FEED YOUR ENTIRE FAMILY FOR A YEAR.
LET THE MEN UP TOP ARGUE OVER WHO RULES WHAT. I'LL BE DOWN HERE...
QUIETLY RULING THEM ALL.
OKAY, I TAKE IT BACK. THAT'S A PRETTY AWESOME PLAN.
WOULD YOU MAYBE RECONSIDER THAT WHOLE CONCUBINE THING?

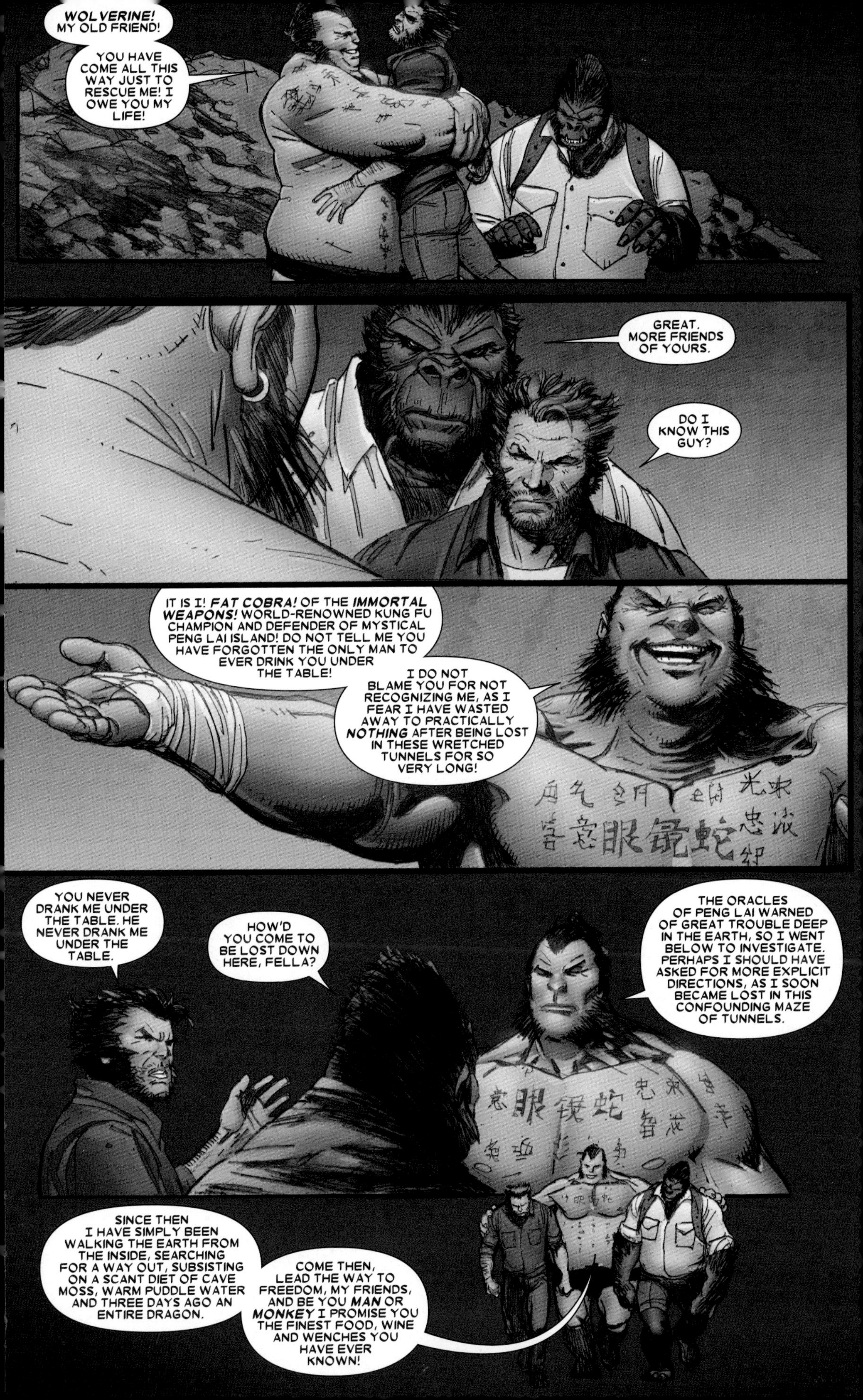
WOLVERINE! MY OLD FRIEND!
YOU HAVE COME ALL THIS WAY JUST TO RESCUE ME! I OWE YOU MY LIFE!
GREAT. MORE FRIENDS OF YOURS.
DO I KNOW THIS GUY?
IT IS I! FAT COBRA! OF THE IMMORTAL WEAPONS! WORLD-RENOWNED KUNG FU CHAMPION AND DEFENDER OF MYSTICAL PENG LAI ISLAND! DO NOT TELL ME YOU HAVE FORGOTTEN THE ONLY MAN TO EVER DRINK YOU UNDER THE TABLE!
I DO NOT BLAME YOU FOR NOT RECOGNIZING ME, AS I FEAR I HAVE WASTED AWAY TO PRACTICALLY NOTHING AFTER BEING LOST IN THESE WRETCHED TUNNELS FOR SO VERY LONG!
YOU NEVER DRANK ME UNDER THE TABLE. HE NEVER DRANK ME UNDER THE TABLE.
HOW'D YOU COME TO BE LOST DOWN HERE, FELLA?
THE ORACLES OF PENG LAI WARNED OF GREAT TROUBLE DEEP IN THE EARTH, SO I WENT BELOW TO INVESTIGATE. PERHAPS I SHOULD HAVE ASKED FOR MORE EXPLICIT DIRECTIONS, AS I SOON BECAME LOST IN THIS CONFOUNDING MAZE OF TUNNELS.
SINCE THEN I HAVE SIMPLY BEEN WALKING THE EARTH FROM THE INSIDE, SEARCHING FOR A WAY OUT, SUBSISTING ON A SCANT DIET OF CAVE MOSS, WARM PUDDLE WATER AND THREE DAYS AGO AN ENTIRE DRAGON.
COME THEN, LEAD THE WAY TO FREEDOM, MY FRIENDS, AND BE YOU MAN OR MONKEY I PROMISE YOU THE FINEST FOOD, WINE AND WENCHES YOU HAVE EVER KNOWN!

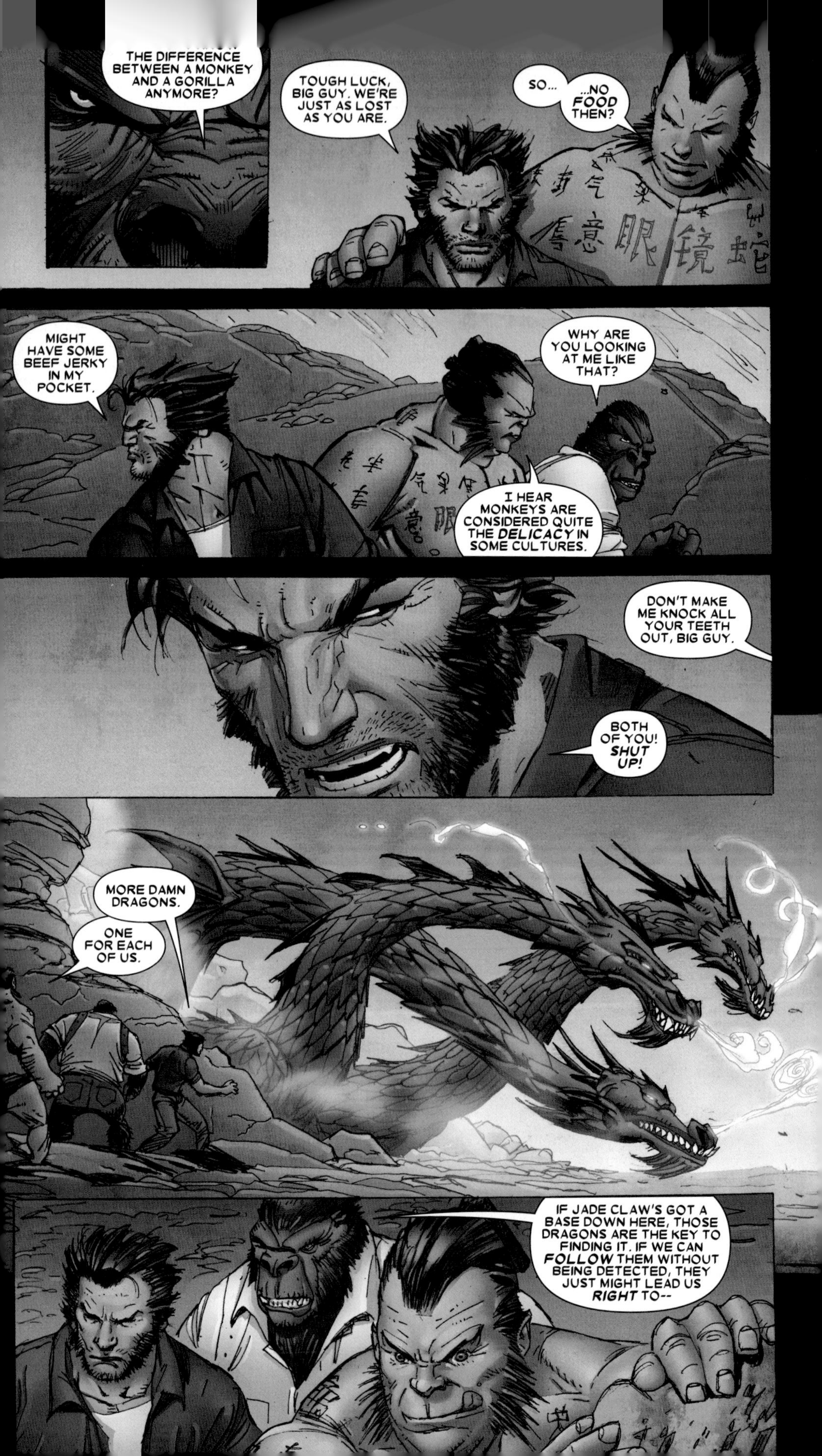
THE DIFFERENCE BETWEEN A MONKEY AND A GORILLA ANYMORE?
TOUGH LUCK, BIG GUY. WE'RE JUST AS LOST AS YOU ARE.
SO...
...NO FOOD THEN?
MIGHT HAVE SOME BEEF JERKY IN MY POCKET.
WHY ARE YOU LOOKING AT ME LIKE THAT?
I HEAR MONKEYS ARE CONSIDERED QUITE THE DELICACY IN SOME CULTURES.
DON'T MAKE ME KNOCK ALL YOUR TEETH OUT, BIG GUY.
BOTH OF YOU! SHUT UP!
MORE DAMN DRAGONS.
ONE FOR EACH OF US.
IF JADE CLAW'S GOT A BASE DOWN HERE, THOSE DRAGONS ARE THE KEY TO FINDING IT. IF WE CAN FOLLOW THEM WITHOUT BEING DETECTED, THEY JUST MIGHT LEAD US RIGHT TO--

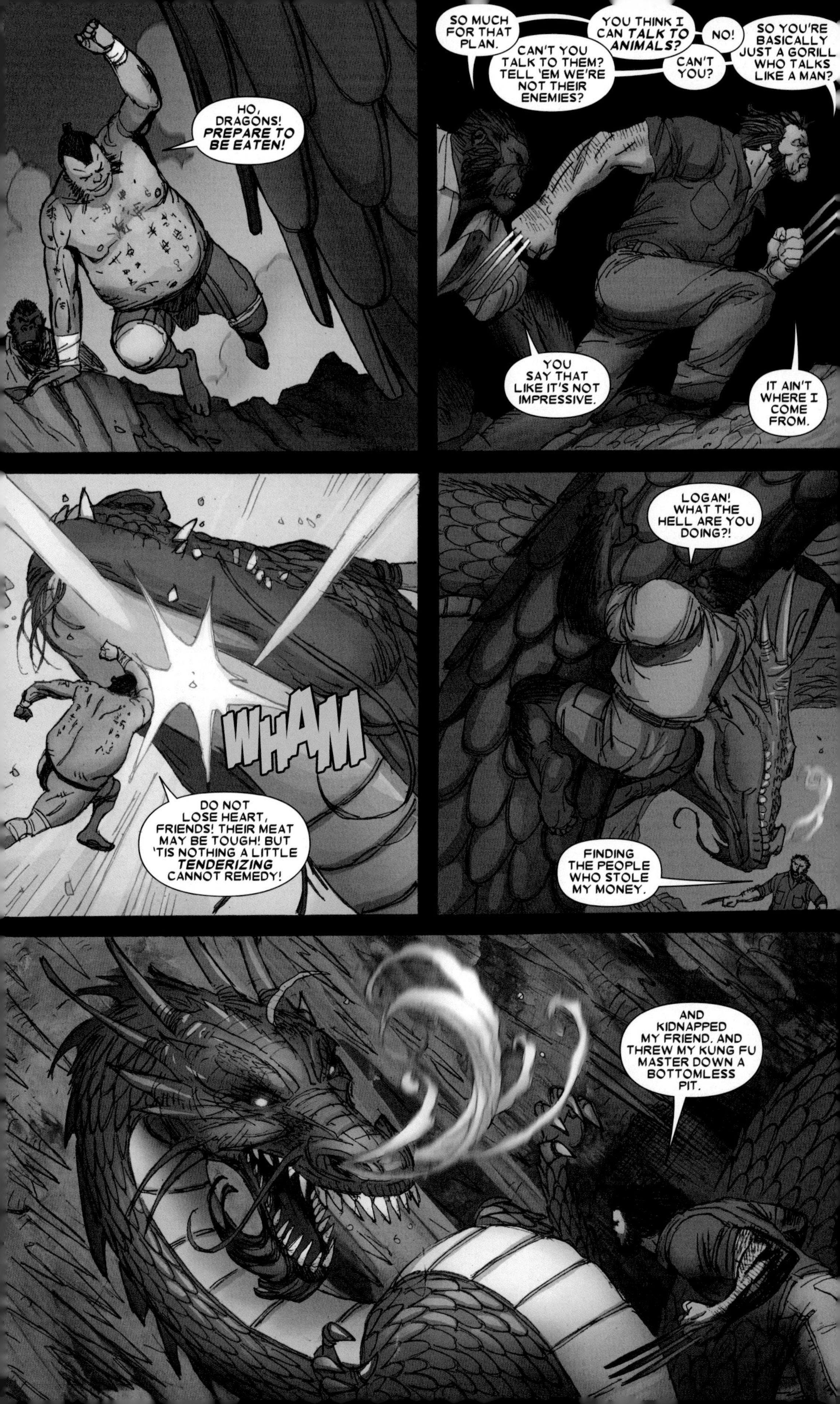
HO, DRAGONS! PREPARE TO BE EATEN!
SO MUCH FOR THAT PLAN.
CAN'T YOU TALK TO THEM? TELL 'EM WE'RE NOT THEIR ENEMIES?
YOU THINK I CAN TALK TO ANIMALS?
CAN'T YOU?
NO!
SO YOU'RE BASICALLY JUST A GORILL WHO TALKS LIKE A MAN?
YOU SAY THAT LIKE IT'S NOT IMPRESSIVE.
IT AIN'T WHERE I COME FROM.
WHAM
DO NOT LOSE HEART, FRIENDS! THEIR MEAT MAY BE TOUGH! BUT 'TIS NOTHING A LITTLE TENDERIZING CANNOT REMEDY!
LOGAN! WHAT THE HELL ARE YOU DOING?!
FINDING THE PEOPLE WHO STOLE MY MONEY.
AND KIDNAPPED MY FRIEND. AND THREW MY KUNG FU MASTER DOWN A BOTTOMLESS PIT.

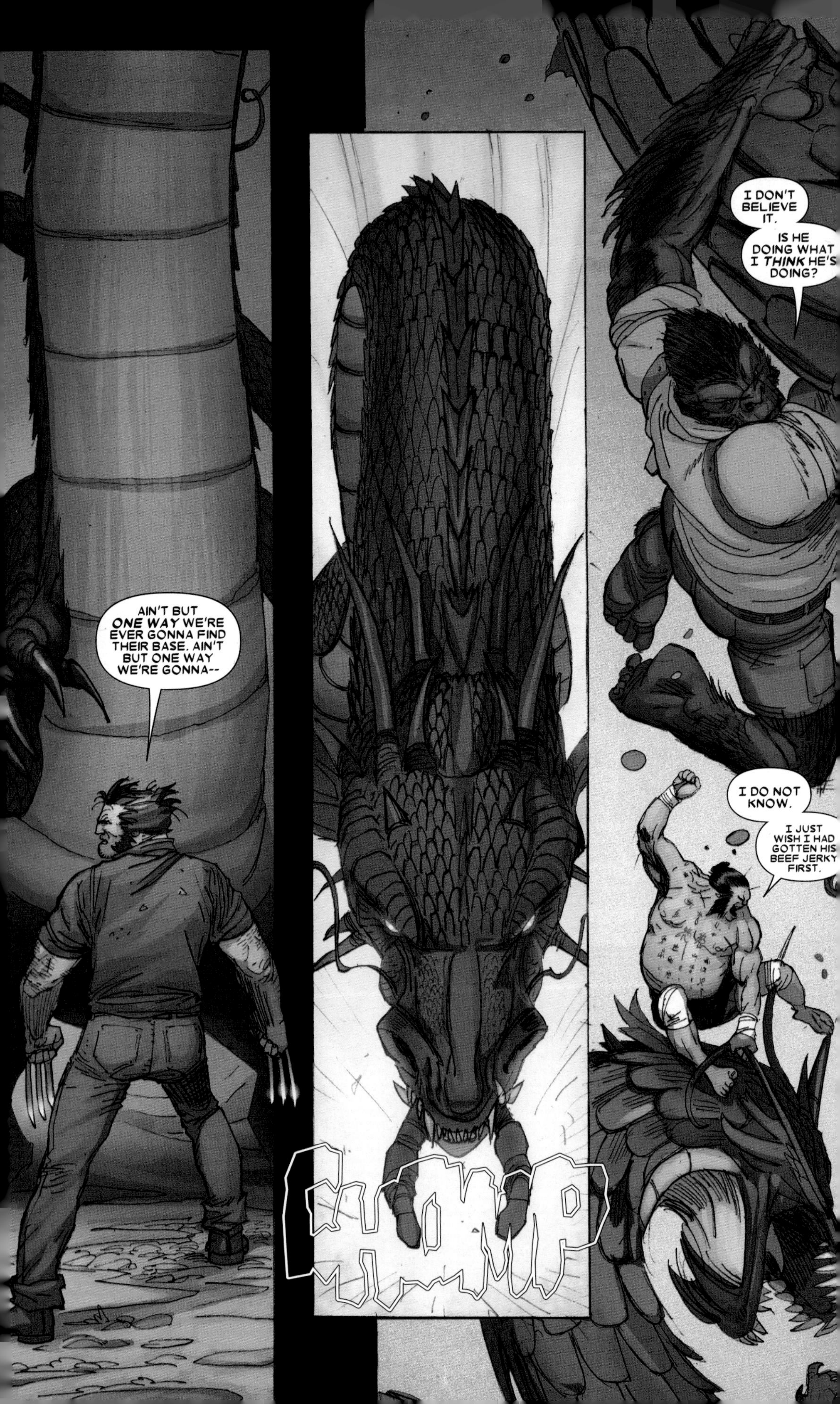
AIN'T BUT ONE WAY WE'RE EVER GONNA FIND THEIR BASE. AIN'T BUT ONE WAY WE'RE GONNA--
CHOMP
I DON'T BELIEVE IT.
IS HE DOING WHAT I THINK HE'S DOING?
I DO NOT KNOW.
I JUST WISH I HAD GOTTEN HIS BEEF JERKY FIRST.

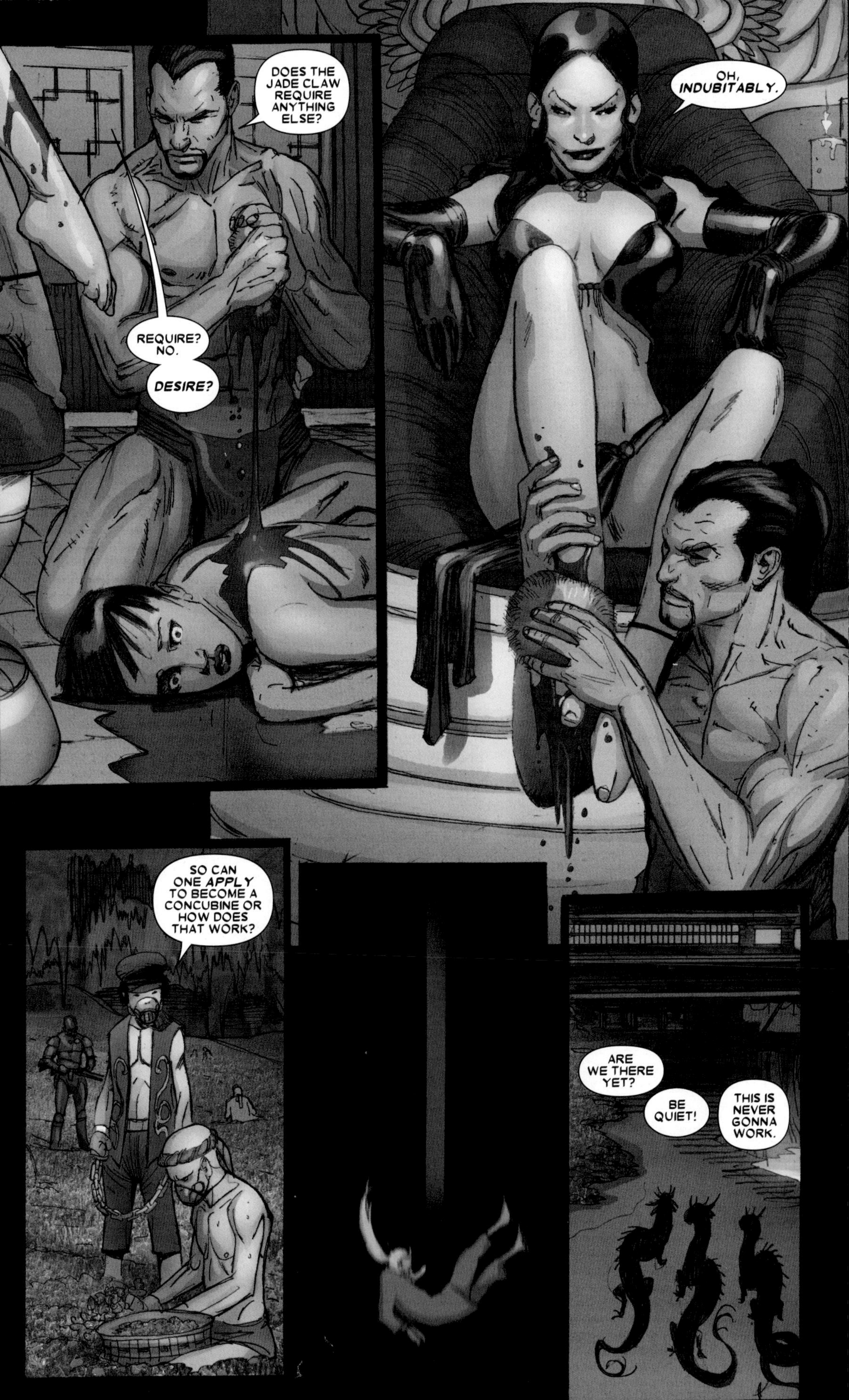
DOES THE JADE CLAW REQUIRE ANYTHING ELSE?
REQUIRE? NO.
DESIRE?
OH, *INDUBITABLY*.
SO CAN ONE *APPLY* TO BECOME A CONCUBINE OR HOW DOES THAT WORK?
ARE WE THERE YET?
BE QUIET!
THIS IS NEVER GONNA WORK.

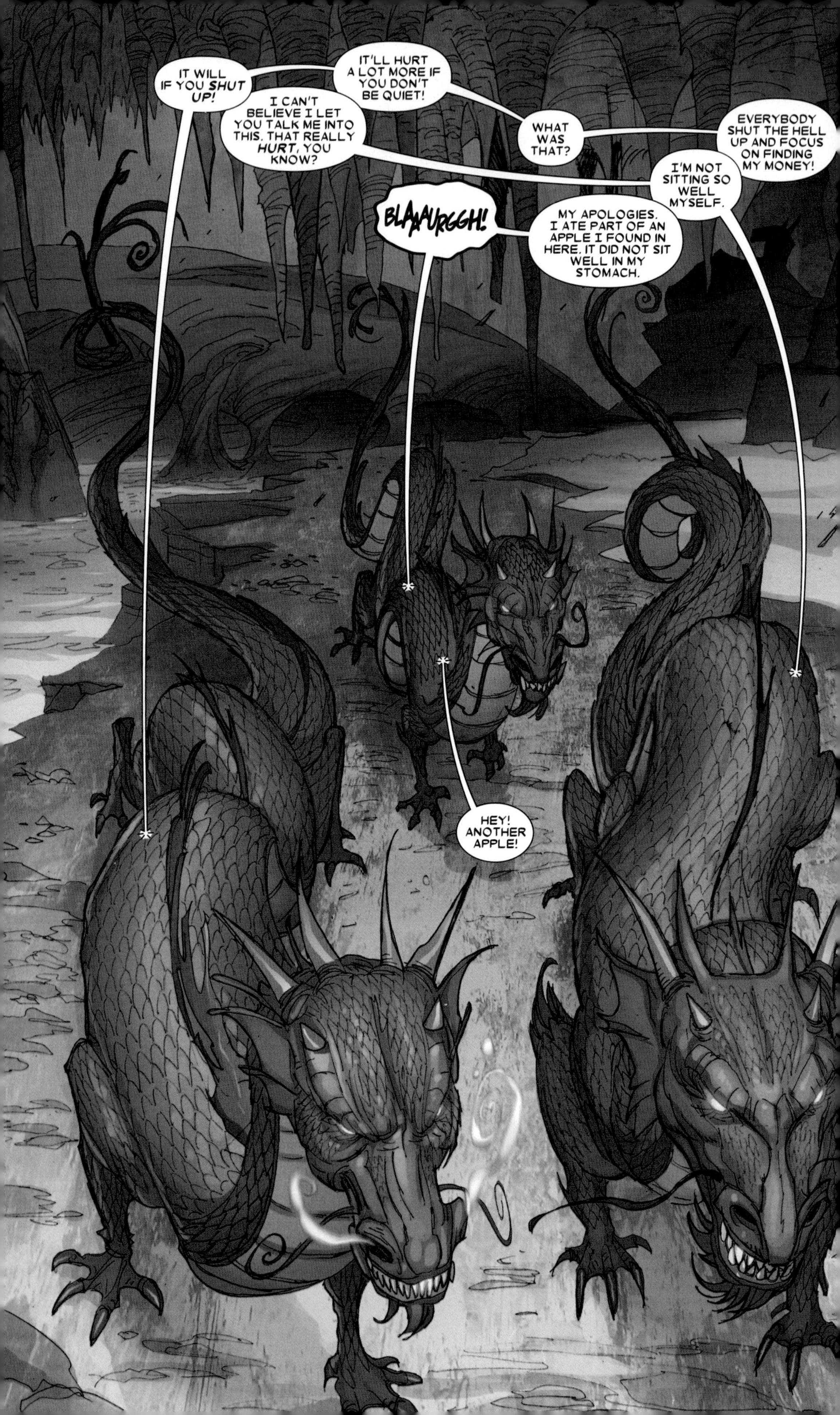
IT WILL IF YOU SHUT UP!
IT'LL HURT A LOT MORE IF YOU DON'T BE QUIET!
I CAN'T BELIEVE I LET YOU TALK ME INTO THIS. THAT REALLY HURT, YOU KNOW?
WHAT WAS THAT?
EVERYBODY SHUT THE HELL UP AND FOCUS ON FINDING MY MONEY!
I'M NOT SITTING SO WELL MYSELF.
BLAAAURGGH!
MY APOLOGIES. I ATE PART OF AN APPLE I FOUND IN HERE. IT DID NOT SIT WELL IN MY STOMACH.
HEY! ANOTHER APPLE!

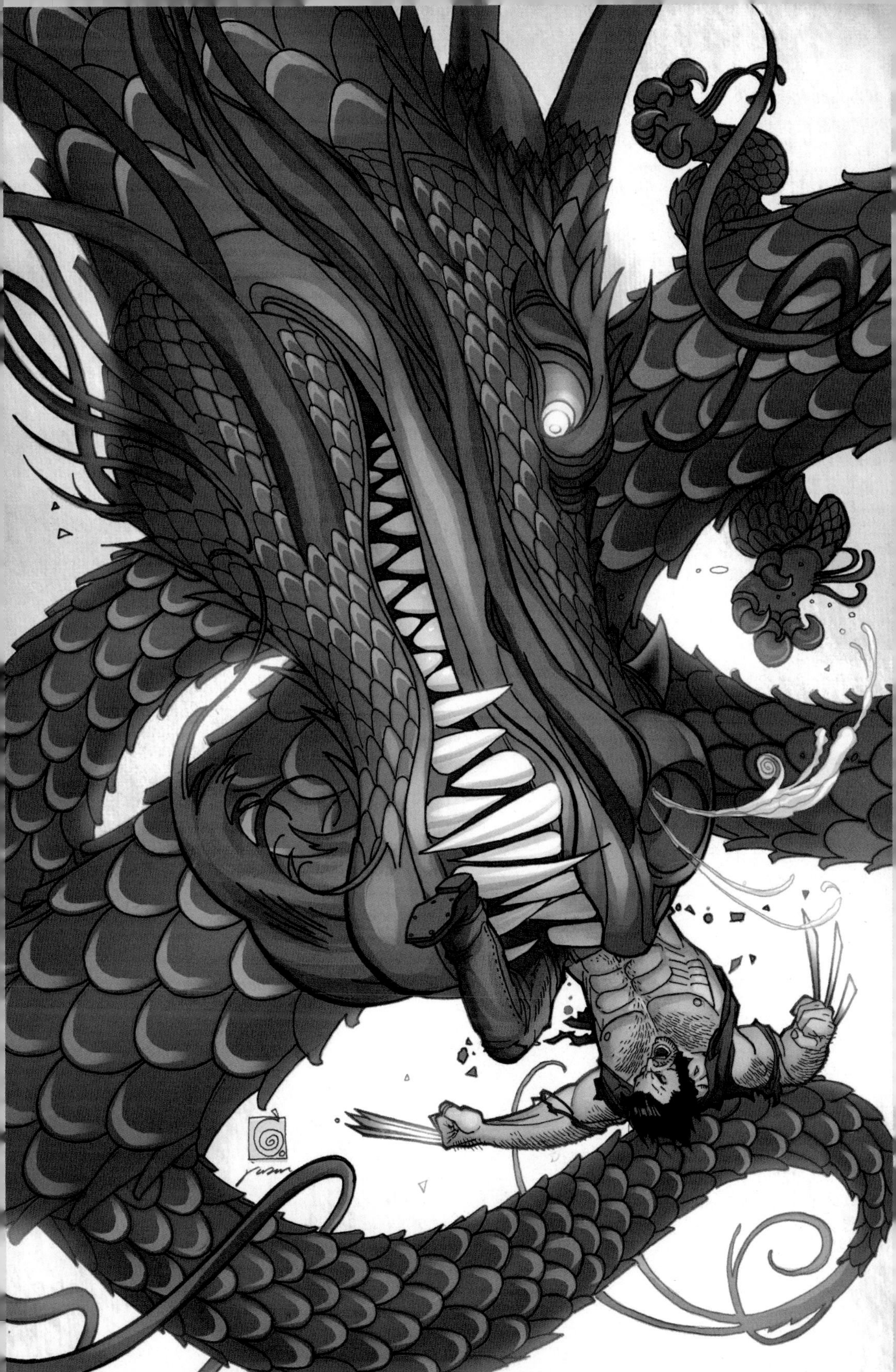

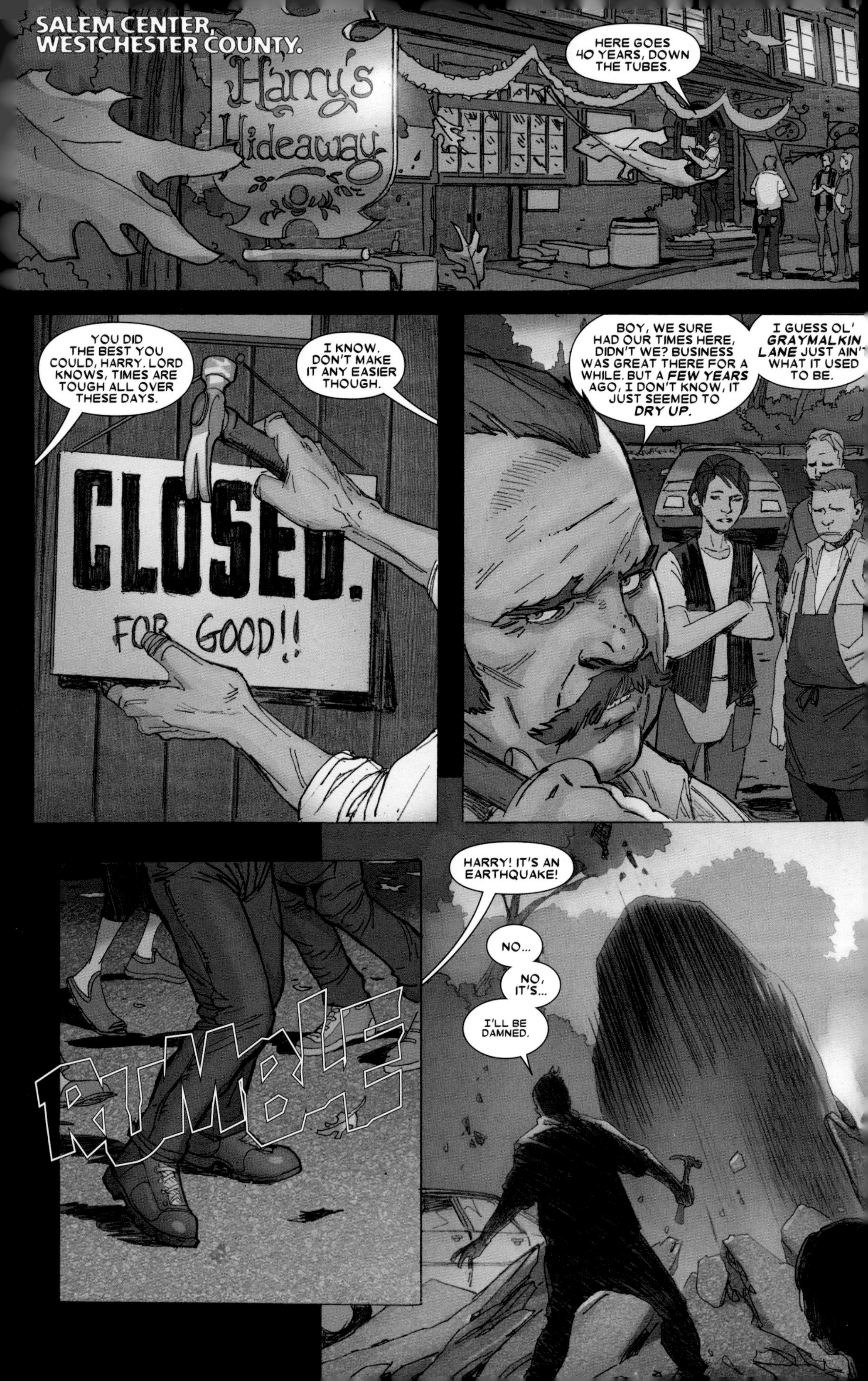
SALEM CENTER, WESTCHESTER COUNTY.
Harry's Hideaway
HERE GOES 40 YEARS, DOWN THE TUBES.
YOU DID THE BEST YOU COULD, HARRY. LORD KNOWS, TIMES ARE TOUGH ALL OVER THESE DAYS.
I KNOW. DON'T MAKE IT ANY EASIER THOUGH.
CLOSED. FOR GOOD!!
BOY, WE SURE HAD OUR TIMES HERE, DIDN'T WE? BUSINESS WAS GREAT THERE FOR A WHILE. BUT A FEW YEARS AGO, I DON'T KNOW, IT JUST SEEMED TO DRY UP.
I GUESS OL' GRAYMALKIN LANE JUST AIN'T WHAT IT USED TO BE.
RUMBLE
HARRY! IT'S AN EARTHQUAKE!
NO...
NO, IT'S...
I'LL BE DAMNED.

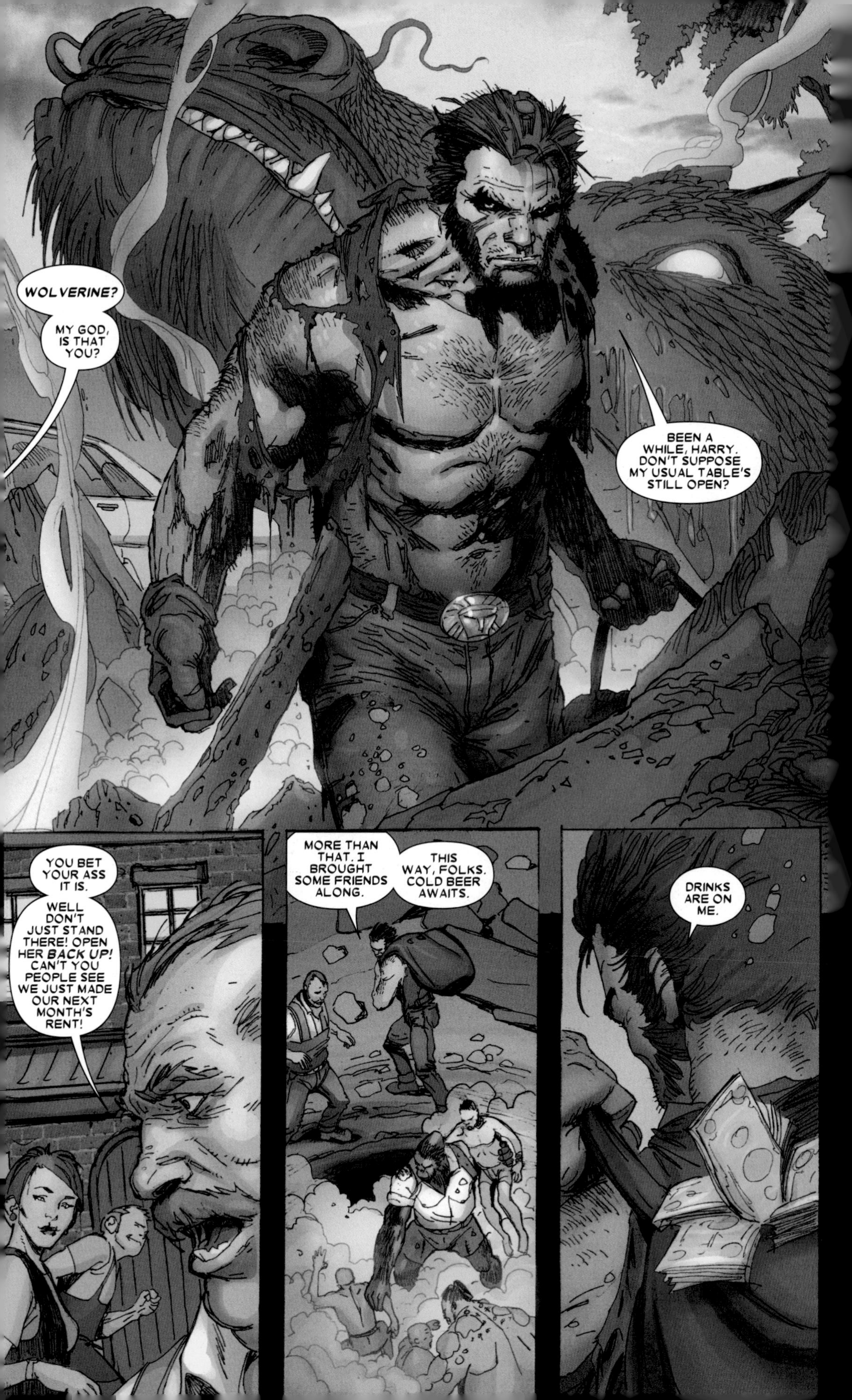

WOLVERINE?
MY GOD, IS THAT YOU?
BEEN A WHILE, HARRY. DON'T SUPPOSE MY USUAL TABLE'S STILL OPEN?
YOU BET YOUR ASS IT IS.
WELL DON'T JUST STAND THERE! OPEN HER BACK UP! CAN'T YOU PEOPLE SEE WE JUST MADE OUR NEXT MONTH'S RENT!
MORE THAN THAT. I BROUGHT SOME FRIENDS ALONG.
THIS WAY, FOLKS. COLD BEER AWAITS.
DRINKS ARE ON ME.

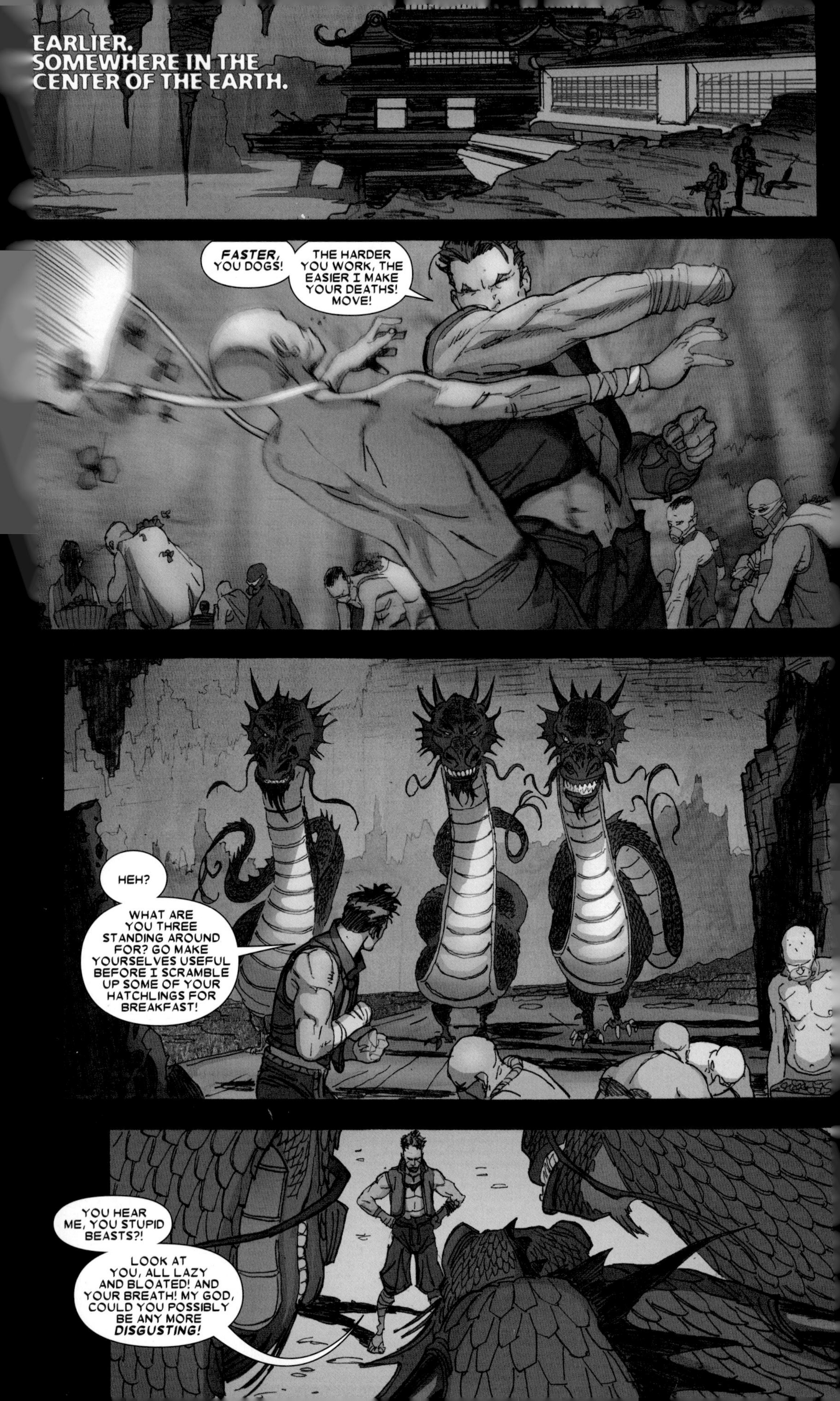
EARLIER. SOMEWHERE IN THE CENTER OF THE EARTH.
FASTER, YOU DOGS!
THE HARDER YOU WORK, THE EASIER I MAKE YOUR DEATHS! MOVE!
HEH?
WHAT ARE YOU THREE STANDING AROUND FOR? GO MAKE YOURSELVES USEFUL BEFORE I SCRAMBLE UP SOME OF YOUR HATCHLINGS FOR BREAKFAST!
YOU HEAR ME, YOU STUPID BEASTS?!
LOOK AT YOU, ALL LAZY AND BLOATED! AND YOUR BREATH! MY GOD, COULD YOU POSSIBLY BE ANY MORE DISGUSTING!

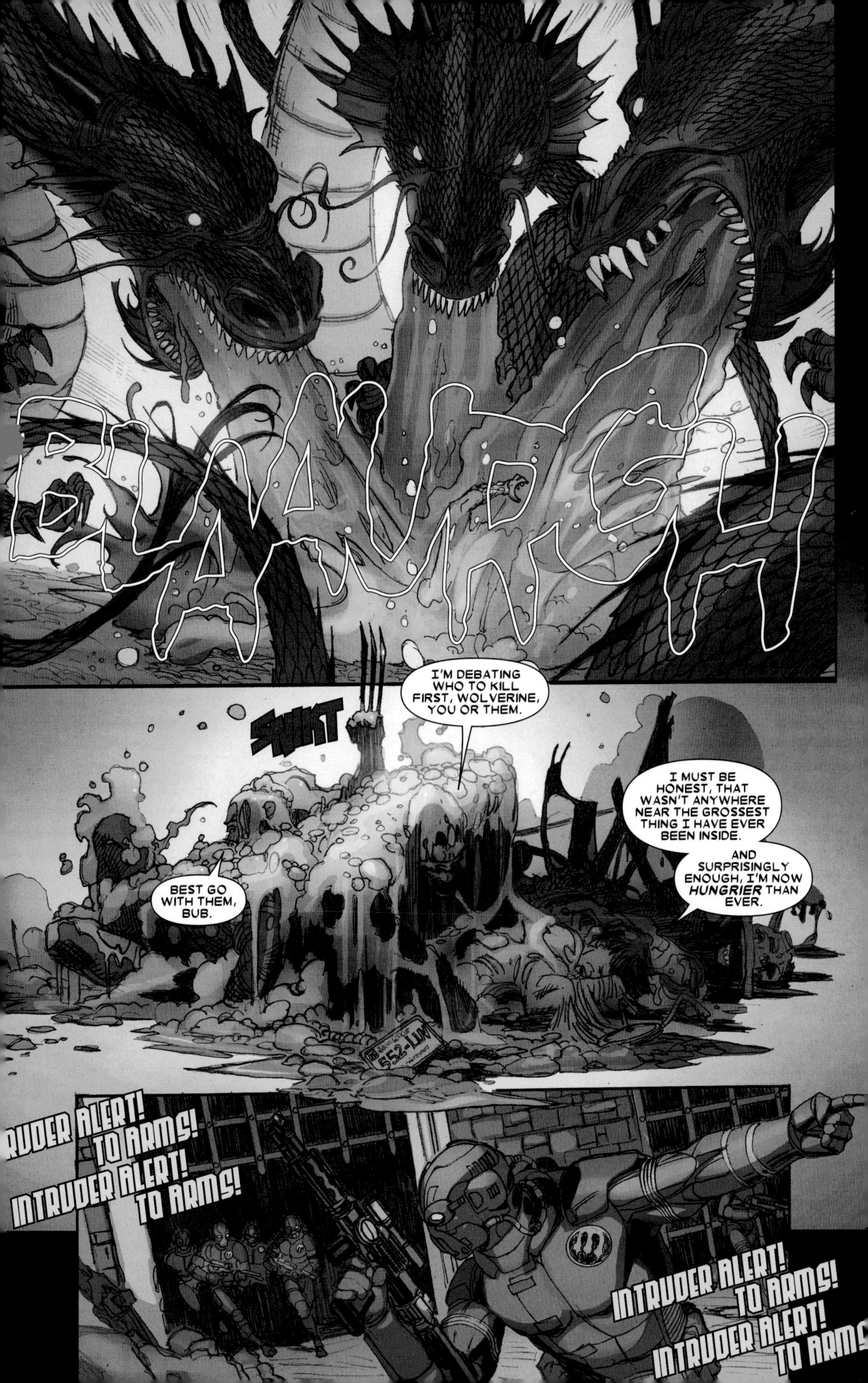
SNIKT
I'M DEBATING WHO TO KILL FIRST, WOLVERINE, YOU OR THEM.
BEST GO WITH THEM, BUB.
I MUST BE HONEST, THAT WASN'T ANYWHERE NEAR THE GROSSEST THING I HAVE EVER BEEN INSIDE.
AND SURPRISINGLY ENOUGH, I'M NOW HUNGRIER THAN EVER.
RUDER ALERT! TO ARMS! INTRUDER ALERT! TO ARMS!
INTRUDER ALERT! TO ARMS! INTRUDER ALERT! TO ARM

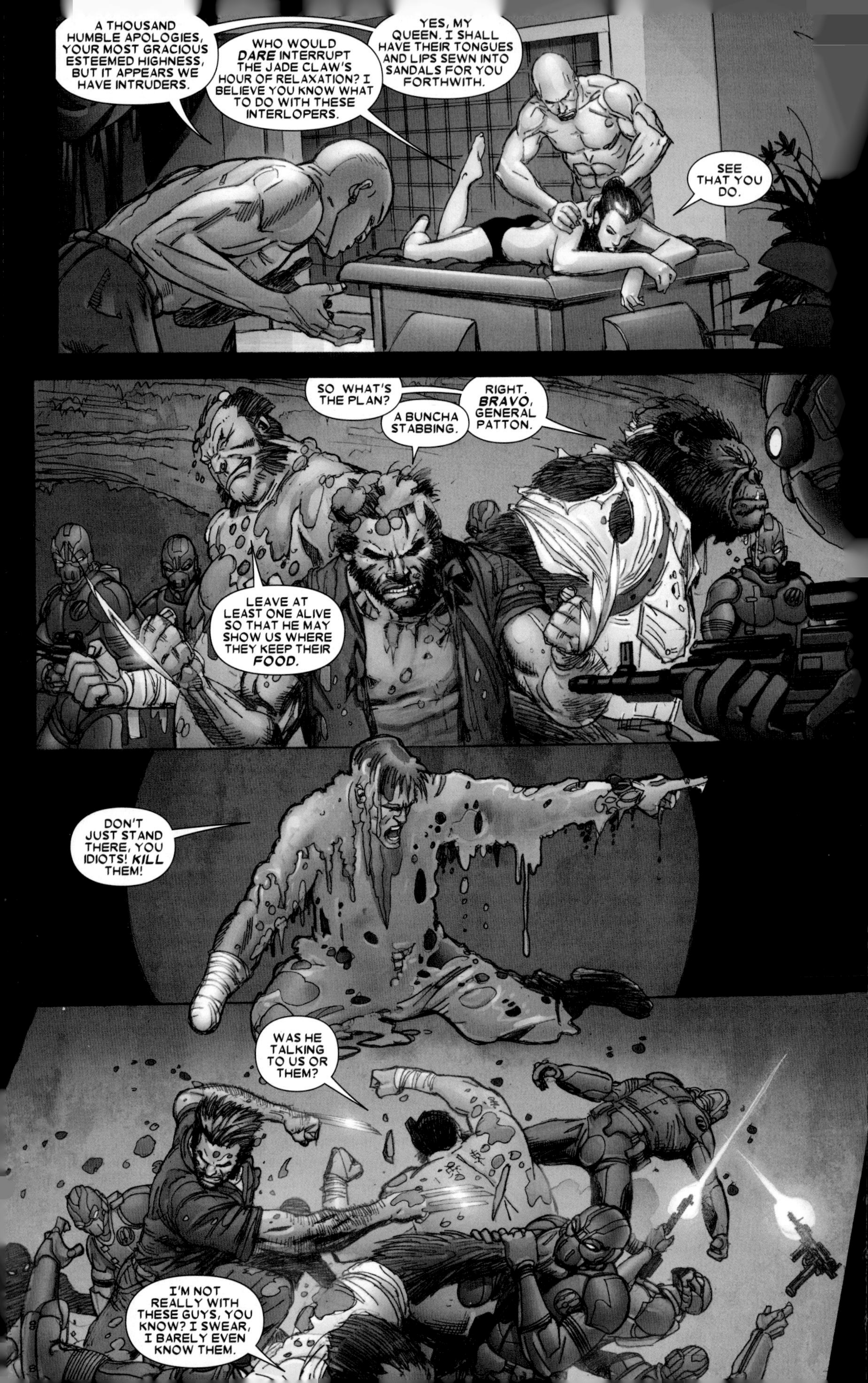
A THOUSAND HUMBLE APOLOGIES, YOUR MOST GRACIOUS ESTEEMED HIGHNESS, BUT IT APPEARS WE HAVE INTRUDERS.
WHO WOULD DARE INTERRUPT THE JADE CLAW'S HOUR OF RELAXATION? I BELIEVE YOU KNOW WHAT TO DO WITH THESE INTERLOPERS.
YES, MY QUEEN. I SHALL HAVE THEIR TONGUES AND LIPS SEWN INTO SANDALS FOR YOU FORTHWITH.
SEE THAT YOU DO.
SO WHAT'S THE PLAN?
A BUNCHA STABBING.
RIGHT. BRAVO, GENERAL PATTON.
LEAVE AT LEAST ONE ALIVE SO THAT HE MAY SHOW US WHERE THEY KEEP THEIR FOOD.
DON'T JUST STAND THERE, YOU IDIOTS! KILL THEM!
WAS HE TALKING TO US OR THEM?
I'M NOT REALLY WITH THESE GUYS, YOU KNOW? I SWEAR, I BARELY EVEN KNOW THEM.

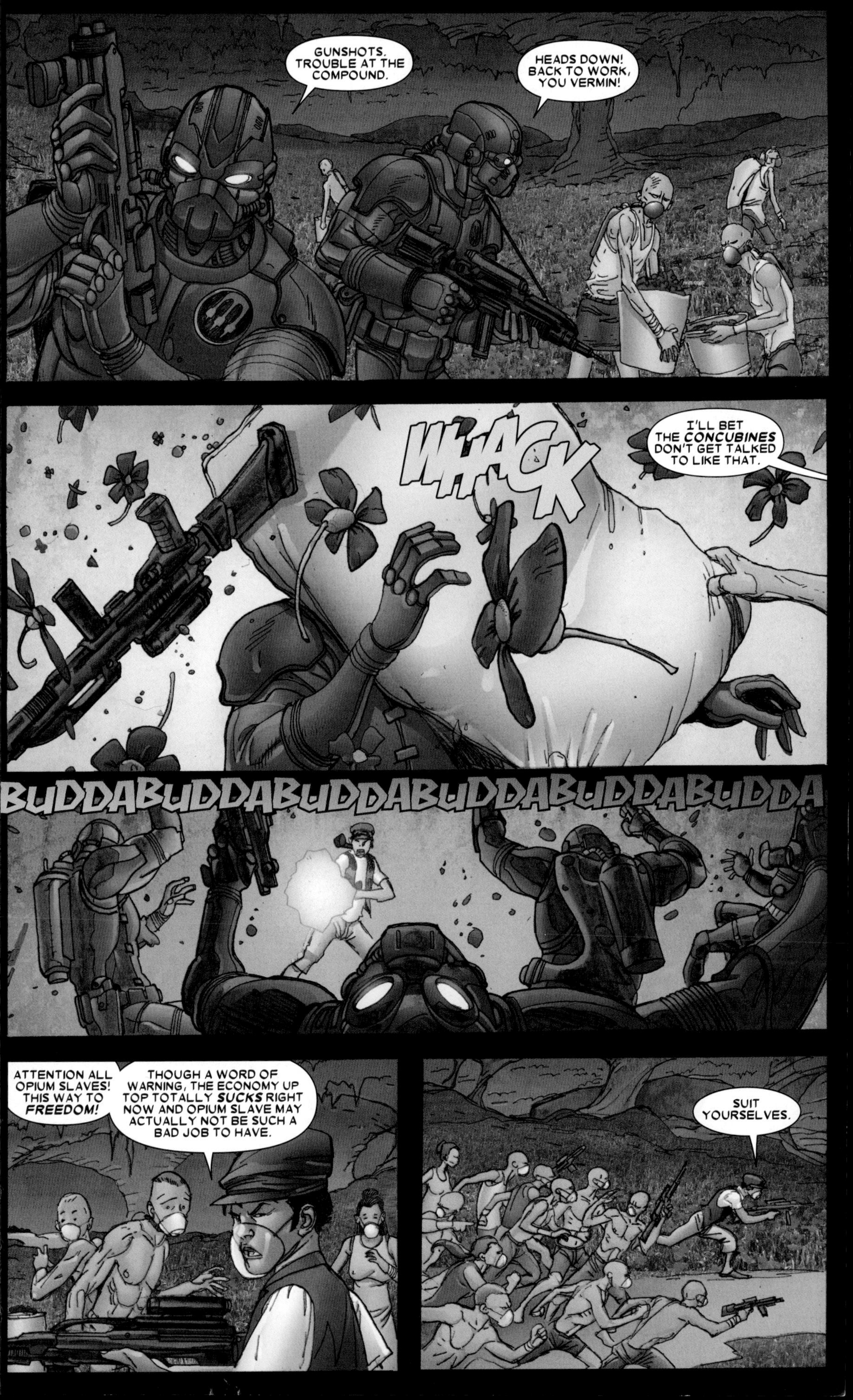
GUNSHOTS. TROUBLE AT THE COMPOUND.
HEADS DOWN! BACK TO WORK, YOU VERMIN!
WHACK
I'LL BET THE CONCUBINES DON'T GET TALKED TO LIKE THAT.
BUDDABUDDABUDDABUDDABUDDABUDDA
ATTENTION ALL OPIUM SLAVES! THIS WAY TO FREEDOM!
THOUGH A WORD OF WARNING, THE ECONOMY UP TOP TOTALLY SUCKS RIGHT NOW AND OPIUM SLAVE MAY ACTUALLY NOT BE SUCH A BAD JOB TO HAVE.
SUIT YOURSELVES.

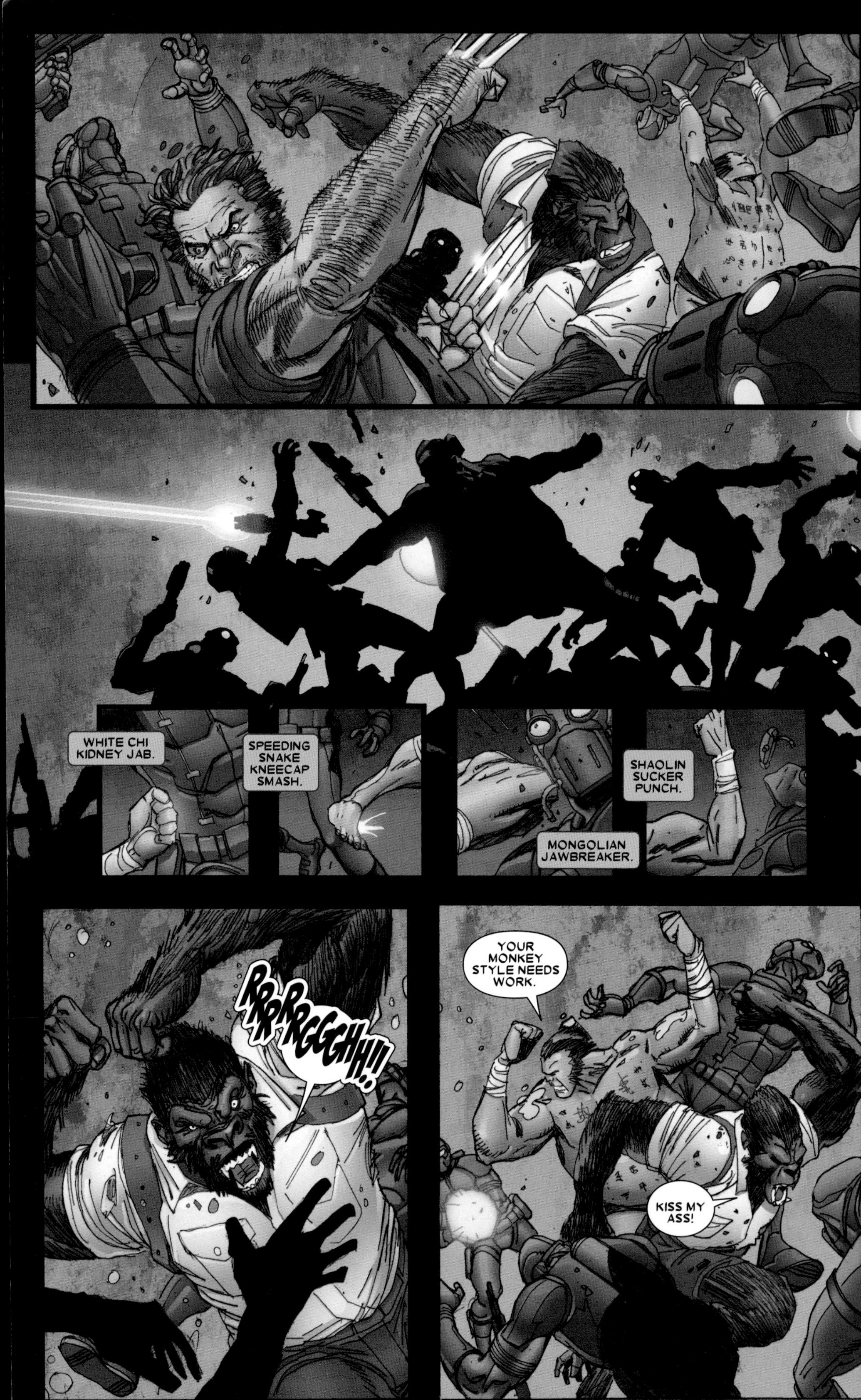
WHITE CHI KIDNEY JAB.
SPEEDING SNAKE KNEECAP SMASH.
MONGOLIAN JAWBREAKER.
SHAOLIN SUCKER PUNCH.
RRRRRGGGHH!!
YOUR MONKEY STYLE NEEDS WORK.
KISS MY ASS!

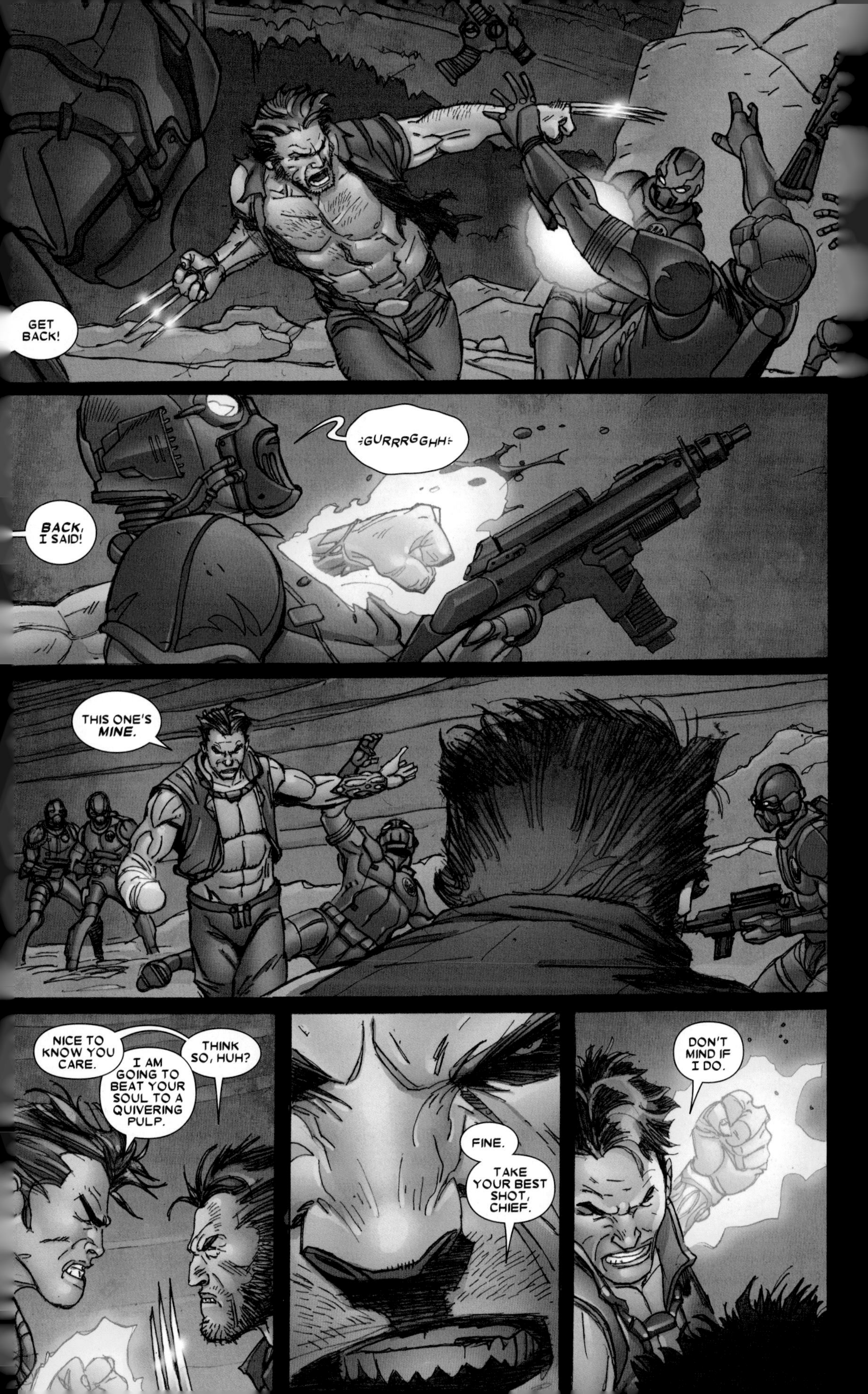
GET BACK!
=GURRRGGHH=
BACK, I SAID!
THIS ONE'S MINE.
NICE TO KNOW YOU CARE.
THINK SO, HUH?
I AM GOING TO BEAT YOUR SOUL TO A QUIVERING PULP.
FINE.
TAKE YOUR BEST SHOT, CHIEF.
DON'T MIND IF I DO.

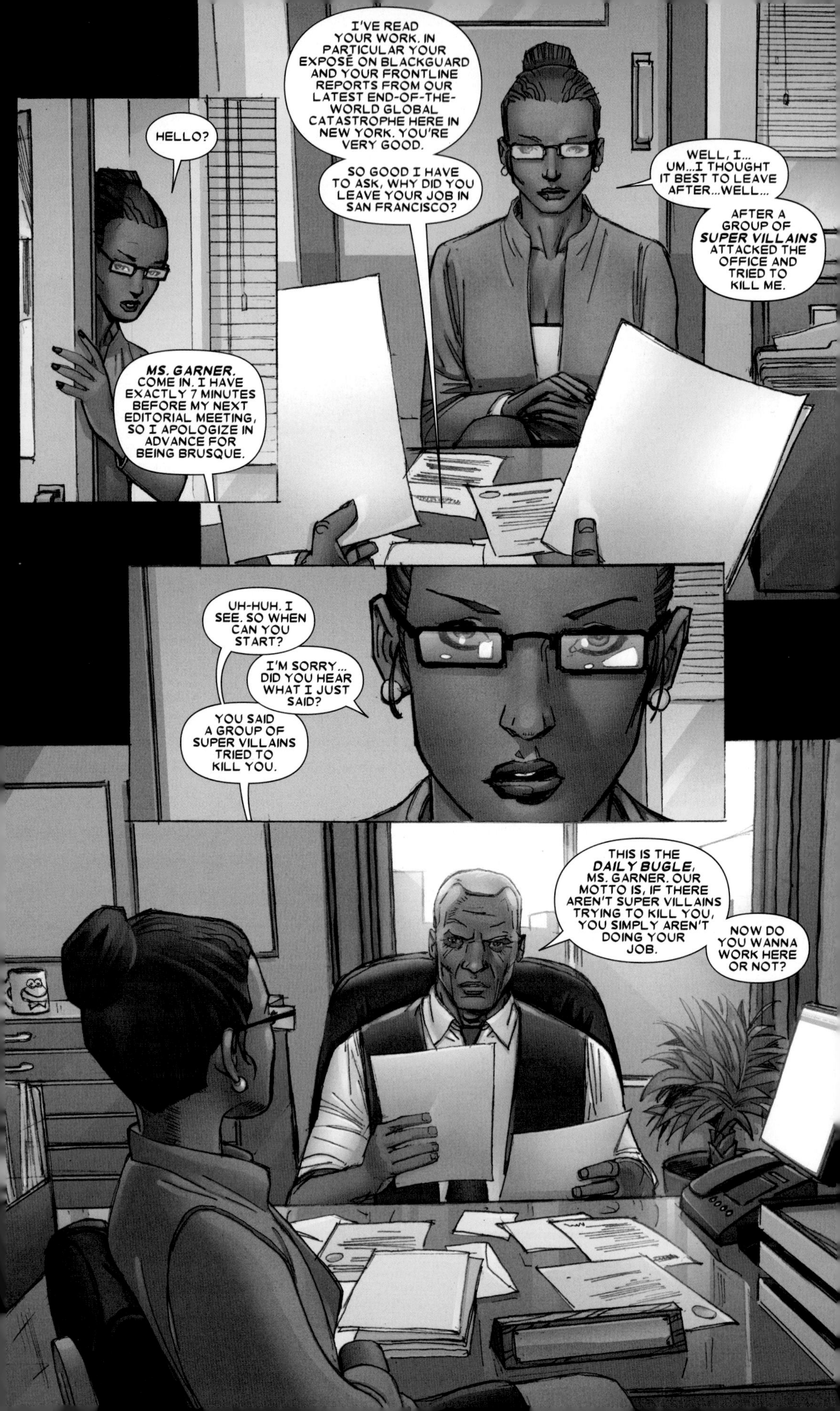
HELLO?
MS. GARNER. COME IN. I HAVE EXACTLY 7 MINUTES BEFORE MY NEXT EDITORIAL MEETING, SO I APOLOGIZE IN ADVANCE FOR BEING BRUSQUE.
I'VE READ YOUR WORK. IN PARTICULAR YOUR EXPOSÉ ON BLACKGUARD AND YOUR FRONTLINE REPORTS FROM OUR LATEST END-OF-THE-WORLD GLOBAL CATASTROPHE HERE IN NEW YORK. YOU'RE VERY GOOD.
SO GOOD I HAVE TO ASK, WHY DID YOU LEAVE YOUR JOB IN SAN FRANCISCO?
WELL, I... UM...I THOUGHT IT BEST TO LEAVE AFTER...WELL...
AFTER A GROUP OF SUPER VILLAINS ATTACKED THE OFFICE AND TRIED TO KILL ME.
UH-HUH. I SEE. SO WHEN CAN YOU START?
I'M SORRY... DID YOU HEAR WHAT I JUST SAID?
YOU SAID A GROUP OF SUPER VILLAINS TRIED TO KILL YOU.
THIS IS THE DAILY BUGLE, MS. GARNER. OUR MOTTO IS, IF THERE AREN'T SUPER VILLAINS TRYING TO KILL YOU, YOU SIMPLY AREN'T DOING YOUR JOB.
NOW DO YOU WANNA WORK HERE OR NOT?

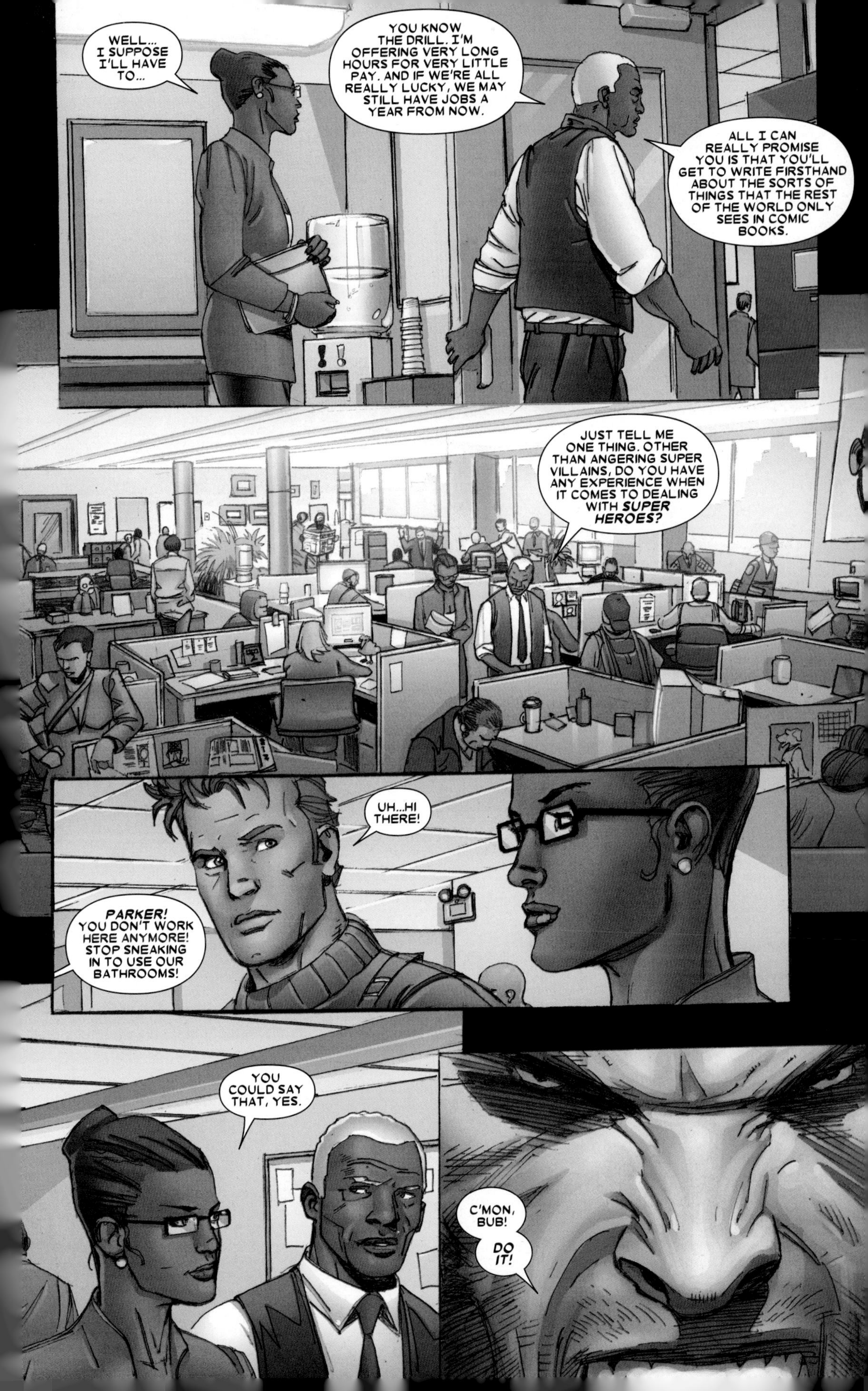

WELL... I SUPPOSE I'LL HAVE TO...
YOU KNOW THE DRILL. I'M OFFERING VERY LONG HOURS FOR VERY LITTLE PAY. AND IF WE'RE ALL REALLY LUCKY, WE MAY STILL HAVE JOBS A YEAR FROM NOW.
ALL I CAN REALLY PROMISE YOU IS THAT YOU'LL GET TO WRITE FIRSTHAND ABOUT THE SORTS OF THINGS THAT THE REST OF THE WORLD ONLY SEES IN COMIC BOOKS.
JUST TELL ME ONE THING. OTHER THAN ANGERING SUPER VILLAINS, DO YOU HAVE ANY EXPERIENCE WHEN IT COMES TO DEALING WITH *SUPER HEROES?*
UH...HI THERE!
PARKER! YOU DON'T WORK HERE ANYMORE! STOP SNEAKING IN TO USE OUR BATHROOMS!
YOU COULD SAY THAT, YES.
C'MON, BUB!
DO IT!

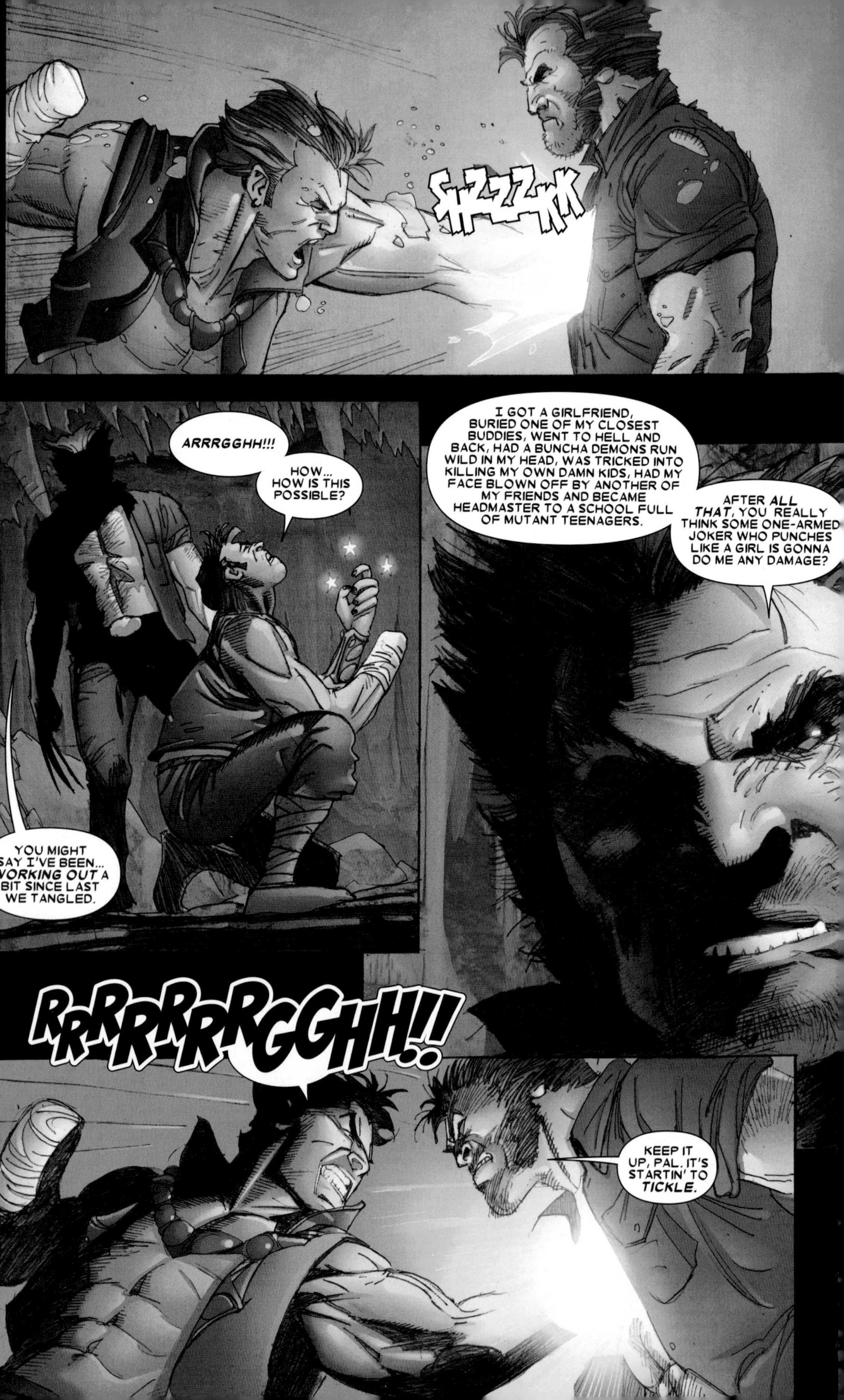
SHZZZKK
ARRRGGHH!!!
HOW... HOW IS THIS POSSIBLE?
YOU MIGHT SAY I'VE BEEN... WORKING OUT A BIT SINCE LAST WE TANGLED.
I GOT A GIRLFRIEND, BURIED ONE OF MY CLOSEST BUDDIES, WENT TO HELL AND BACK, HAD A BUNCHA DEMONS RUN WILD IN MY HEAD, WAS TRICKED INTO KILLING MY OWN DAMN KIDS, HAD MY FACE BLOWN OFF BY ANOTHER OF MY FRIENDS AND BECAME HEADMASTER TO A SCHOOL FULL OF MUTANT TEENAGERS.
AFTER ALL THAT, YOU REALLY THINK SOME ONE-ARMED JOKER WHO PUNCHES LIKE A GIRL IS GONNA DO ME ANY DAMAGE?
RRRRRRGGHH!!!
KEEP IT UP, PAL. IT'S STARTIN' TO TICKLE.

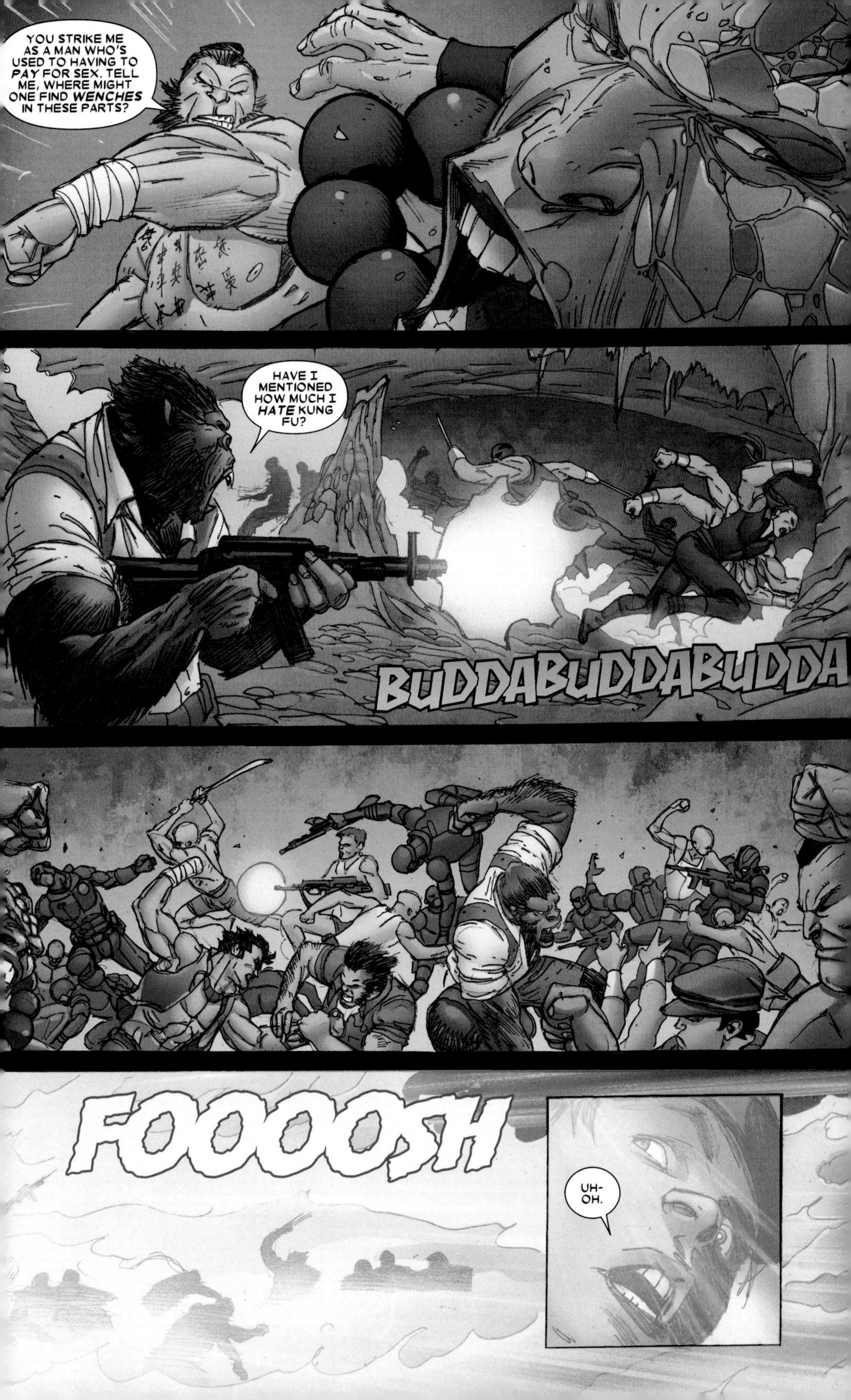
YOU STRIKE ME AS A MAN WHO'S USED TO HAVING TO PAY FOR SEX. TELL ME, WHERE MIGHT ONE FIND WENCHES IN THESE PARTS?
HAVE I MENTIONED HOW MUCH I HATE KUNG FU?
BUDDABUDDABUDDA
FOOOOSH
UH-OH.

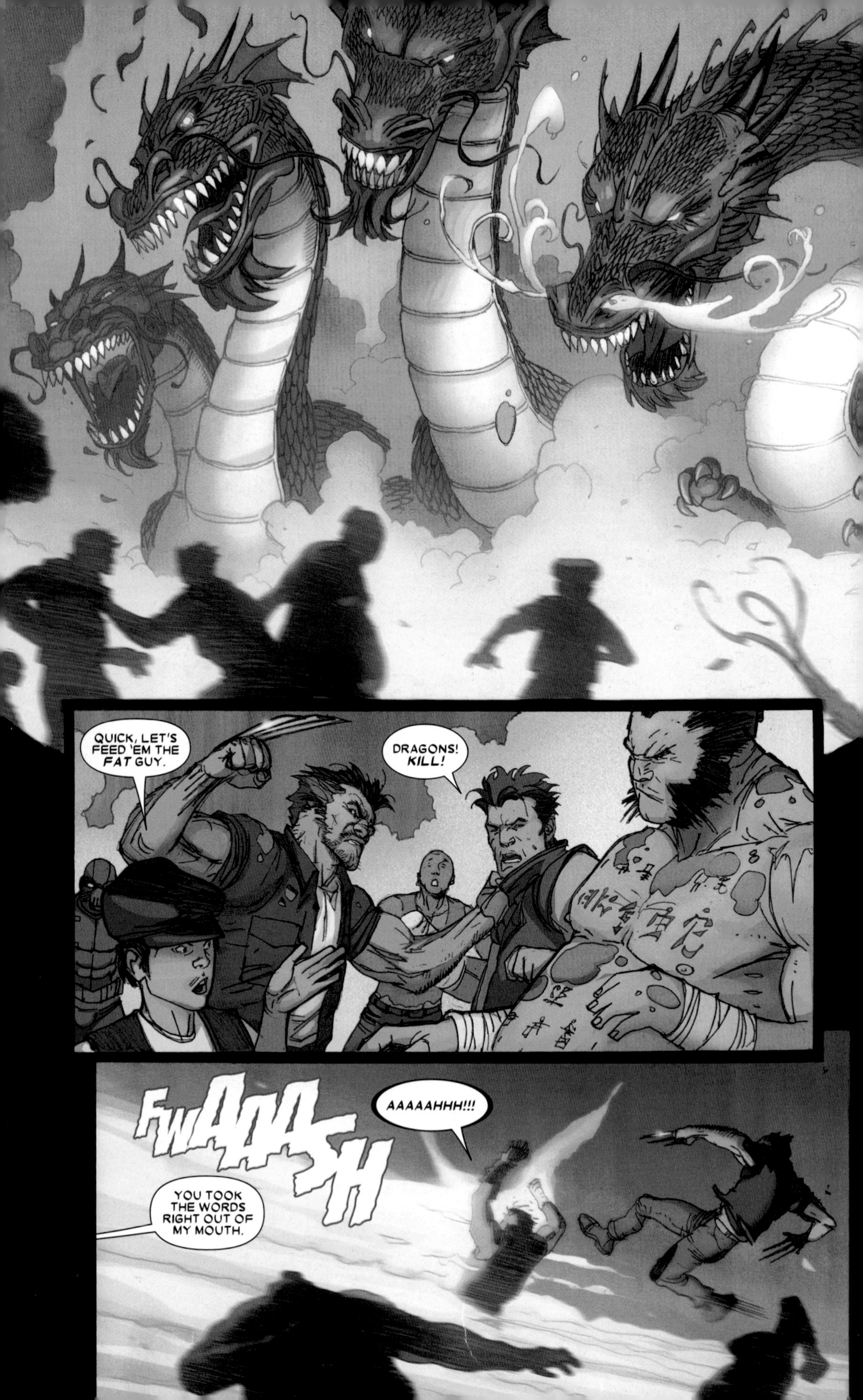
QUICK, LET'S FEED 'EM THE FAT GUY.
DRAGONS! KILL!
FWAAASH
AAAAAHHH!!!
YOU TOOK THE WORDS RIGHT OUT OF MY MOUTH.

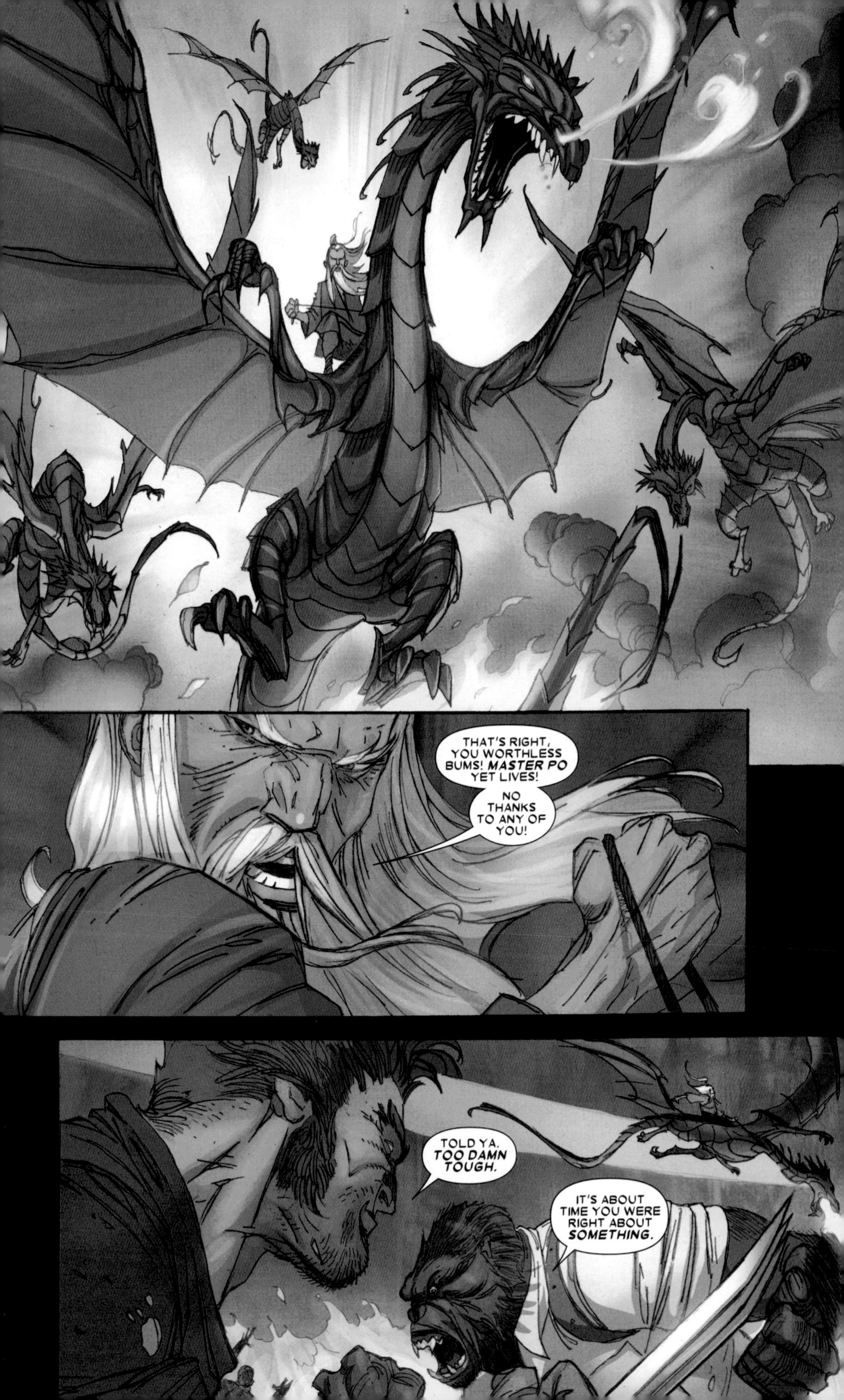
THAT'S RIGHT, YOU WORTHLESS BUMS! MASTER PO YET LIVES!
NO THANKS TO ANY OF YOU!
TOLD YA. TOO DAMN TOUGH.
IT'S ABOUT TIME YOU WERE RIGHT ABOUT SOMETHING.

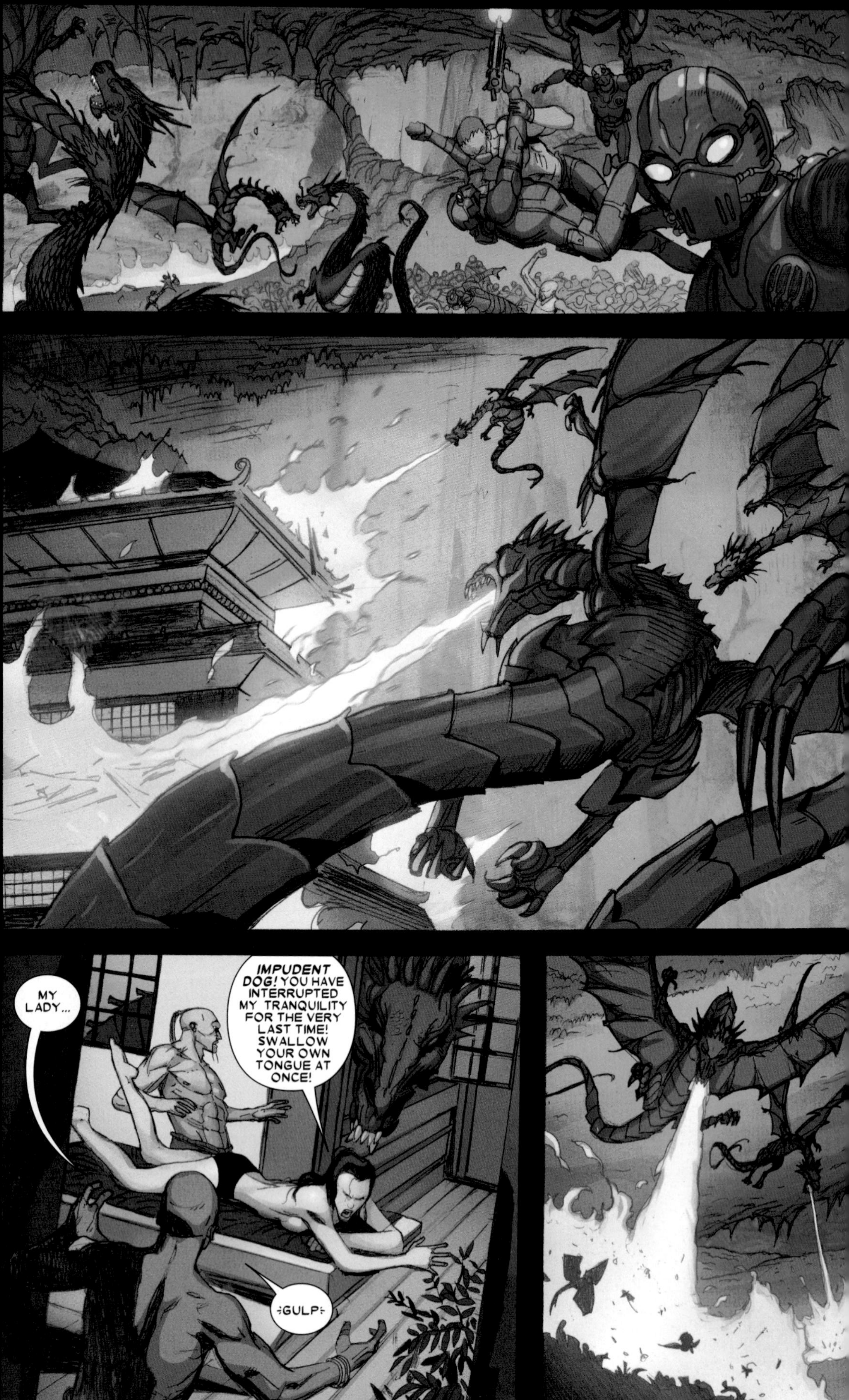
MY LADY...
IMPUDENT DOG! YOU HAVE INTERRUPTED MY TRANQUILITY FOR THE VERY LAST TIME! SWALLOW YOUR OWN TONGUE AT ONCE!
GULP

JADE CLAW'S FINISHED. RECKON YOU KNOW WHAT'S NEXT.

YOU DONE PUNCHED YOUR LAST SOUL, BUB.

SNIKT

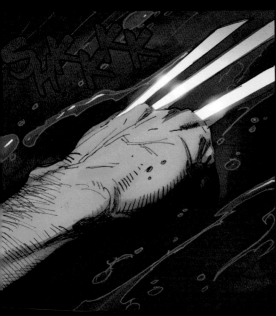

AAAARRGHH!

THE REST IS ALL YOURS, MASTER.

PLEASE...

YOU WOULDN'T HIT A MAN WITH NO ARMS, WOULD YOU?

NO.

KRAK

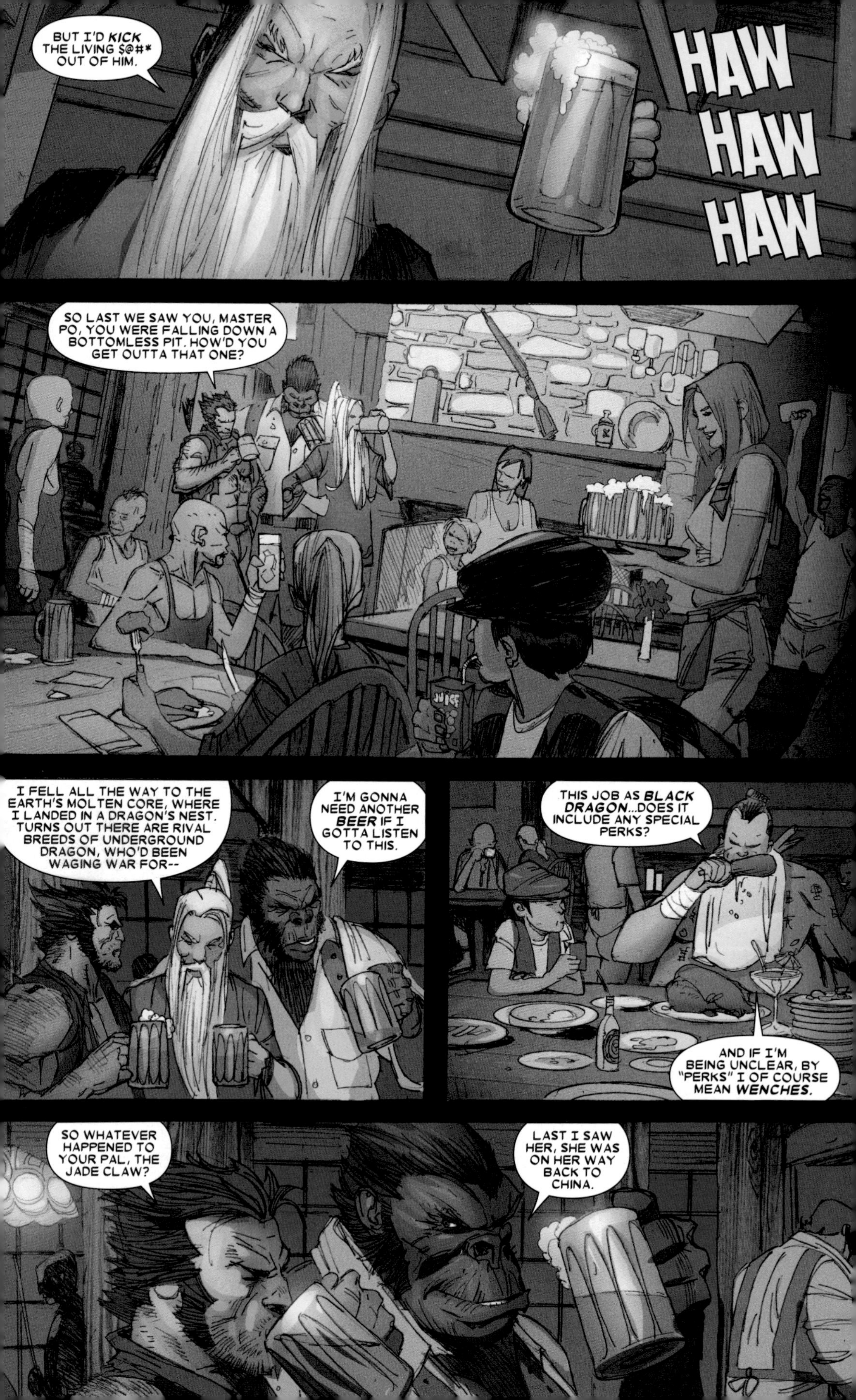
BUT I'D KICK THE LIVING $@#* OUT OF HIM.
HAW HAW HAW
SO LAST WE SAW YOU, MASTER PO, YOU WERE FALLING DOWN A BOTTOMLESS PIT. HOW'D YOU GET OUTTA THAT ONE?
JUICE
I FELL ALL THE WAY TO THE EARTH'S MOLTEN CORE, WHERE I LANDED IN A DRAGON'S NEST. TURNS OUT THERE ARE RIVAL BREEDS OF UNDERGROUND DRAGON, WHO'D BEEN WAGING WAR FOR--
I'M GONNA NEED ANOTHER BEER IF I GOTTA LISTEN TO THIS.
THIS JOB AS BLACK DRAGON...DOES IT INCLUDE ANY SPECIAL PERKS?
AND IF I'M BEING UNCLEAR, BY "PERKS" I OF COURSE MEAN WENCHES.
SO WHATEVER HAPPENED TO YOUR PAL, THE JADE CLAW?
LAST I SAW HER, SHE WAS ON HER WAY BACK TO CHINA.

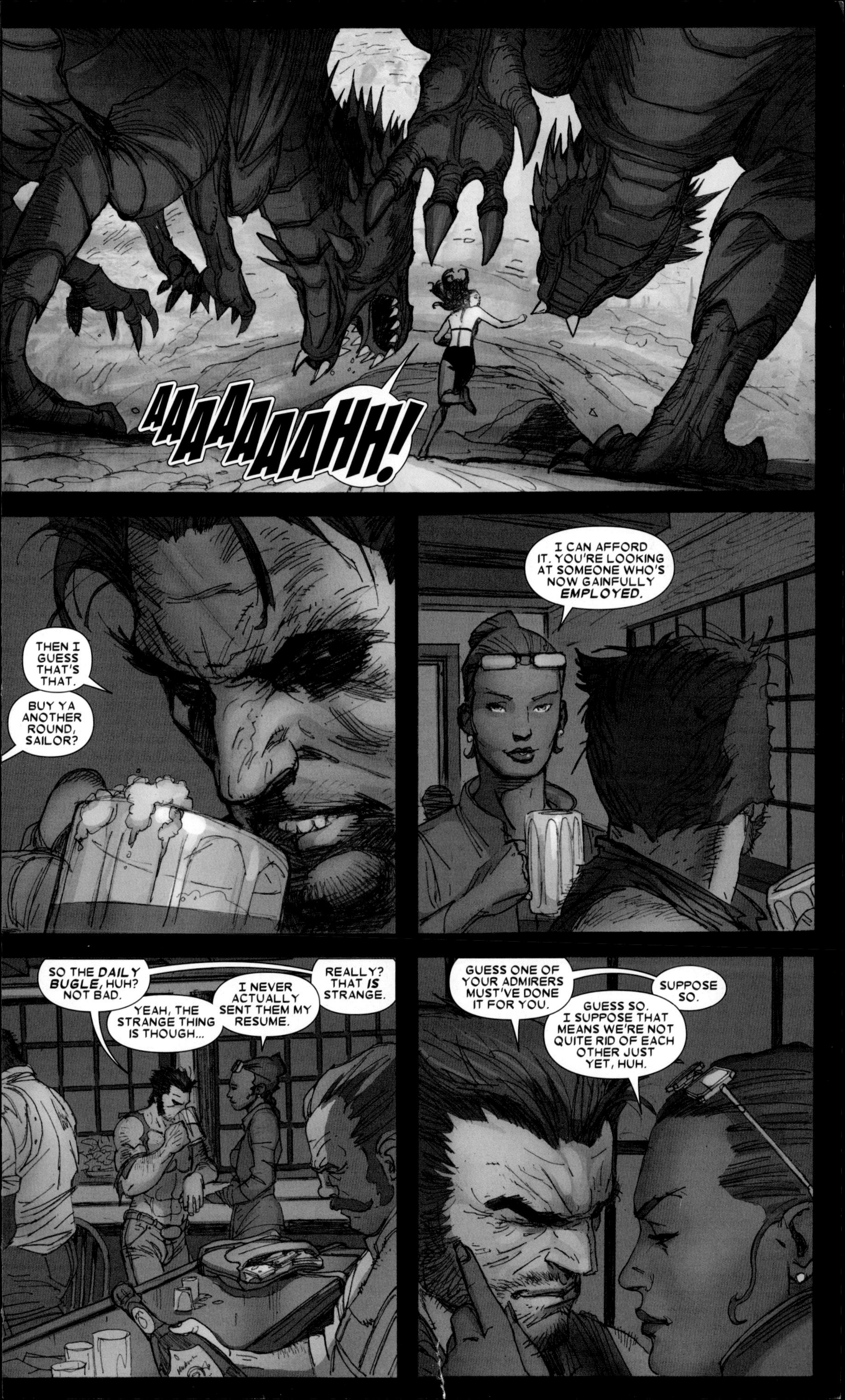
AAAAAAAAHH!
THEN I GUESS THAT'S THAT.
BUY YA ANOTHER ROUND, SAILOR?
I CAN AFFORD IT. YOU'RE LOOKING AT SOMEONE WHO'S NOW GAINFULLY EMPLOYED.
SO THE DAILY BUGLE, HUH? NOT BAD.
YEAH, THE STRANGE THING IS THOUGH...
I NEVER ACTUALLY SENT THEM MY RESUME.
REALLY? THAT IS STRANGE.
GUESS ONE OF YOUR ADMIRERS MUST'VE DONE IT FOR YOU.
SUPPOSE SO.
GUESS SO. I SUPPOSE THAT MEANS WE'RE NOT QUITE RID OF EACH OTHER JUST YET, HUH.

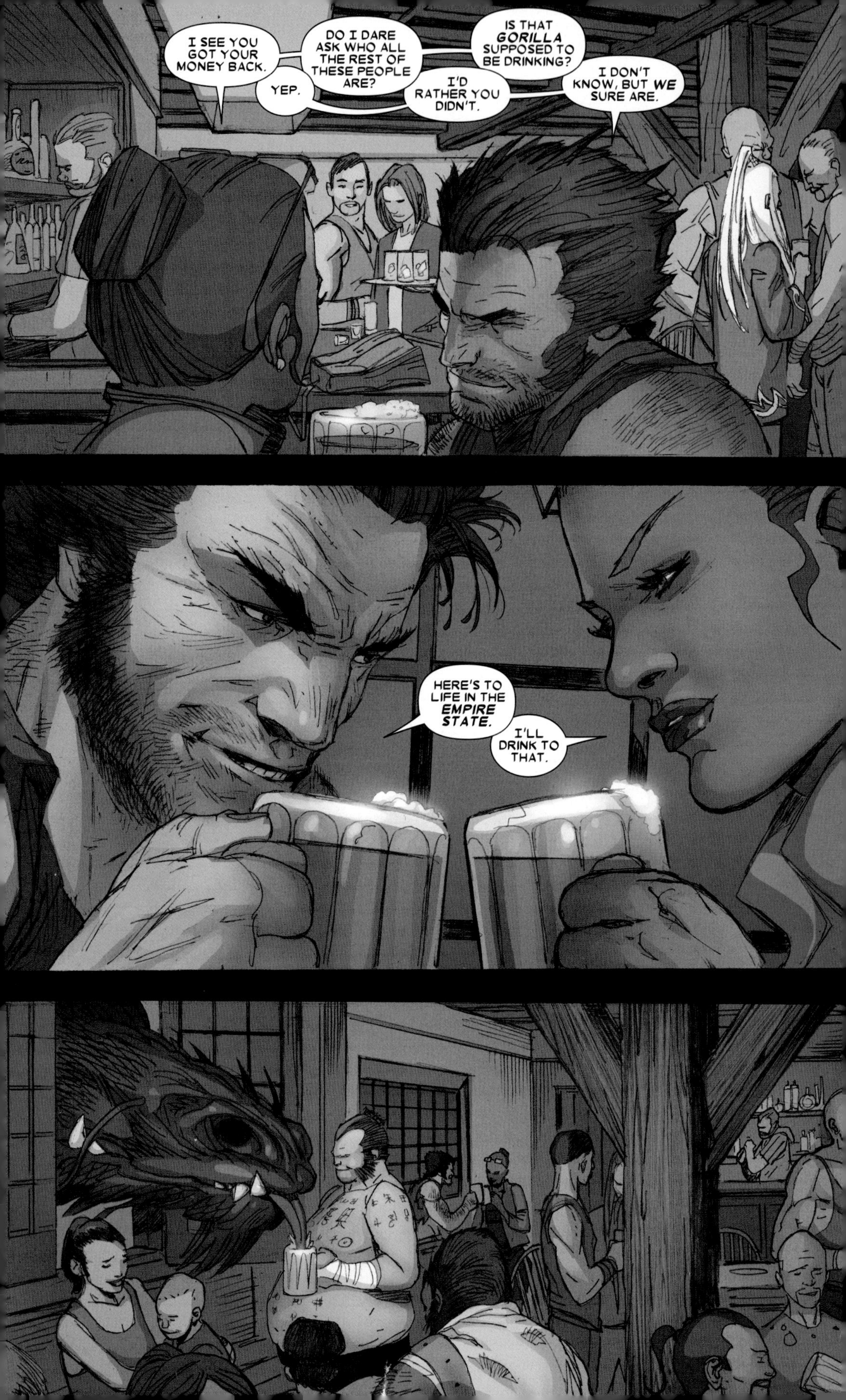
I SEE YOU GOT YOUR MONEY BACK.
YEP.
DO I DARE ASK WHO ALL THE REST OF THESE PEOPLE ARE?
I'D RATHER YOU DIDN'T.
IS THAT *GORILLA* SUPPOSED TO BE DRINKING?
I DON'T KNOW, BUT *WE* SURE ARE.
HERE'S TO LIFE IN THE *EMPIRE STATE.*
I'LL DRINK TO THAT.

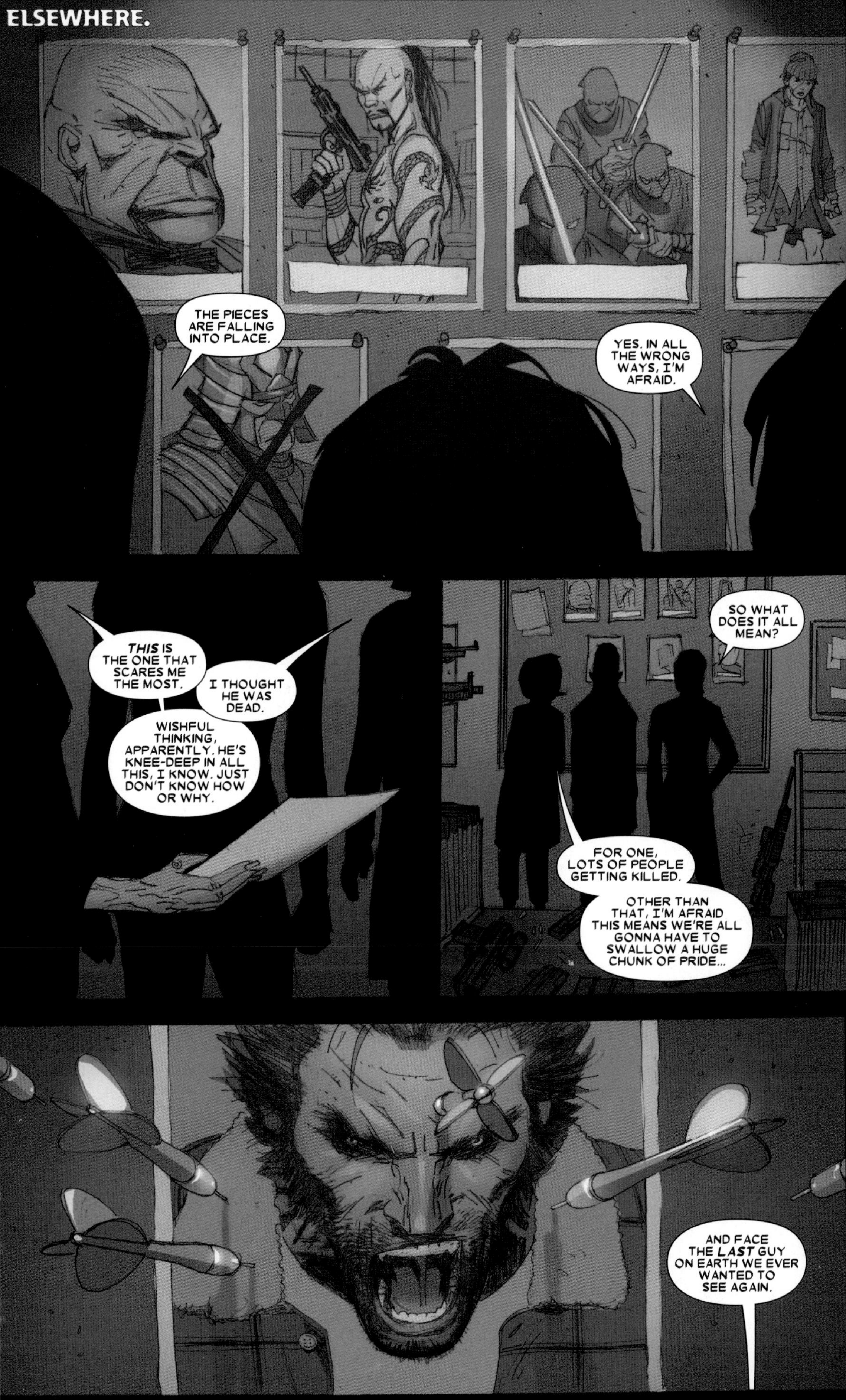
ELSEWHERE.
THE PIECES ARE FALLING INTO PLACE.
YES. IN ALL THE WRONG WAYS, I'M AFRAID.
THIS IS THE ONE THAT SCARES ME THE MOST.
I THOUGHT HE WAS DEAD.
WISHFUL THINKING, APPARENTLY. HE'S KNEE-DEEP IN ALL THIS, I KNOW. JUST DON'T KNOW HOW OR WHY.
SO WHAT DOES IT ALL MEAN?
FOR ONE, LOTS OF PEOPLE GETTING KILLED.
OTHER THAN THAT, I'M AFRAID THIS MEANS WE'RE ALL GONNA HAVE TO SWALLOW A HUGE CHUNK OF PRIDE...
AND FACE THE *LAST* GUY ON EARTH WE EVER WANTED TO SEE AGAIN.

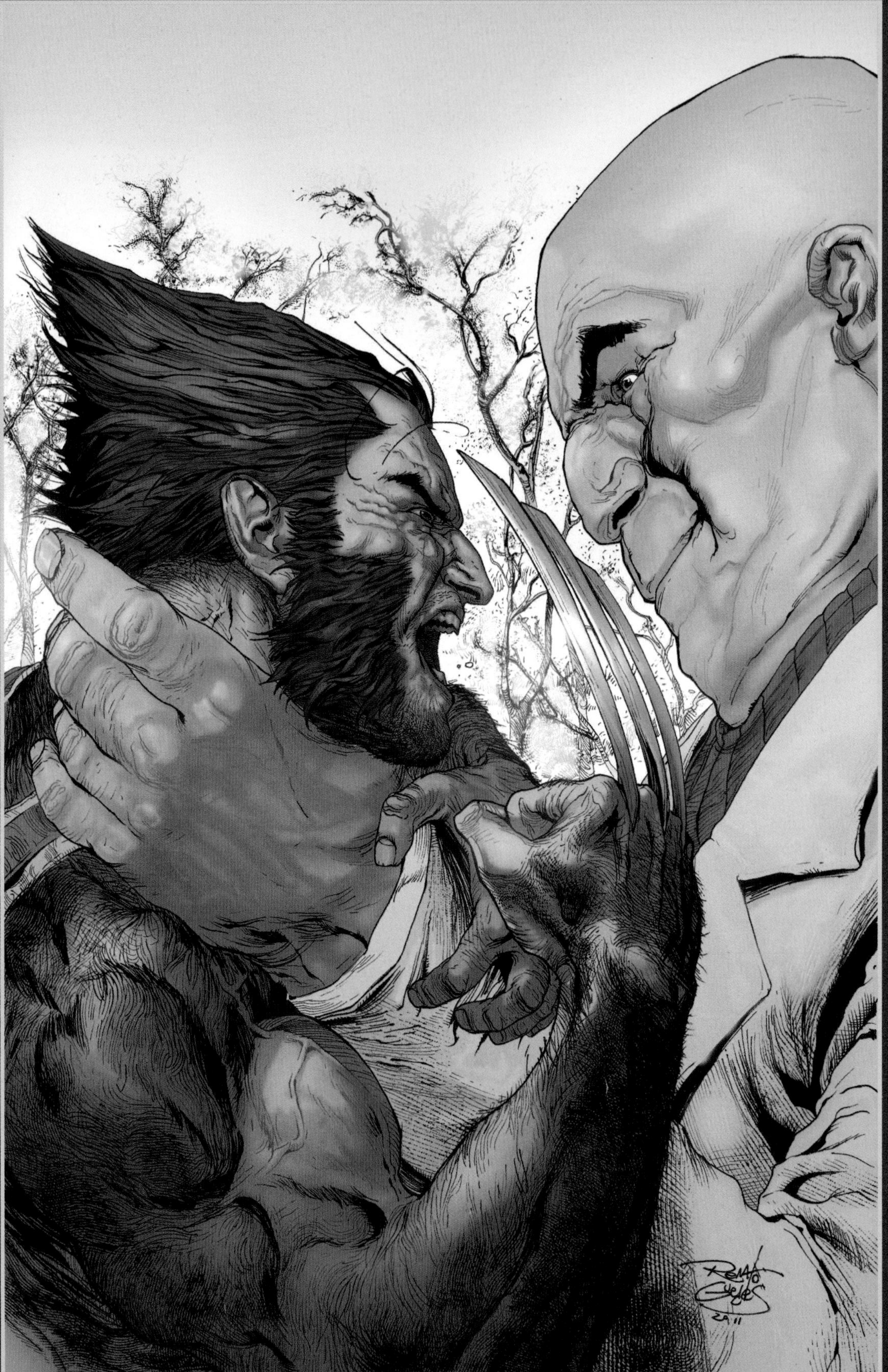

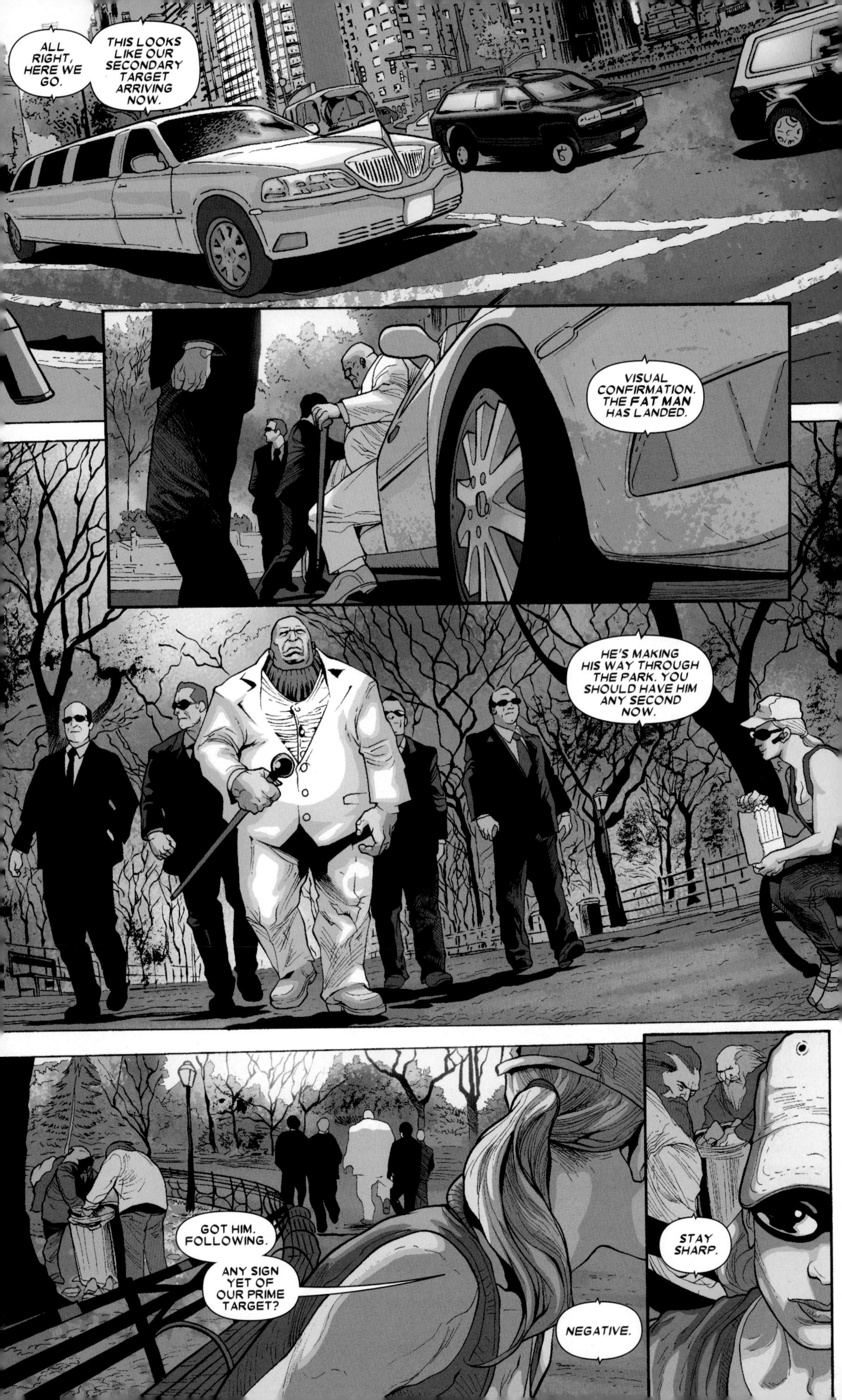
ALL RIGHT, HERE WE GO.
THIS LOOKS LIKE OUR SECONDARY TARGET ARRIVING NOW.
VISUAL CONFIRMATION. THE FAT MAN HAS LANDED.
HE'S MAKING HIS WAY THROUGH THE PARK. YOU SHOULD HAVE HIM ANY SECOND NOW.
GOT HIM. FOLLOWING.
ANY SIGN YET OF OUR PRIME TARGET?
NEGATIVE.
STAY SHARP.

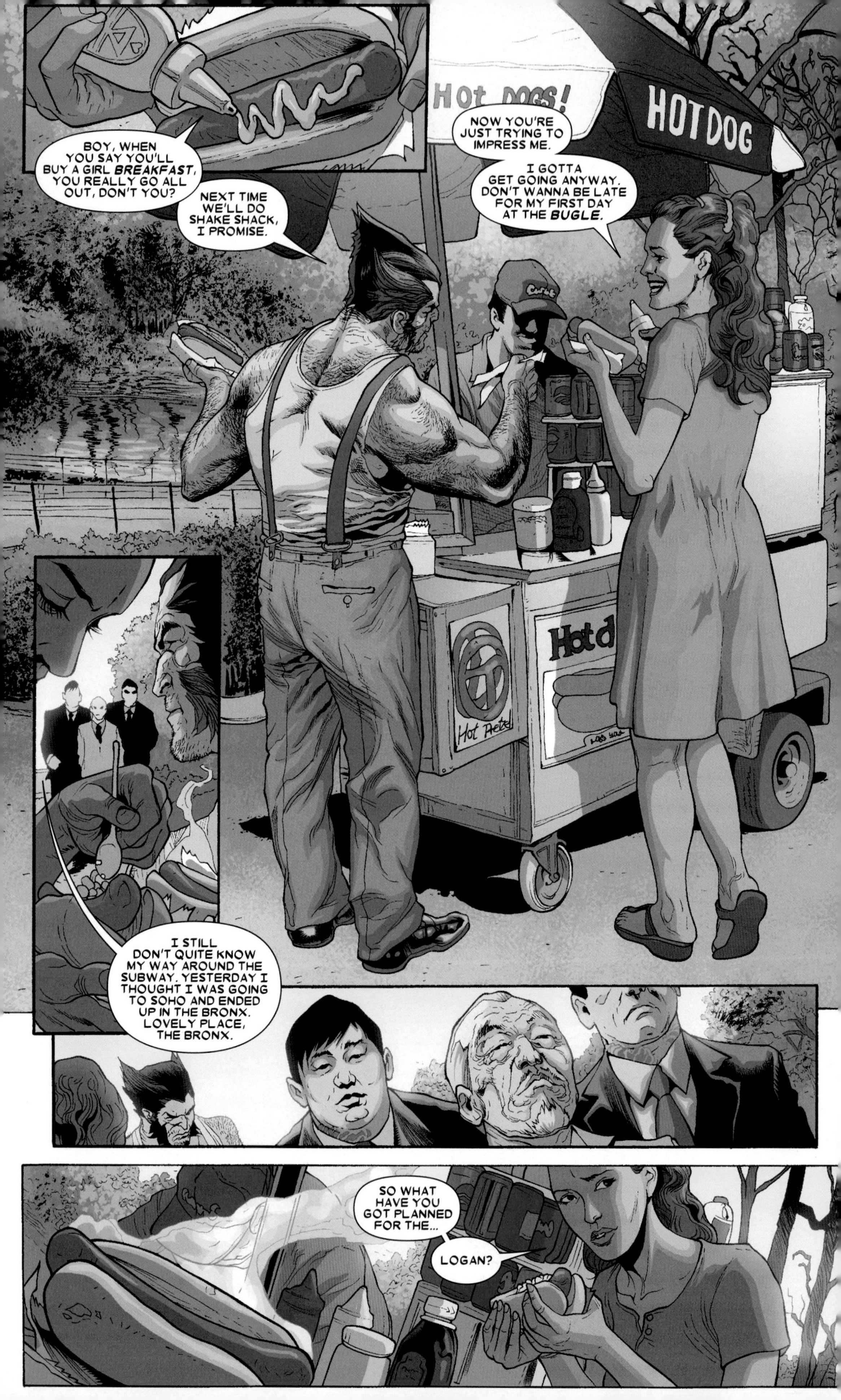
BOY, WHEN YOU SAY YOU'LL BUY A GIRL BREAKFAST, YOU REALLY GO ALL OUT, DON'T YOU?
NEXT TIME WE'LL DO SHAKE SHACK, I PROMISE.
Hot DOGS!
HOT DOG
NOW YOU'RE JUST TRYING TO IMPRESS ME.
I GOTTA GET GOING ANYWAY. DON'T WANNA BE LATE FOR MY FIRST DAY AT THE BUGLE.
Hot d
Hot Pretz
I STILL DON'T QUITE KNOW MY WAY AROUND THE SUBWAY. YESTERDAY I THOUGHT I WAS GOING TO SOHO AND ENDED UP IN THE BRONX. LOVELY PLACE, THE BRONX.
SO WHAT HAVE YOU GOT PLANNED FOR THE...
LOGAN?

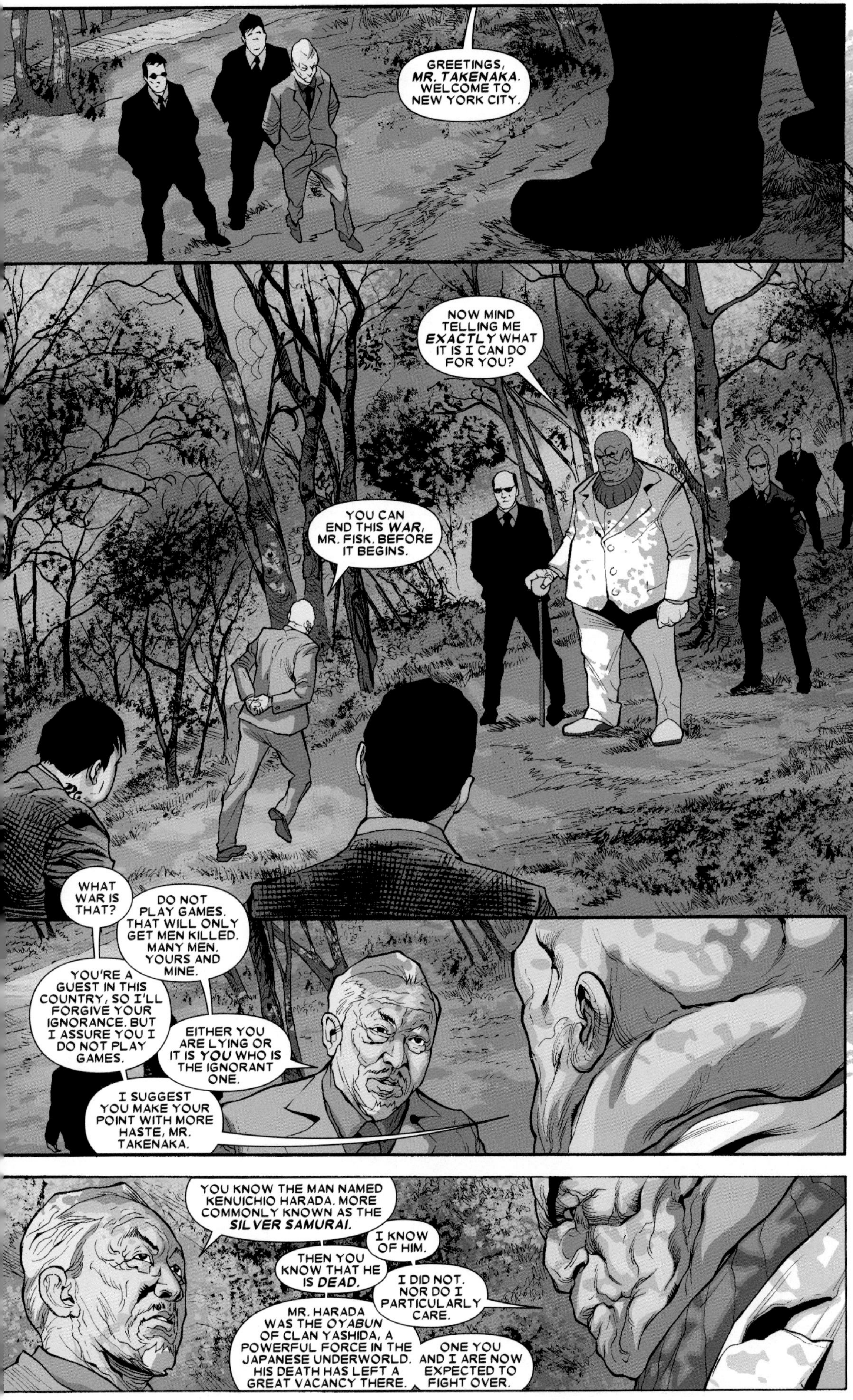
GREETINGS, MR. TAKENAKA. WELCOME TO NEW YORK CITY.
NOW MIND TELLING ME EXACTLY WHAT IT IS I CAN DO FOR YOU?
YOU CAN END THIS WAR, MR. FISK. BEFORE IT BEGINS.
WHAT WAR IS THAT?
DO NOT PLAY GAMES. THAT WILL ONLY GET MEN KILLED. MANY MEN. YOURS AND MINE.
YOU'RE A GUEST IN THIS COUNTRY, SO I'LL FORGIVE YOUR IGNORANCE. BUT I ASSURE YOU I DO NOT PLAY GAMES.
EITHER YOU ARE LYING OR IT IS YOU WHO IS THE IGNORANT ONE.
I SUGGEST YOU MAKE YOUR POINT WITH MORE HASTE, MR. TAKENAKA.
YOU KNOW THE MAN NAMED KENUICHIO HARADA. MORE COMMONLY KNOWN AS THE SILVER SAMURAI.
I KNOW OF HIM.
THEN YOU KNOW THAT HE IS DEAD.
I DID NOT. NOR DO I PARTICULARLY CARE.
MR. HARADA WAS THE OYABUN OF CLAN YASHIDA, A POWERFUL FORCE IN THE JAPANESE UNDERWORLD. HIS DEATH HAS LEFT A GREAT VACANCY THERE.
ONE YOU AND I ARE NOW EXPECTED TO FIGHT OVER.

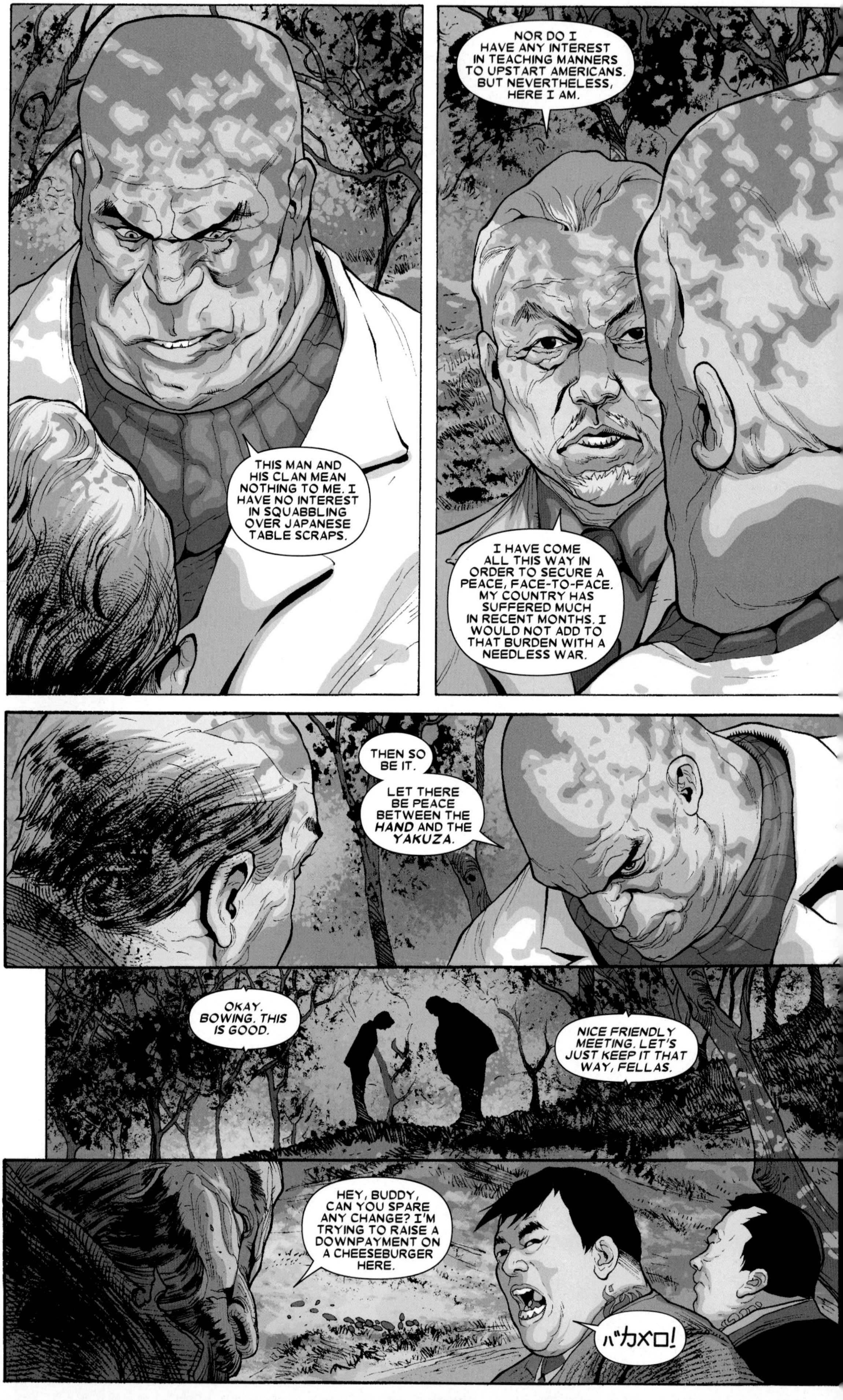
THIS MAN AND HIS CLAN MEAN NOTHING TO ME. I HAVE NO INTEREST IN SQUABBLING OVER JAPANESE TABLE SCRAPS.
NOR DO I HAVE ANY INTEREST IN TEACHING MANNERS TO UPSTART AMERICANS. BUT NEVERTHELESS, HERE I AM.
I HAVE COME ALL THIS WAY IN ORDER TO SECURE A PEACE, FACE-TO-FACE. MY COUNTRY HAS SUFFERED MUCH IN RECENT MONTHS. I WOULD NOT ADD TO THAT BURDEN WITH A NEEDLESS WAR.
THEN SO BE IT.
LET THERE BE PEACE BETWEEN THE *HAND* AND THE *YAKUZA*.
OKAY. BOWING. THIS IS GOOD.
NICE FRIENDLY MEETING. LET'S JUST KEEP IT THAT WAY, FELLAS.
HEY, BUDDY, CAN YOU SPARE ANY CHANGE? I'M TRYING TO RAISE A DOWNPAYMENT ON A CHEESEBURGER HERE.
バカヤロ!

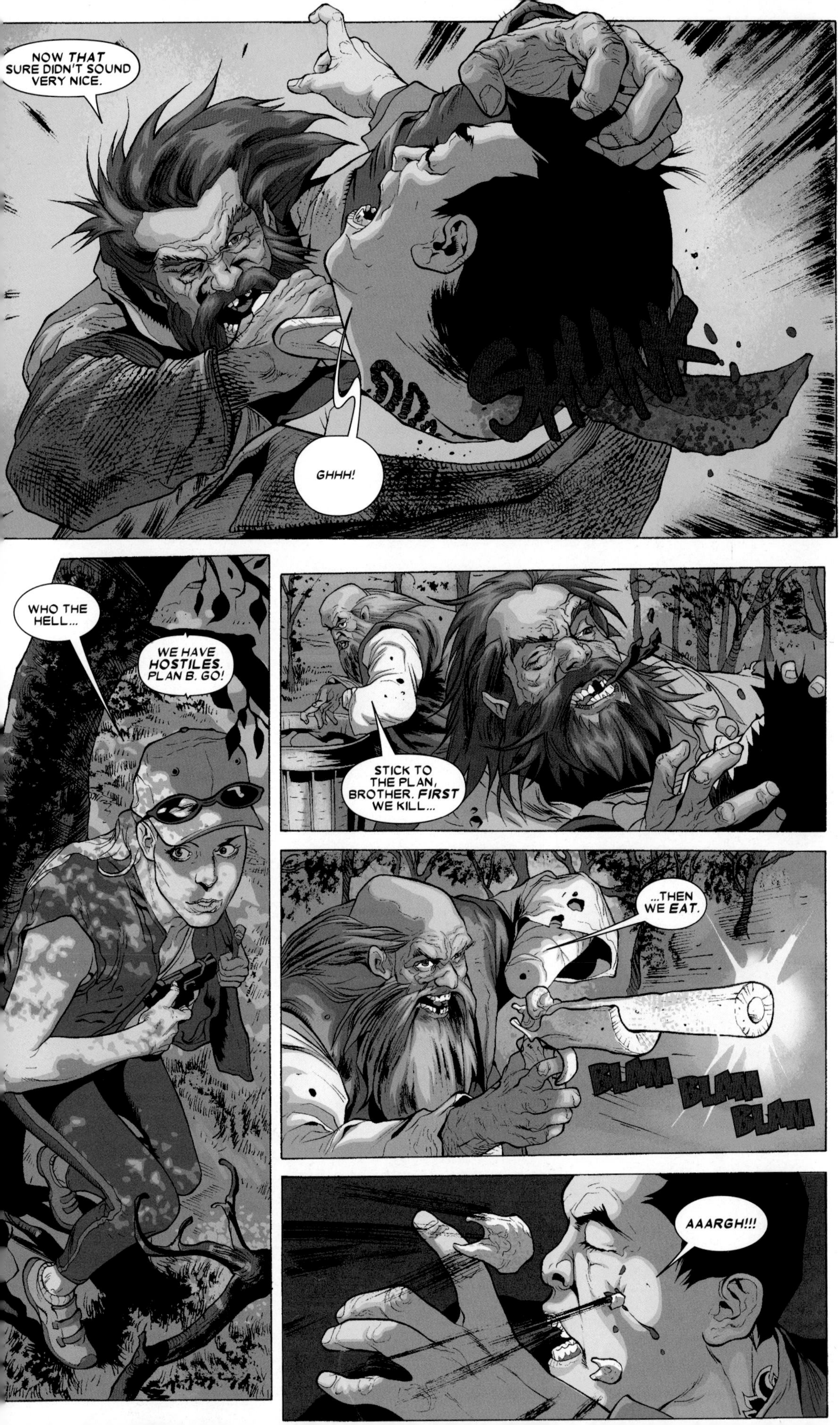
NOW THAT SURE DIDN'T SOUND VERY NICE.
SHUNK
GHHH!
WHO THE HELL...
WE HAVE HOSTILES. PLAN B. GO!
STICK TO THE PLAN, BROTHER. FIRST WE KILL...
...THEN WE EAT.
BLAM BLAM BLAM
AAARGH!!!

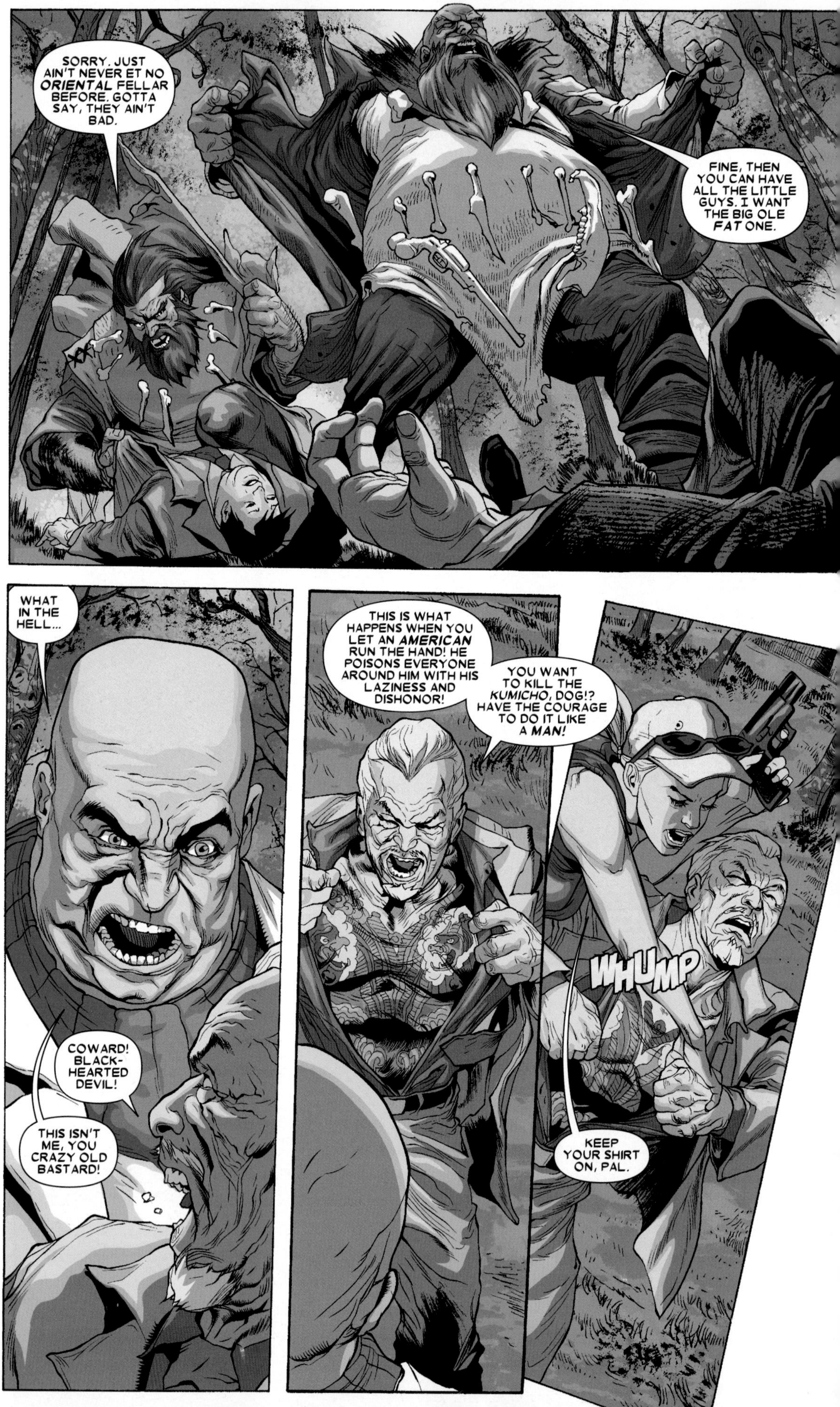
SORRY. JUST AIN'T NEVER ET NO ORIENTAL FELLAR BEFORE. GOTTA SAY, THEY AIN'T BAD.
FINE, THEN YOU CAN HAVE ALL THE LITTLE GUYS. I WANT THE BIG OLE FAT ONE.
WHAT IN THE HELL...
COWARD! BLACK-HEARTED DEVIL!
THIS ISN'T ME, YOU CRAZY OLD BASTARD!
THIS IS WHAT HAPPENS WHEN YOU LET AN AMERICAN RUN THE HAND! HE POISONS EVERYONE AROUND HIM WITH HIS LAZINESS AND DISHONOR!
YOU WANT TO KILL THE KUMICHO, DOG!? HAVE THE COURAGE TO DO IT LIKE A MAN!
WHUMP
KEEP YOUR SHIRT ON, PAL.

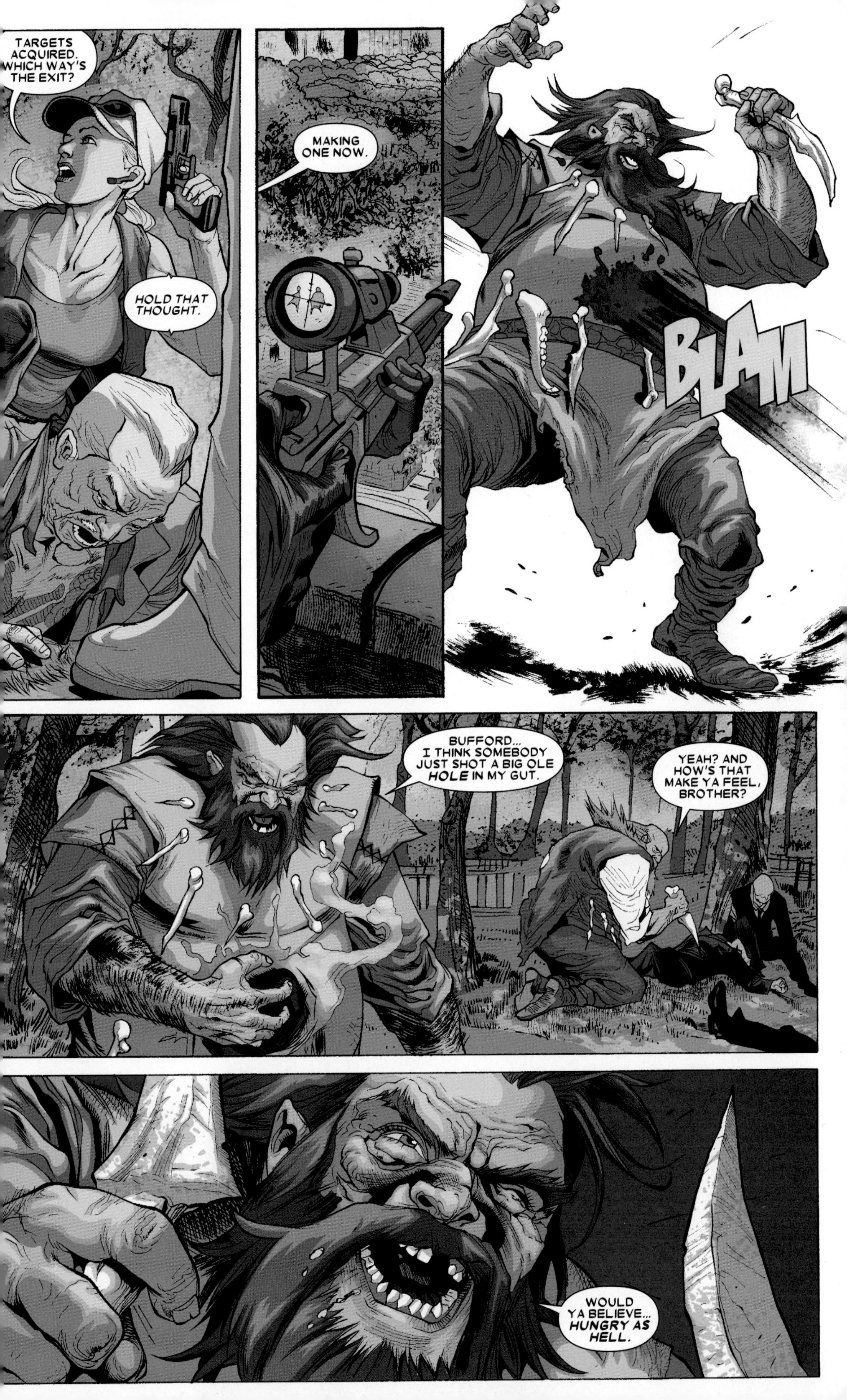
TARGETS ACQUIRED. WHICH WAY'S THE EXIT?
HOLD THAT THOUGHT.
MAKING ONE NOW.
BLAM
BUFFORD... I THINK SOMEBODY JUST SHOT A BIG OLE *HOLE* IN MY GUT.
YEAH? AND HOW'S THAT MAKE YA FEEL, BROTHER?
WOULD YA BELIEVE... *HUNGRY AS HELL.*

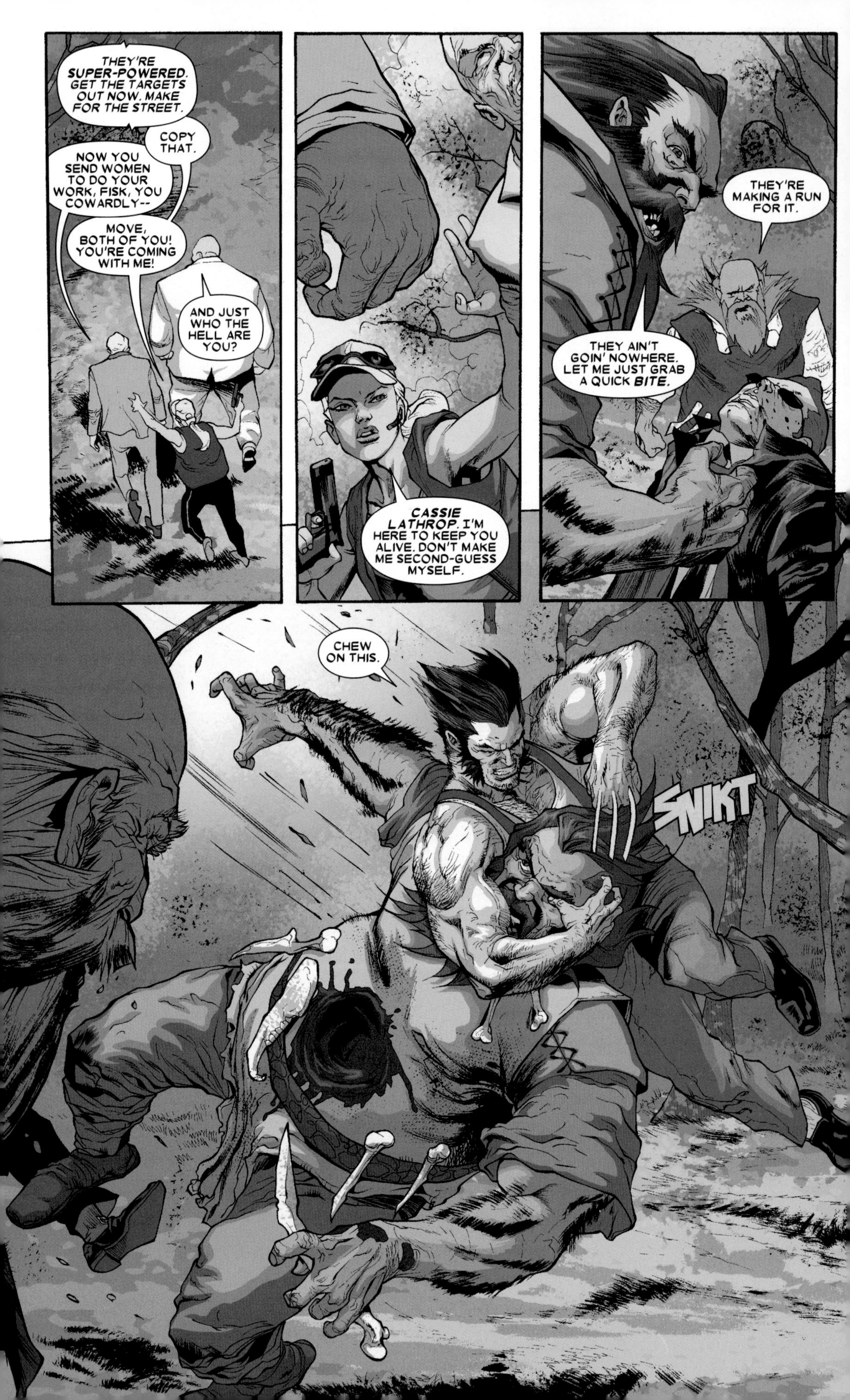
THEY'RE SUPER-POWERED. GET THE TARGETS OUT NOW. MAKE FOR THE STREET.
COPY THAT.
NOW YOU SEND WOMEN TO DO YOUR WORK, FISK, YOU COWARDLY--
MOVE, BOTH OF YOU! YOU'RE COMING WITH ME!
AND JUST WHO THE HELL ARE YOU?
CASSIE LATHROP. I'M HERE TO KEEP YOU ALIVE. DON'T MAKE ME SECOND-GUESS MYSELF.
THEY'RE MAKING A RUN FOR IT.
THEY AIN'T GOIN' NOWHERE. LET ME JUST GRAB A QUICK BITE.
CHEW ON THIS.
SNIKT

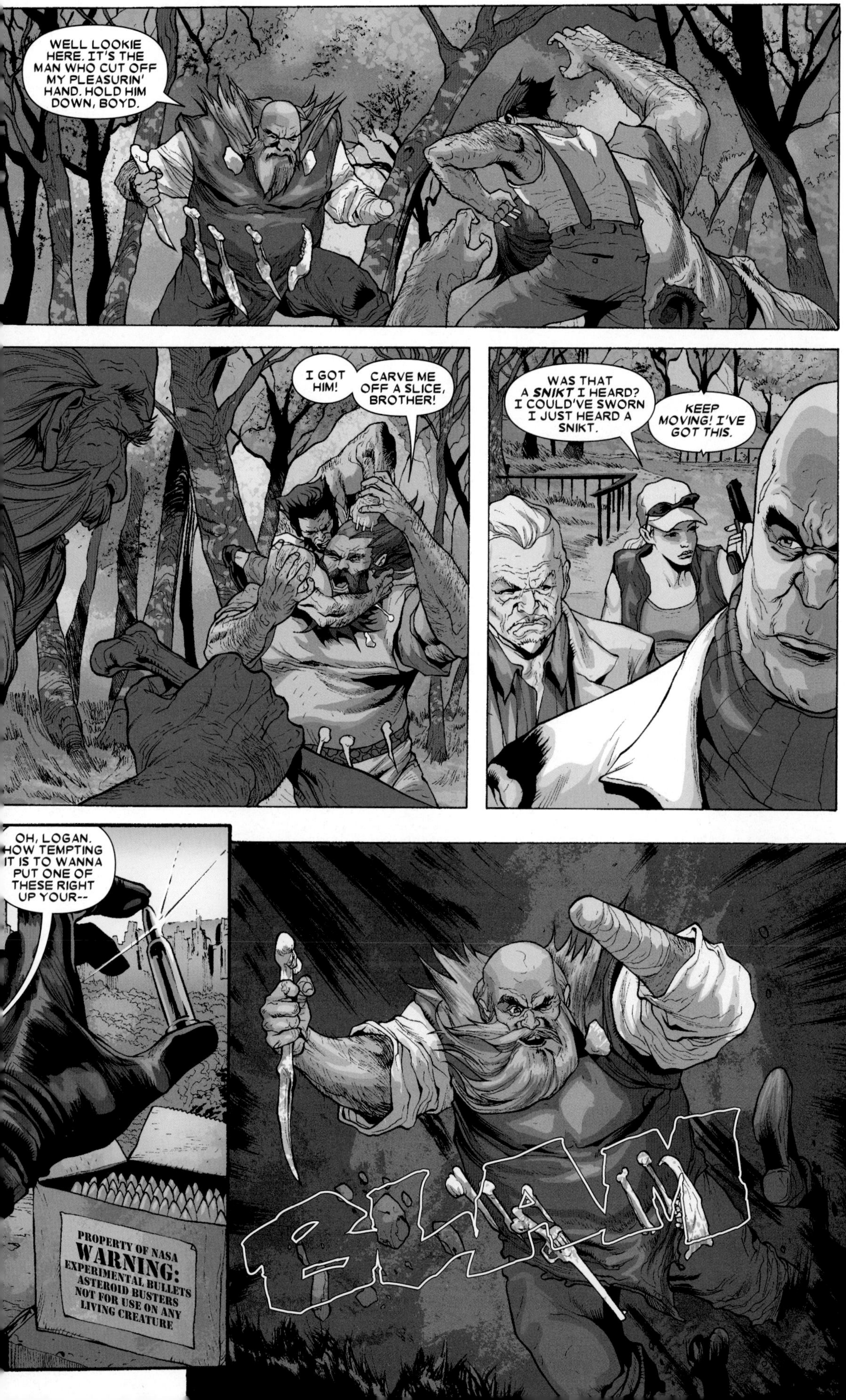
WELL LOOKIE HERE. IT'S THE MAN WHO CUT OFF MY PLEASURIN' HAND. HOLD HIM DOWN, BOYD.
I GOT HIM!
CARVE ME OFF A SLICE, BROTHER!
WAS THAT A SNIKT I HEARD? I COULD'VE SWORN I JUST HEARD A SNIKT.
KEEP MOVING! I'VE GOT THIS.
OH, LOGAN. HOW TEMPTING IT IS TO WANNA PUT ONE OF THESE RIGHT UP YOUR--
PROPERTY OF NASA
WARNING:
EXPERIMENTAL BULLETS
ASTEROID BUSTERS
NOT FOR USE ON ANY
LIVING CREATURE

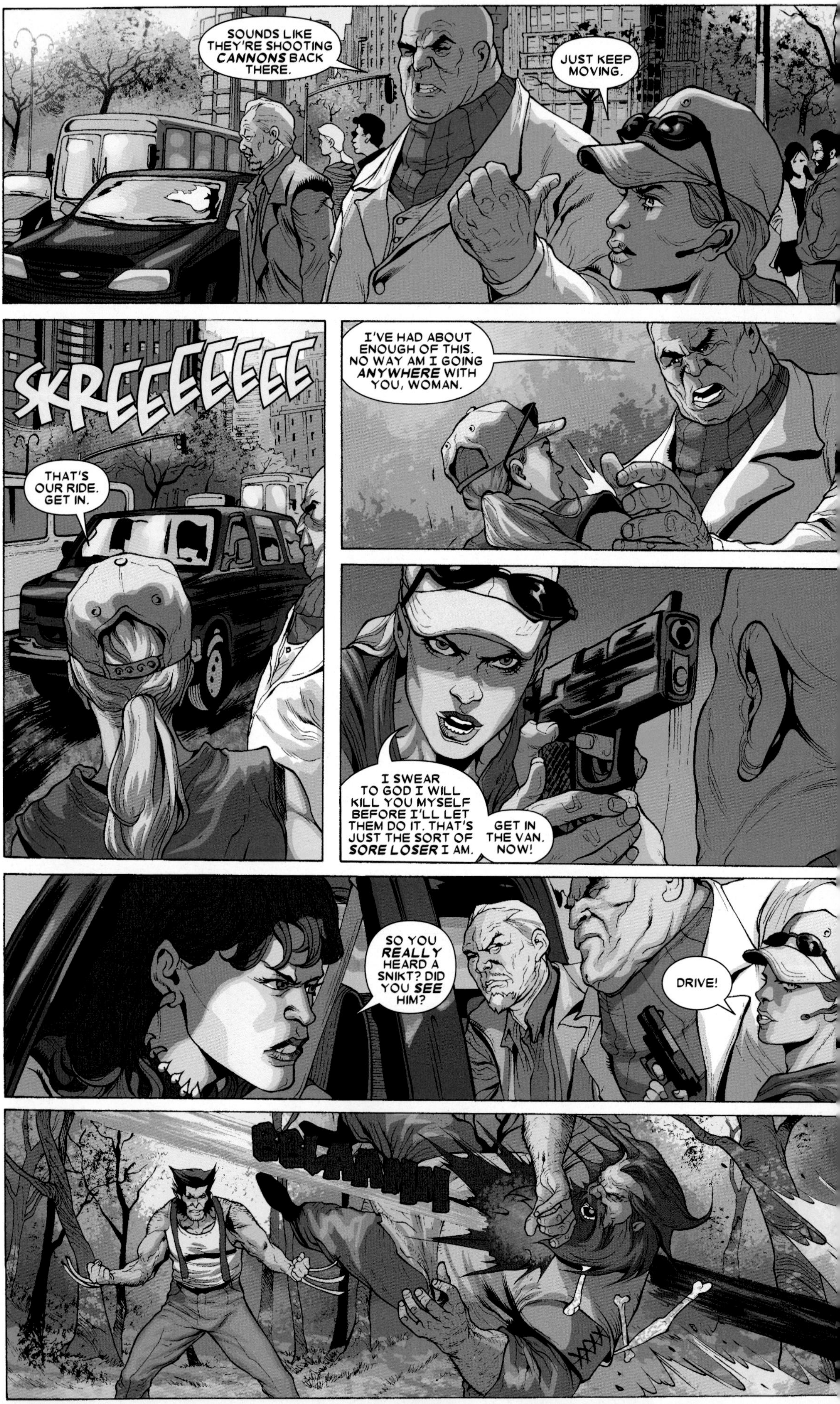
SOUNDS LIKE THEY'RE SHOOTING *CANNONS* BACK THERE.
JUST KEEP MOVING.
SKREEEEEEEE
THAT'S OUR RIDE. GET IN.
I'VE HAD ABOUT ENOUGH OF THIS. NO WAY AM I GOING *ANYWHERE* WITH YOU, WOMAN.
I SWEAR TO GOD I WILL KILL YOU MYSELF BEFORE I'LL LET THEM DO IT. THAT'S JUST THE SORT OF *SORE LOSER* I AM.
GET IN THE VAN. NOW!
SO YOU *REALLY* HEARD A SNIKT? DID YOU *SEE* HIM?
DRIVE!

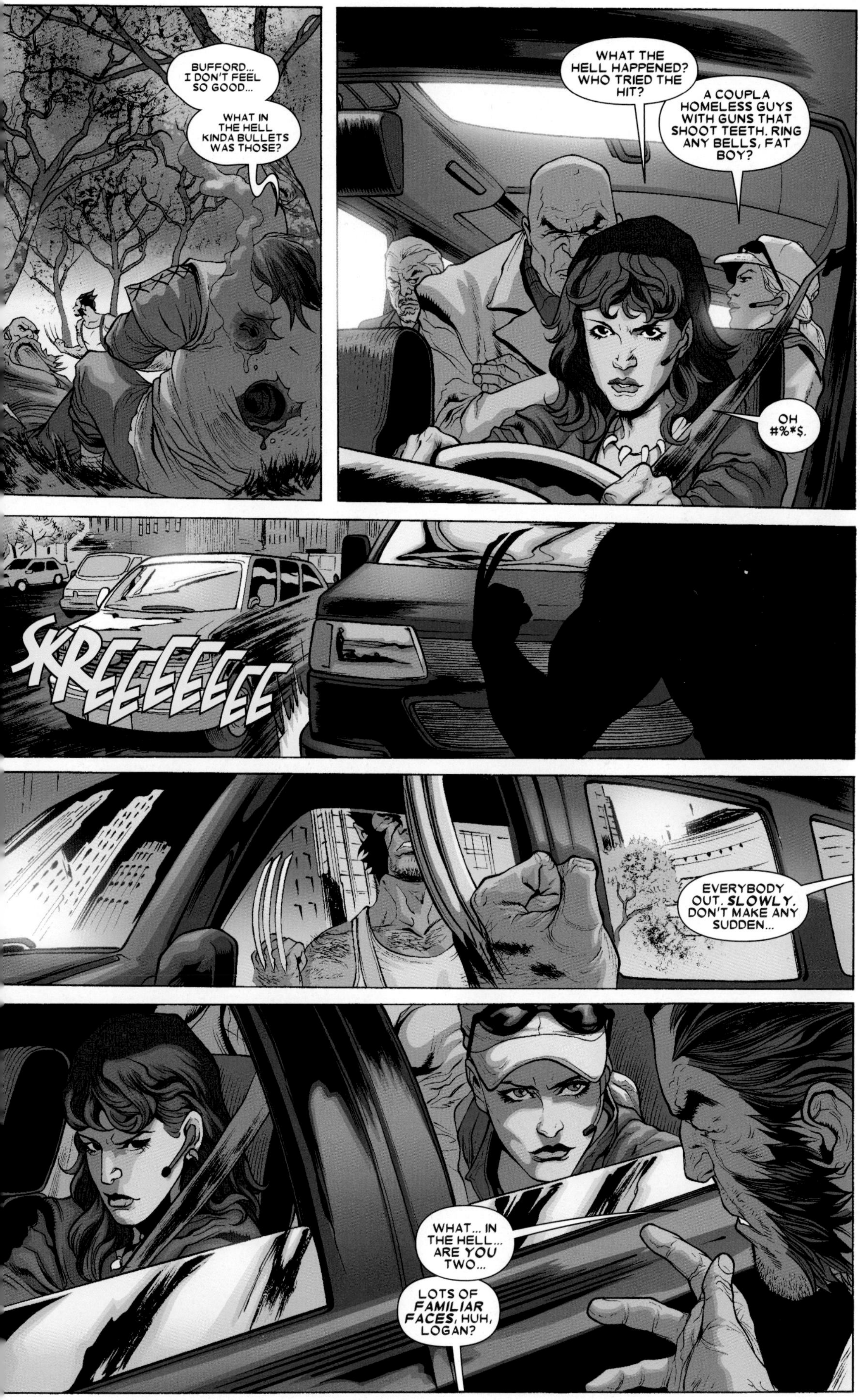
BUFFORD... I DON'T FEEL SO GOOD...
WHAT IN THE HELL KINDA BULLETS WAS THOSE?
WHAT THE HELL HAPPENED? WHO TRIED THE HIT?
A COUPLA HOMELESS GUYS WITH GUNS THAT SHOOT TEETH. RING ANY BELLS, FAT BOY?
OH #%*$.
SKREEEEEEEE
EVERYBODY OUT. SLOWLY. DON'T MAKE ANY SUDDEN...
WHAT... IN THE HELL... ARE YOU TWO...
LOTS OF FAMILIAR FACES, HUH, LOGAN?

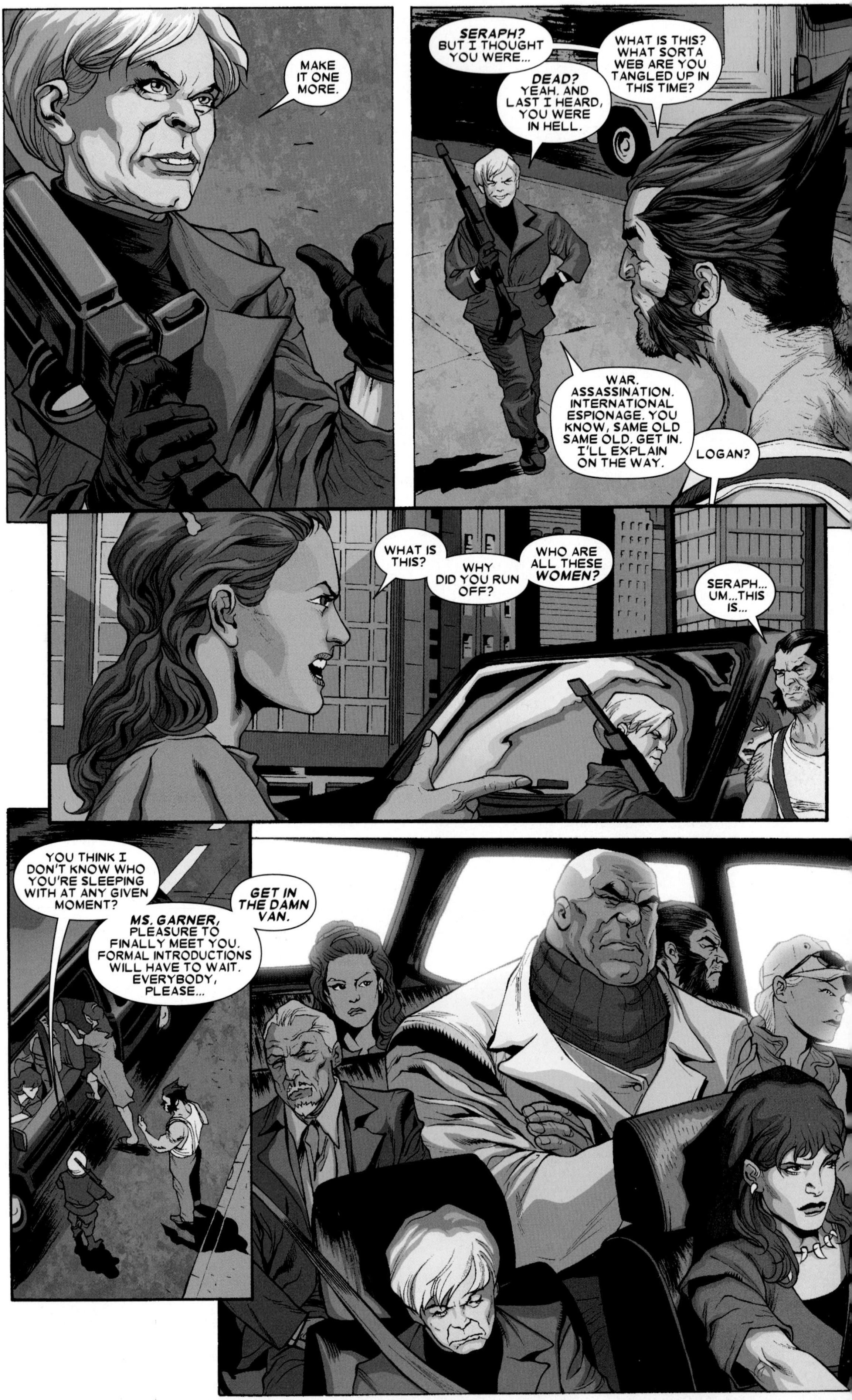
MAKE IT ONE MORE.
SERAPH? BUT I THOUGHT YOU WERE...
DEAD? YEAH. AND LAST I HEARD, YOU WERE IN HELL.
WHAT IS THIS? WHAT SORTA WEB ARE YOU TANGLED UP IN THIS TIME?
WAR. ASSASSINATION. INTERNATIONAL ESPIONAGE. YOU KNOW, SAME OLD SAME OLD. GET IN. I'LL EXPLAIN ON THE WAY.
LOGAN?
WHAT IS THIS?
WHY DID YOU RUN OFF?
WHO ARE ALL THESE WOMEN?
SERAPH... UM...THIS IS...
YOU THINK I DON'T KNOW WHO YOU'RE SLEEPING WITH AT ANY GIVEN MOMENT?
MS. GARNER, PLEASURE TO FINALLY MEET YOU. FORMAL INTRODUCTIONS WILL HAVE TO WAIT. EVERYBODY, PLEASE...
GET IN THE DAMN VAN.

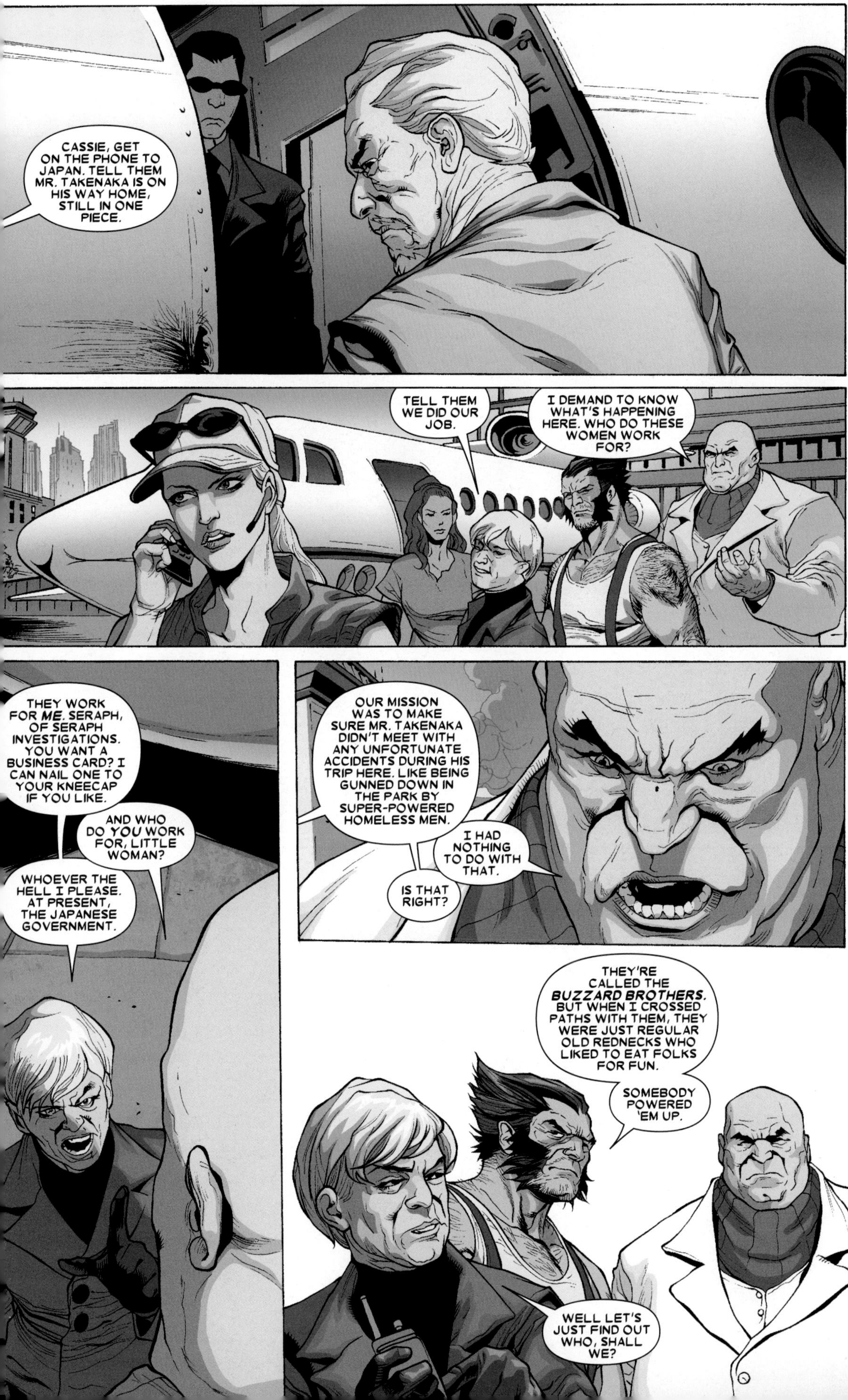
CASSIE, GET ON THE PHONE TO JAPAN. TELL THEM MR. TAKENAKA IS ON HIS WAY HOME, STILL IN ONE PIECE.
TELL THEM WE DID OUR JOB.
I DEMAND TO KNOW WHAT'S HAPPENING HERE. WHO DO THESE WOMEN WORK FOR?
THEY WORK FOR ME. SERAPH, OF SERAPH INVESTIGATIONS. YOU WANT A BUSINESS CARD? I CAN NAIL ONE TO YOUR KNEECAP IF YOU LIKE.
AND WHO DO YOU WORK FOR, LITTLE WOMAN?
WHOEVER THE HELL I PLEASE. AT PRESENT, THE JAPANESE GOVERNMENT.
OUR MISSION WAS TO MAKE SURE MR. TAKENAKA DIDN'T MEET WITH ANY UNFORTUNATE ACCIDENTS DURING HIS TRIP HERE. LIKE BEING GUNNED DOWN IN THE PARK BY SUPER-POWERED HOMELESS MEN.
I HAD NOTHING TO DO WITH THAT.
IS THAT RIGHT?
THEY'RE CALLED THE BUZZARD BROTHERS. BUT WHEN I CROSSED PATHS WITH THEM, THEY WERE JUST REGULAR OLD REDNECKS WHO LIKED TO EAT FOLKS FOR FUN.
SOMEBODY POWERED 'EM UP.
WELL LET'S JUST FIND OUT WHO, SHALL WE?

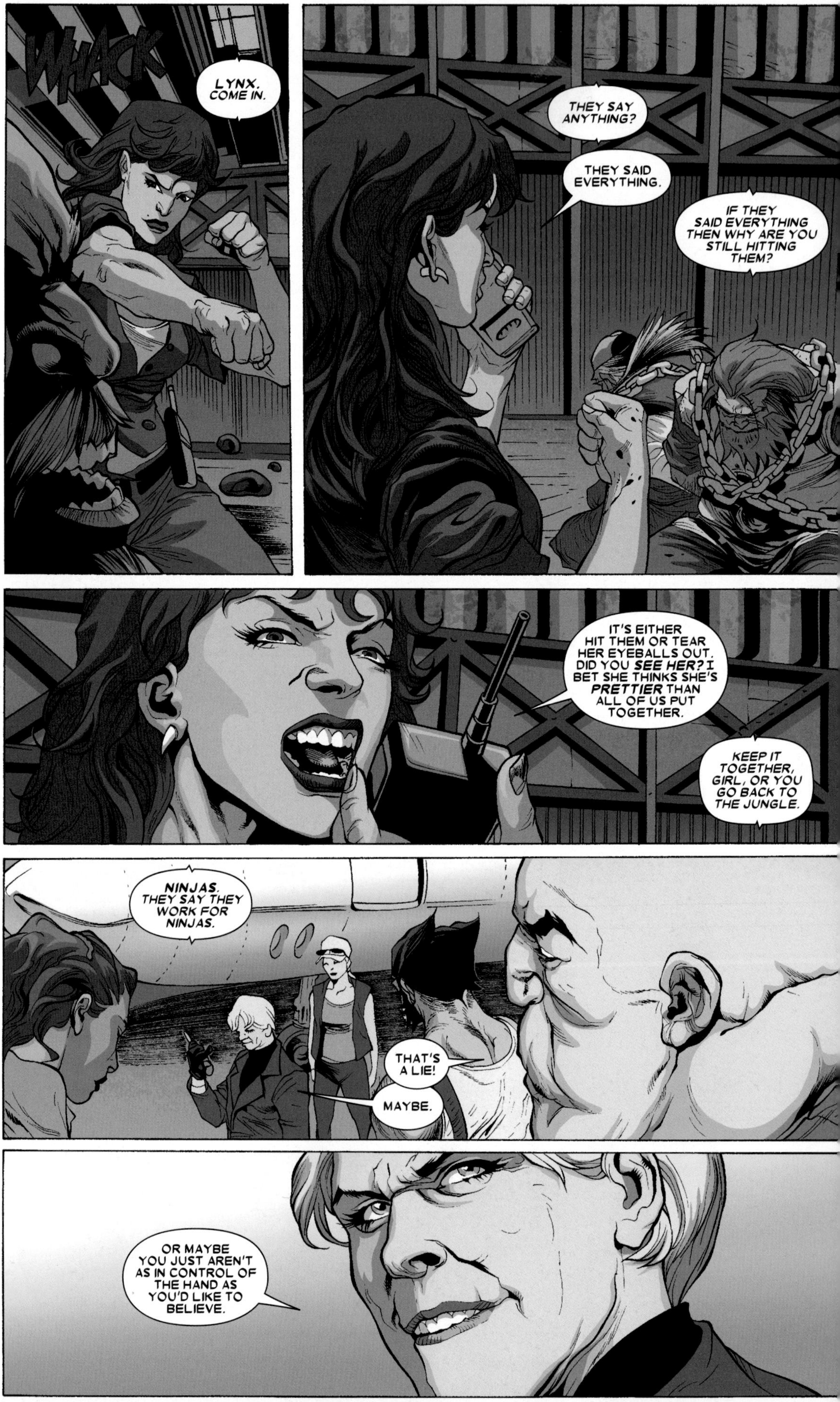
WHACK
LYNX. COME IN.
THEY SAY ANYTHING?
THEY SAID EVERYTHING.
IF THEY SAID EVERYTHING THEN WHY ARE YOU STILL HITTING THEM?
IT'S EITHER HIT THEM OR TEAR HER EYEBALLS OUT. DID YOU SEE HER? I BET SHE THINKS SHE'S PRETTIER THAN ALL OF US PUT TOGETHER.
KEEP IT TOGETHER, GIRL, OR YOU GO BACK TO THE JUNGLE.
NINJAS. THEY SAY THEY WORK FOR NINJAS.
THAT'S A LIE!
MAYBE.
OR MAYBE YOU JUST AREN'T AS IN CONTROL OF THE HAND AS YOU'D LIKE TO BELIEVE.

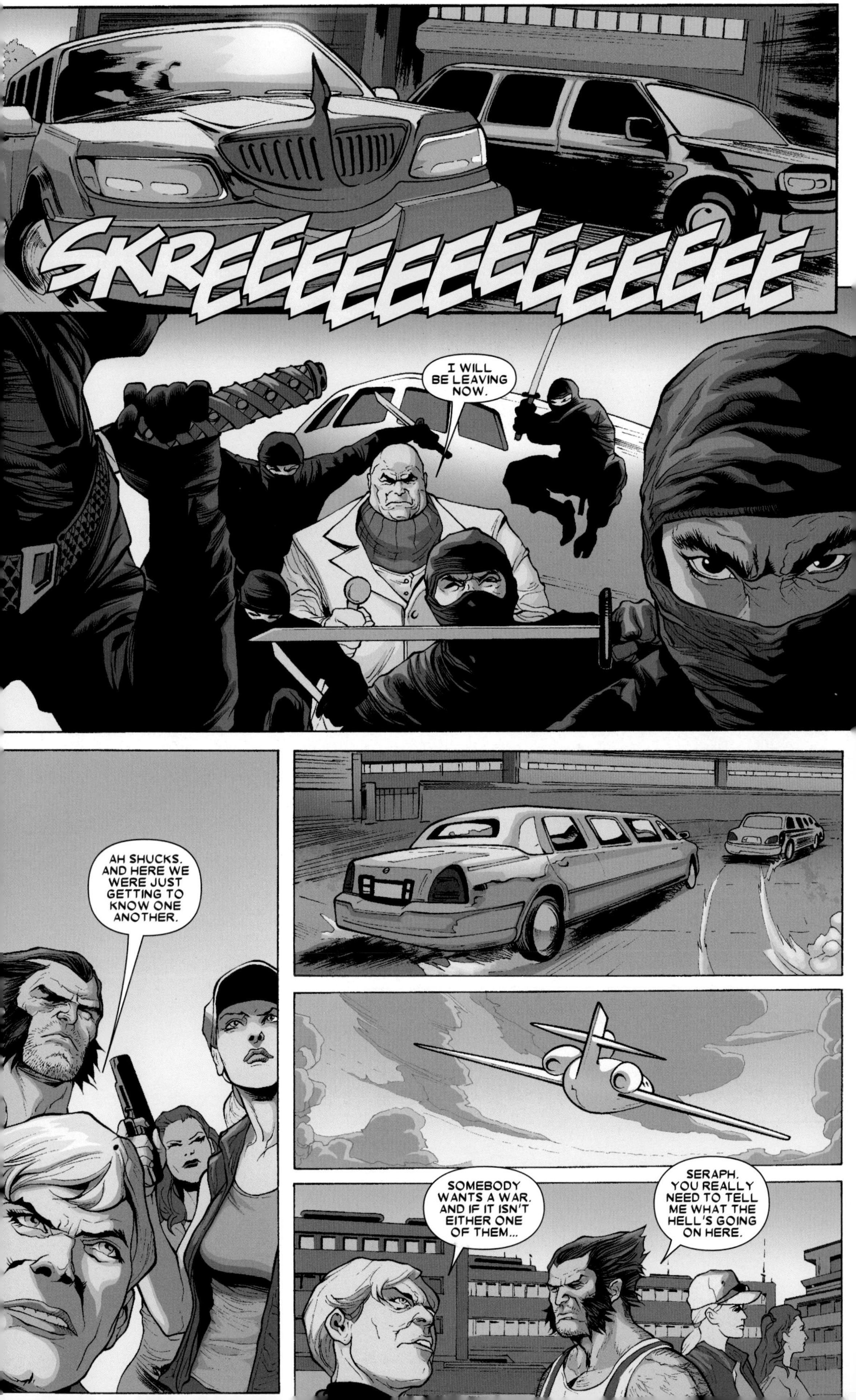
SKREEEEEEEEEEEEEEE
I WILL BE LEAVING NOW.
AH SHUCKS. AND HERE WE WERE JUST GETTING TO KNOW ONE ANOTHER.
SOMEBODY WANTS A WAR. AND IF IT ISN'T EITHER ONE OF THEM...
SERAPH. YOU REALLY NEED TO TELL ME WHAT THE HELL'S GOING ON HERE.

WE DON'T TAKE ORDERS FROM YOU, #&*%@!

CASSIE...

NO, TO HELL WITH HIM! WE CAN'T TRUST HIM!

YOU MIGHT THINK YOU CAN, BUT JUST AS SOON AS YOU LOOK THE OTHER WAY HE'LL UP AND RUN OUT ON YOU!

OH OKAY, I GET IT. THEY'RE ALL *EX-GIRLFRIENDS*, AREN'T THEY?

SERAPH...

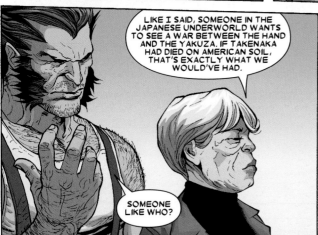

LIKE I SAID, SOMEONE IN THE JAPANESE UNDERWORLD WANTS TO SEE A WAR BETWEEN THE HAND AND THE YAKUZA. IF TAKENAKA HAD DIED ON AMERICAN SOIL, THAT'S EXACTLY WHAT WE WOULD'VE HAD.

SOMEONE LIKE WHO?

SERAPH? LIKE WHO?

I GOT SOME IDEAS.

AND?

AND YOU AREN'T GONNA LIKE 'EM.

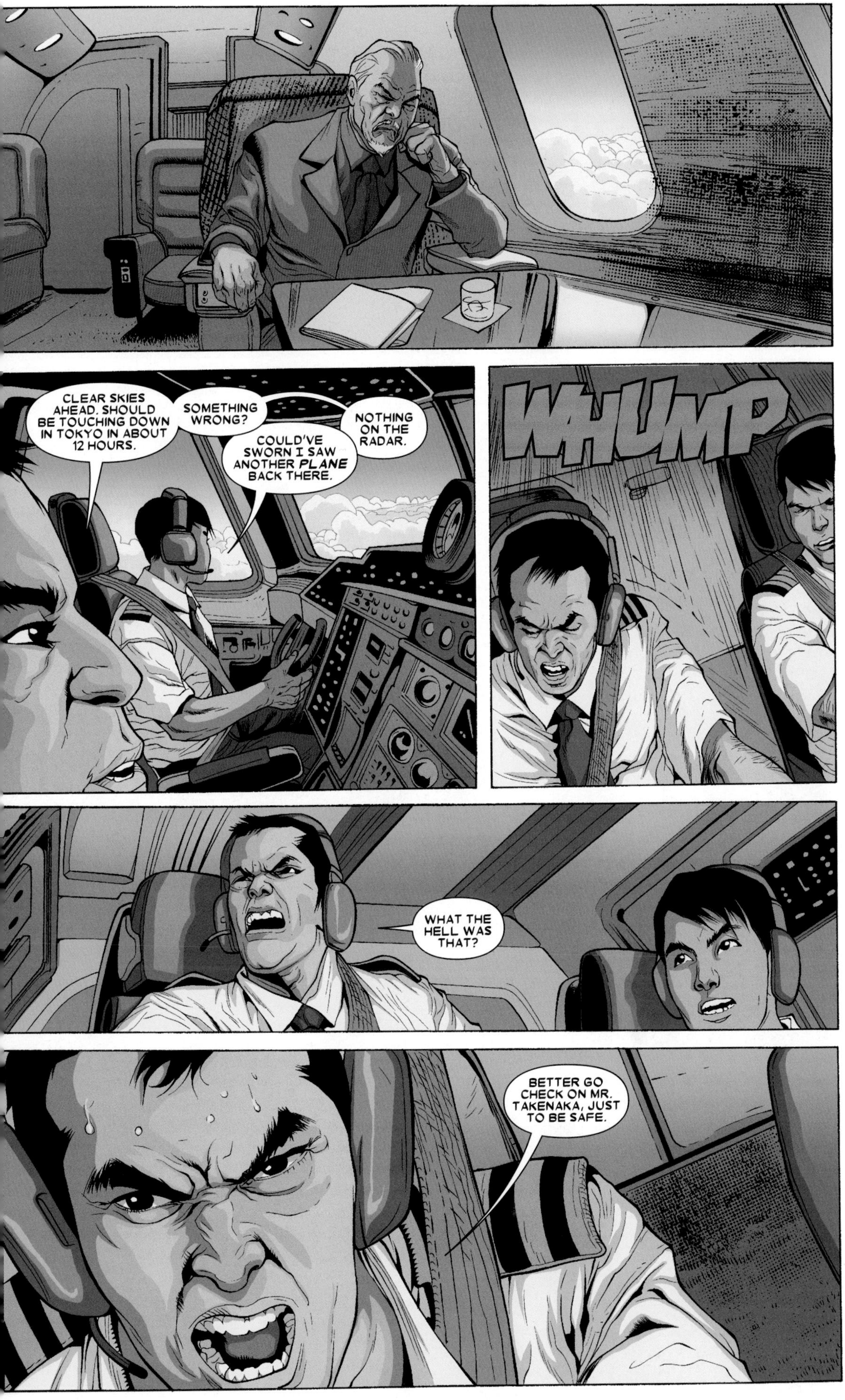

CLEAR SKIES AHEAD. SHOULD BE TOUCHING DOWN IN TOKYO IN ABOUT 12 HOURS.
SOMETHING WRONG?
COULD'VE SWORN I SAW ANOTHER PLANE BACK THERE.
NOTHING ON THE RADAR.
WHUMP
WHAT THE HELL WAS THAT?
BETTER GO CHECK ON MR. TAKENAKA, JUST TO BE SAFE.

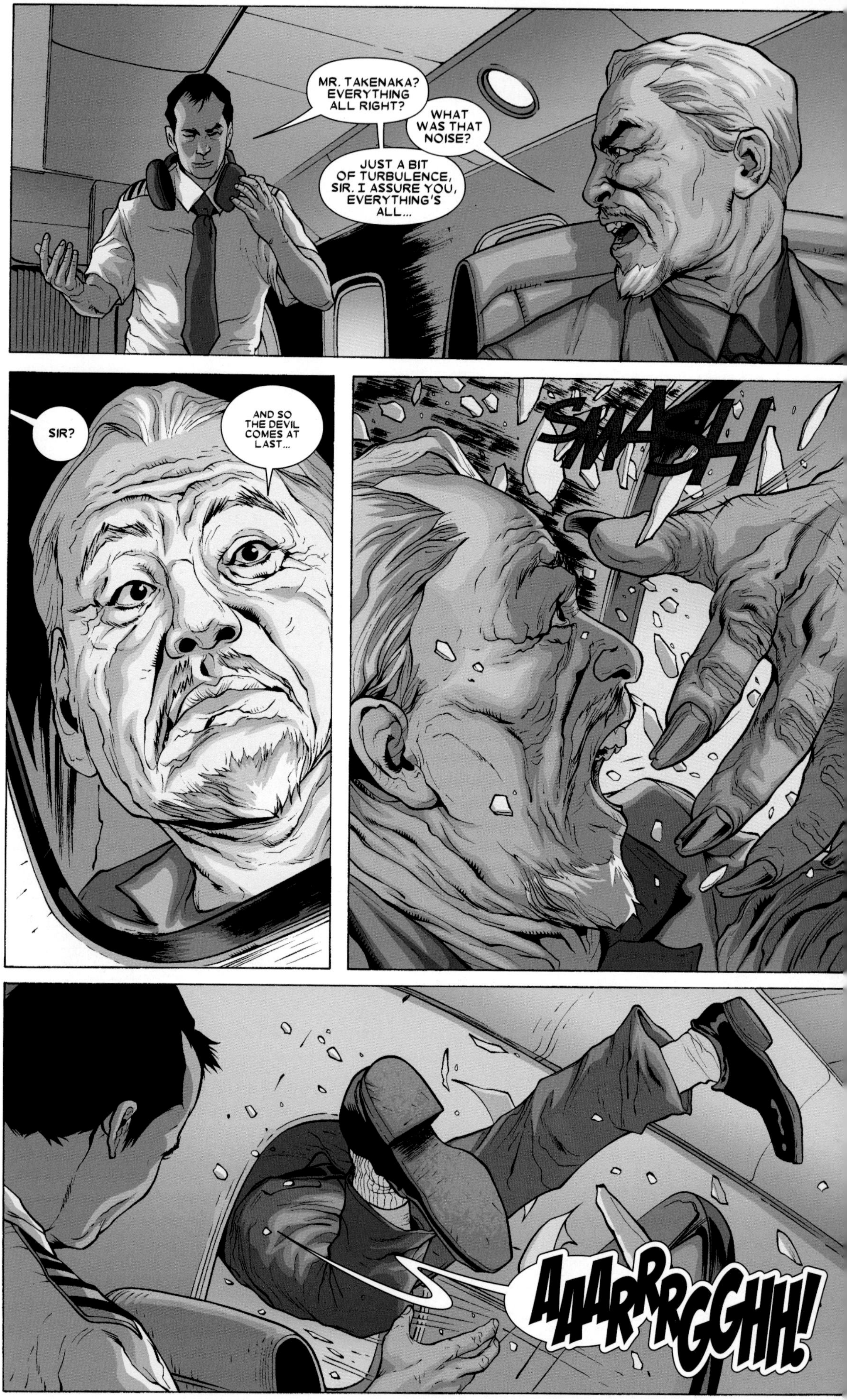
MR. TAKENAKA? EVERYTHING ALL RIGHT?
WHAT WAS THAT NOISE?
JUST A BIT OF TURBULENCE, SIR. I ASSURE YOU, EVERYTHING'S ALL...
SIR?
AND SO THE DEVIL COMES AT LAST...
SMASH
AAARRRGGHH!

HAVE YOU MADE CONTACT WITH THE TARGET, OVER?
OH, YEAH.
I'D SAY SO.
PLEASE CONFIRM THAT TARGET HAS BEEN NEUTRALIZED.
TARGET'S TAKING A NOSE DIVE FROM 30,000 FEET. THAT NEUTRALIZED ENOUGH FOR YA?
I TOLD YA I'D DELIVER, DIDN'T I?
YOU WANTED A WAR?

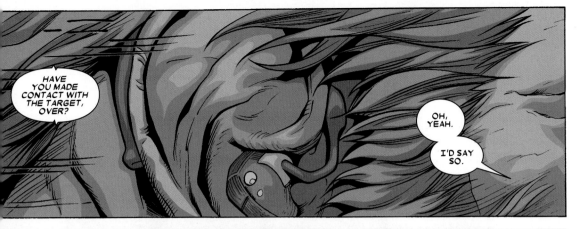

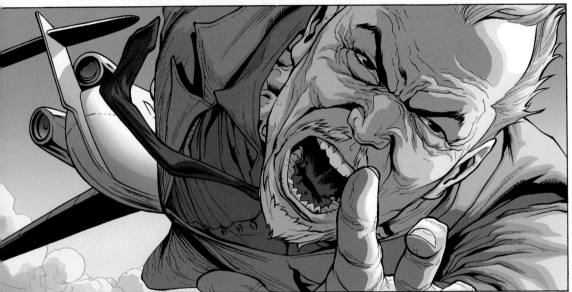

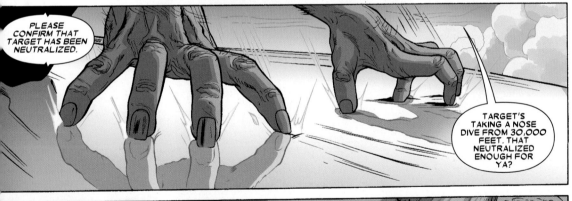

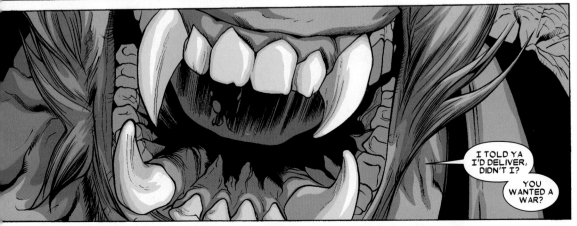

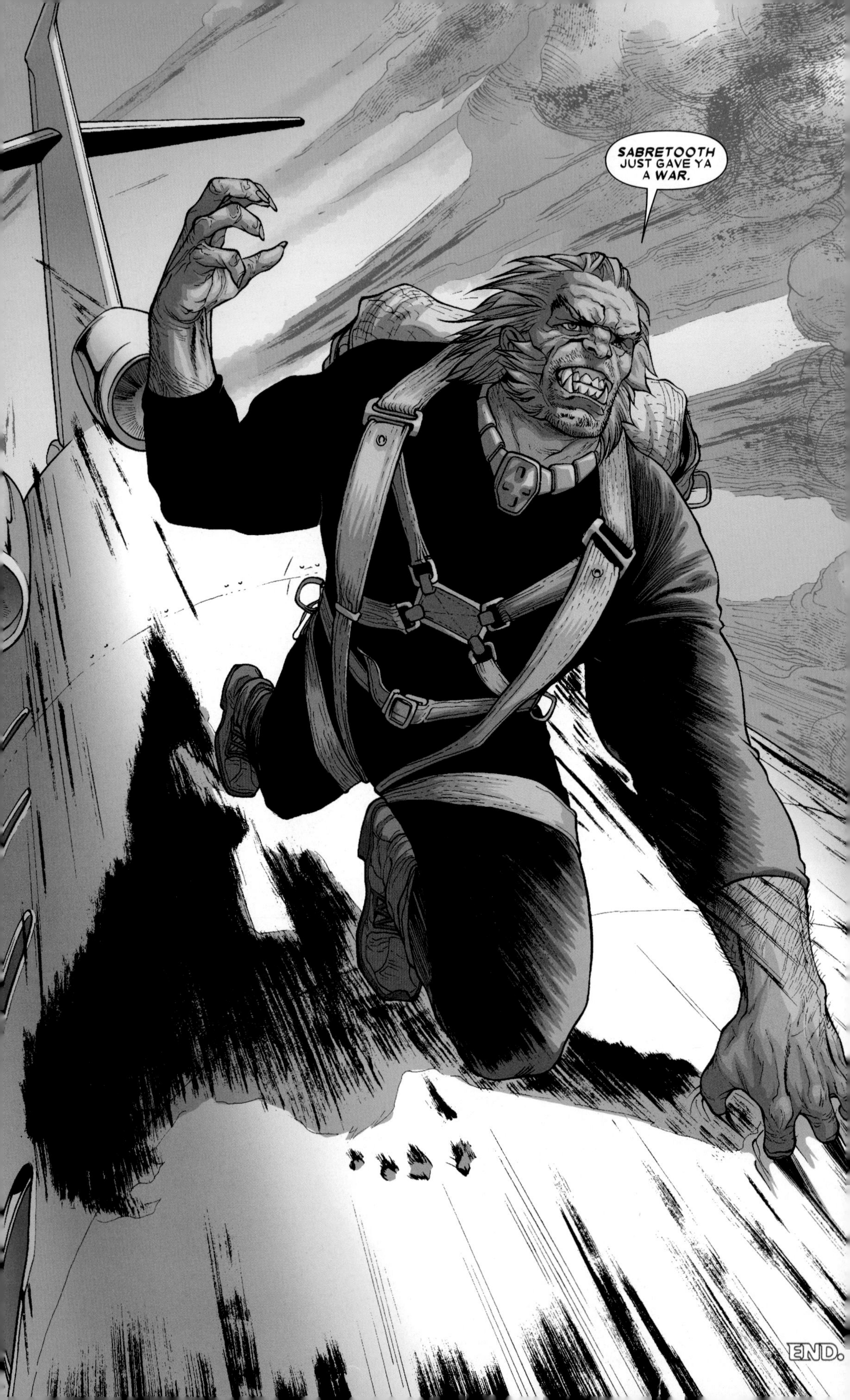
SABRETOOTH JUST GAVE YA A WAR.
END.

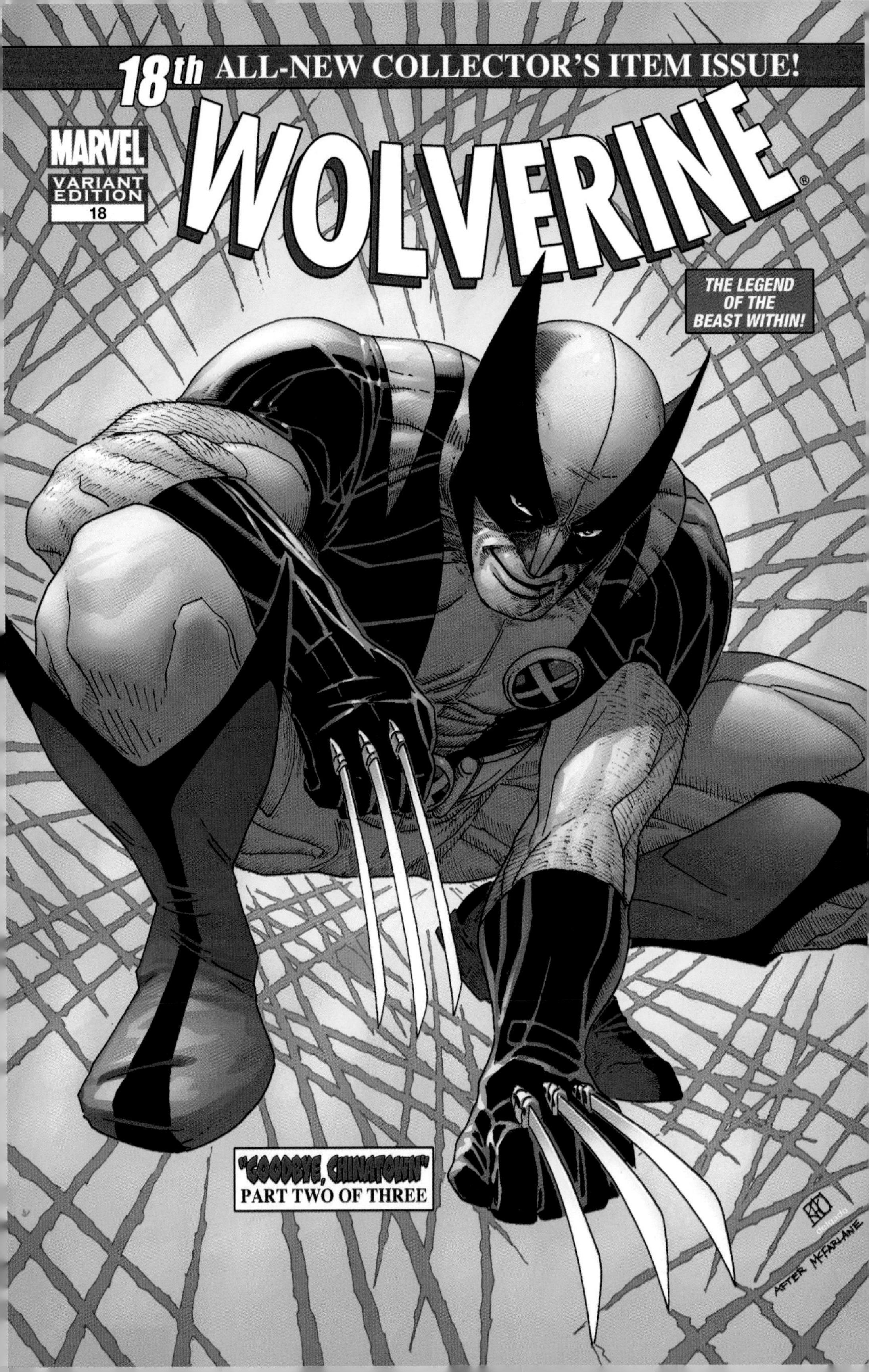
18th ALL-NEW COLLECTOR'S ITEM ISSUE!
MARVEL
VARIANT EDITION
18
WOLVERINE
THE LEGEND OF THE BEAST WITHIN!
"GOODBYE, CHINATOWN"
PART TWO OF THREE
AFTER McFARLANE

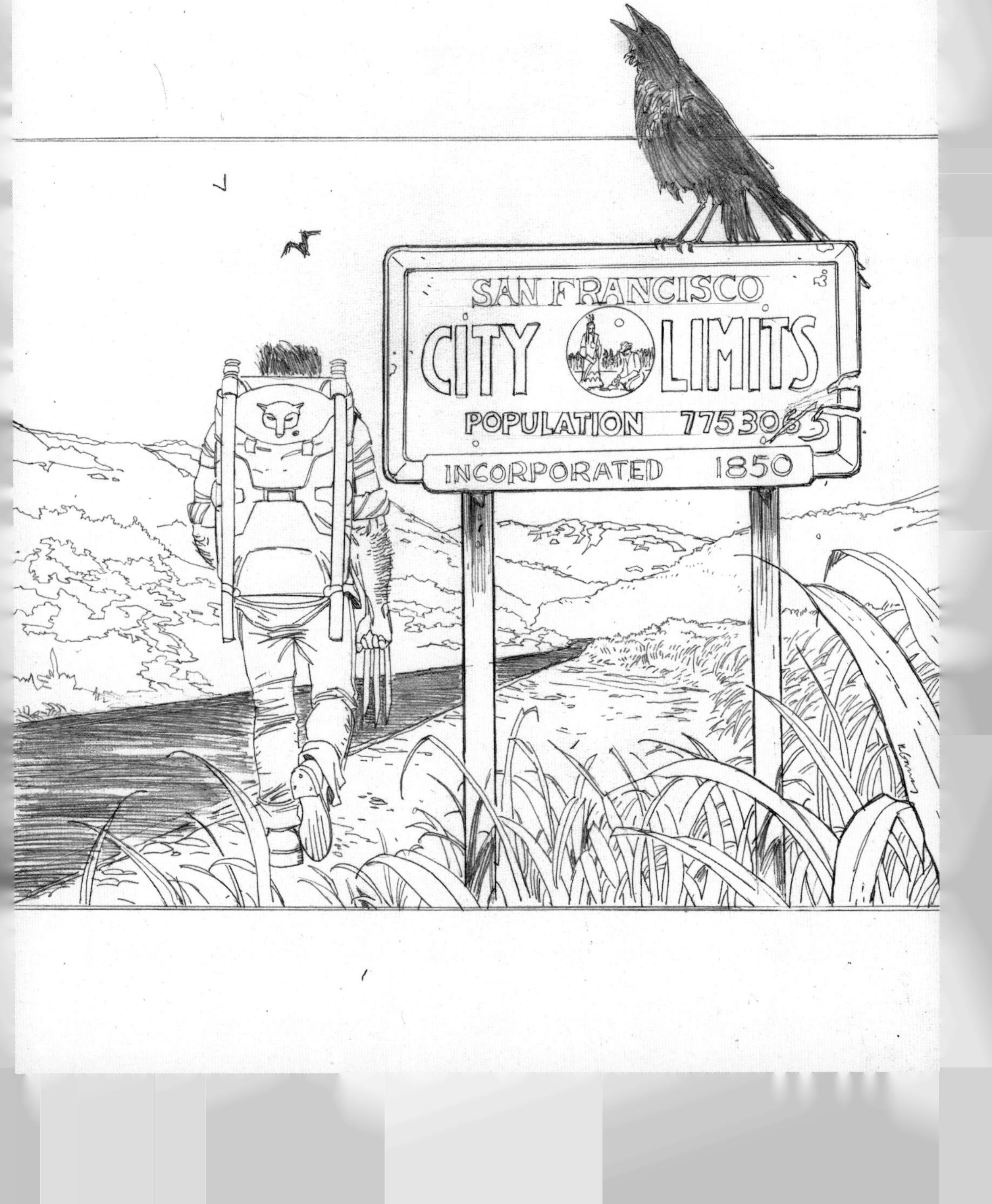
SAN FRANCISCO
CITY LIMITS
POPULATION 77530
INCORPORATED 1850

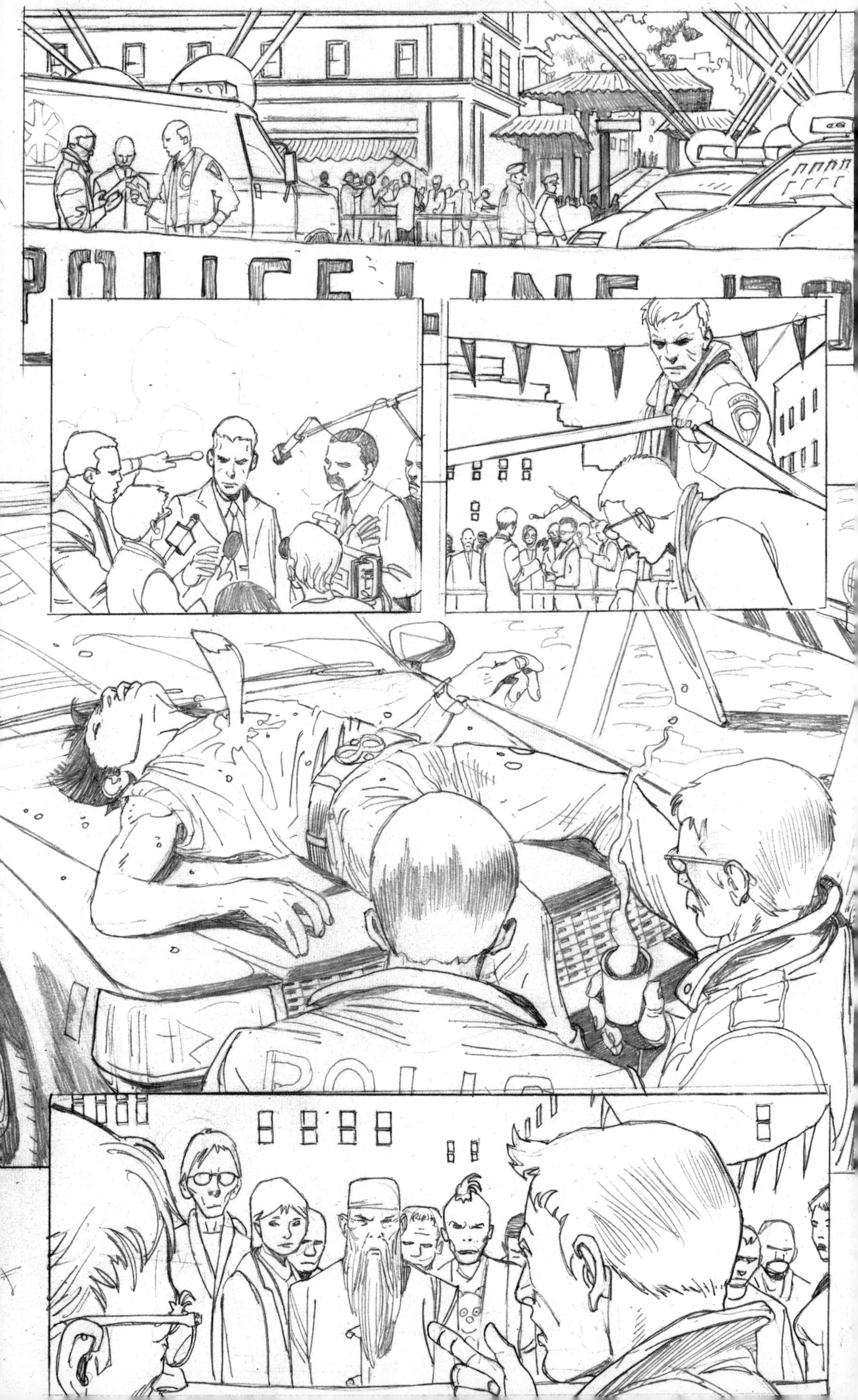

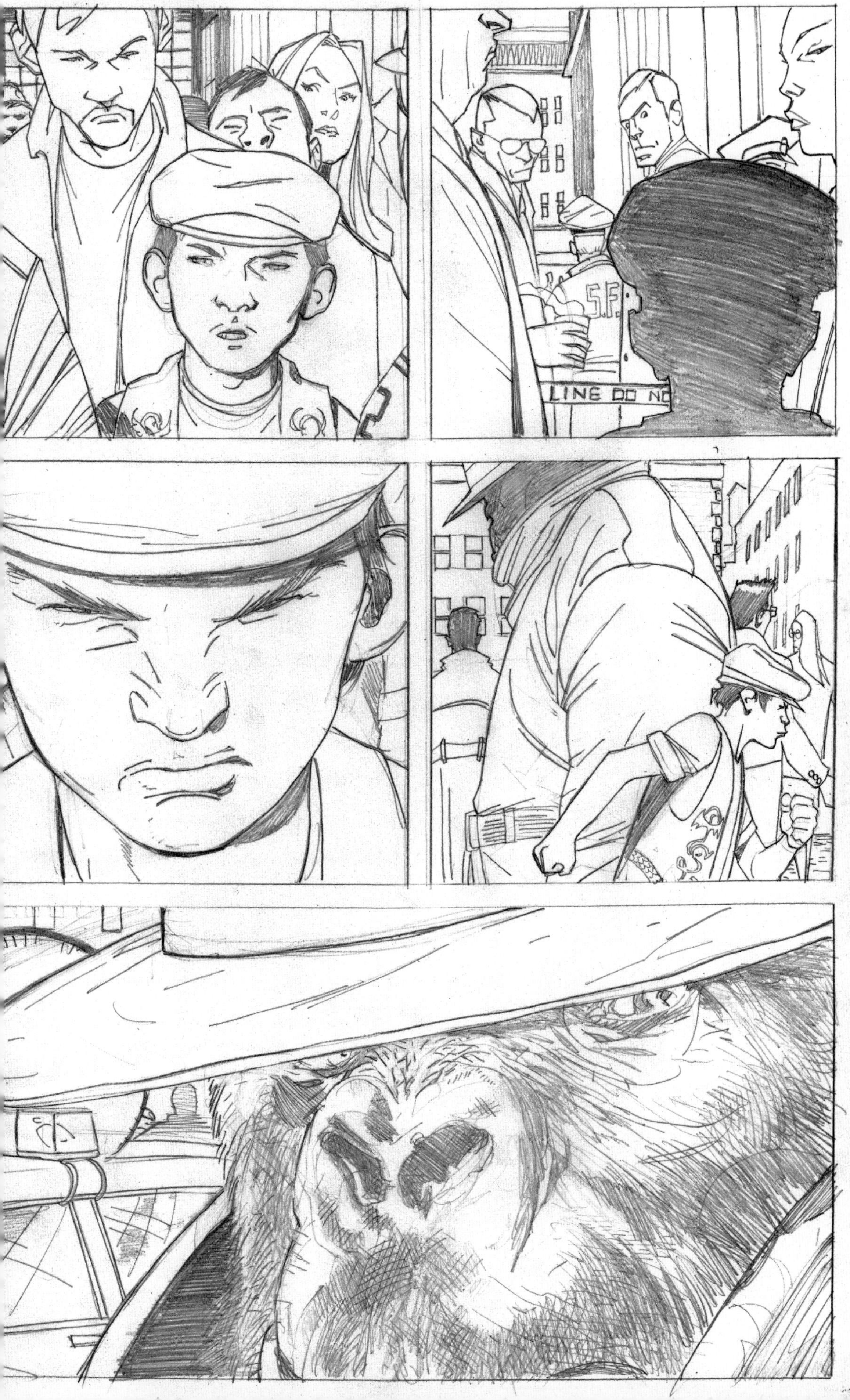
S.F.
LINE DO NO

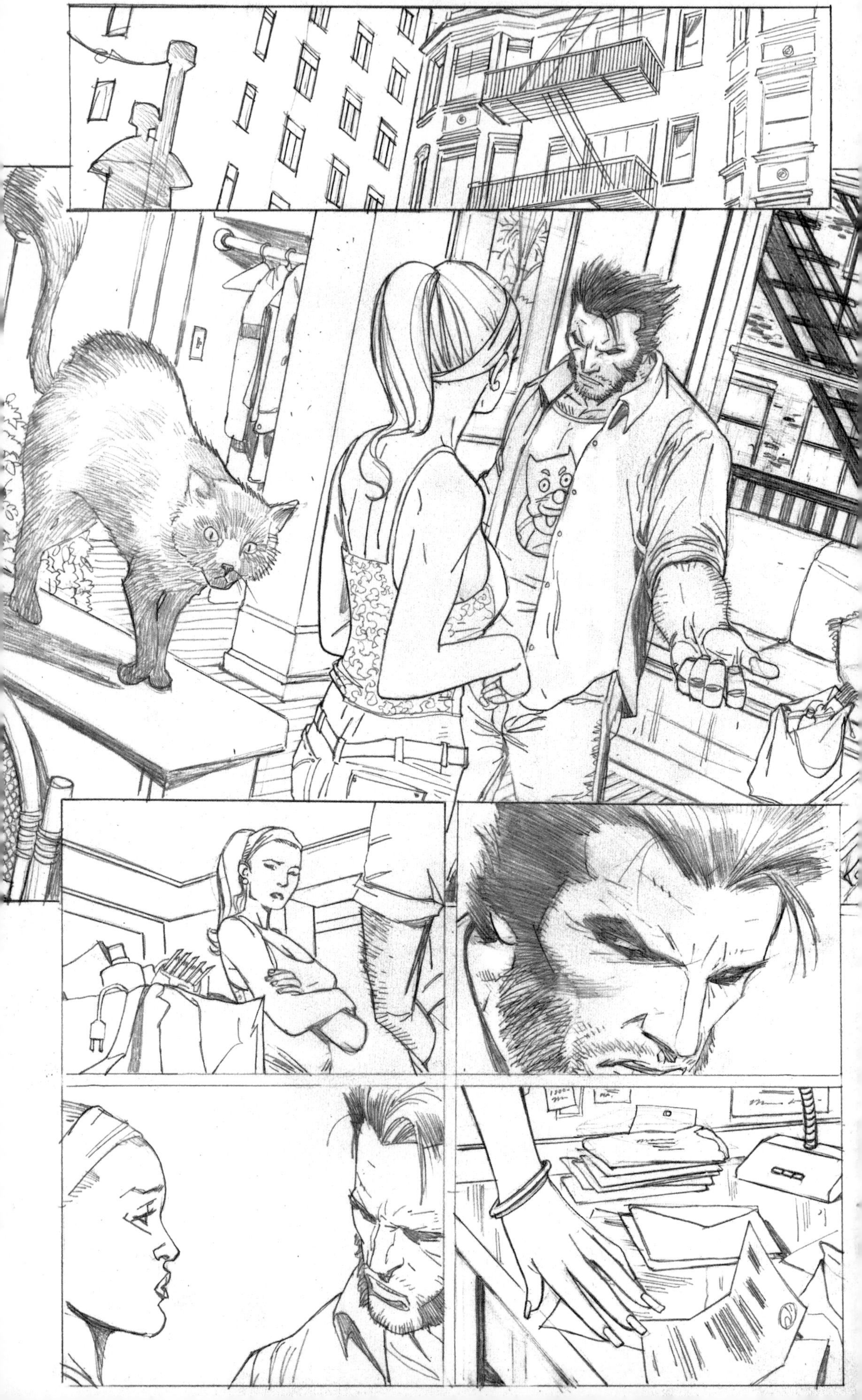

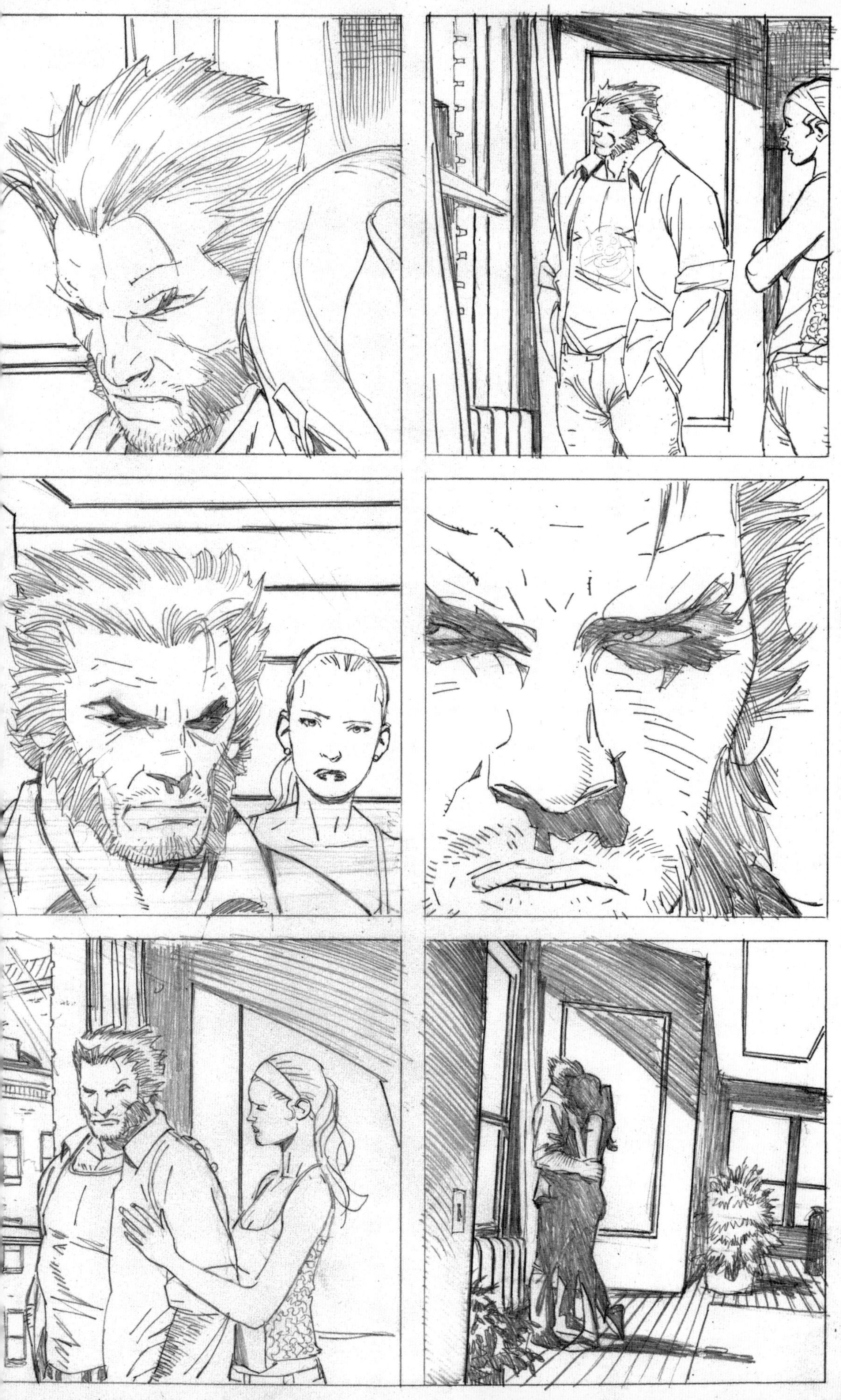

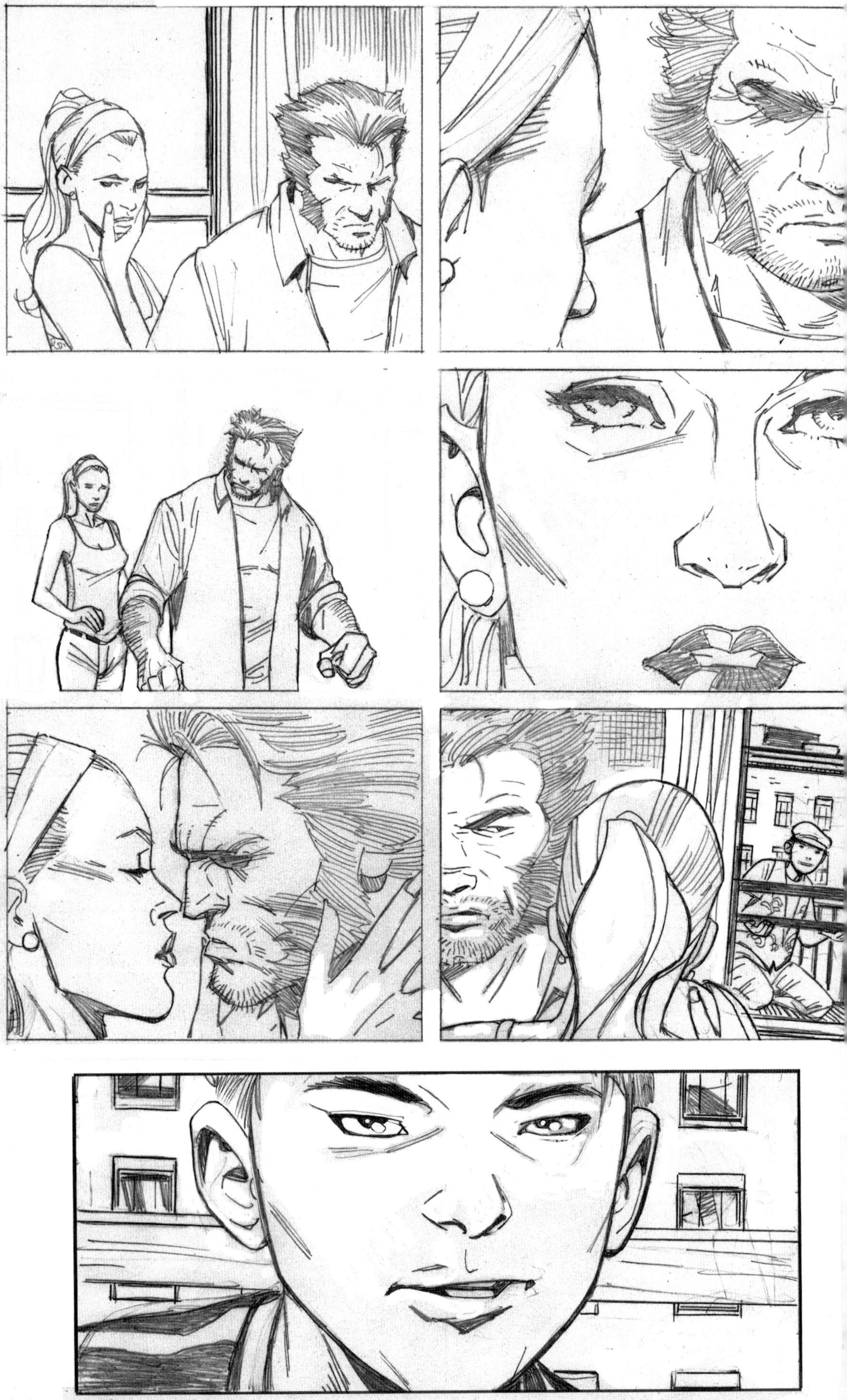

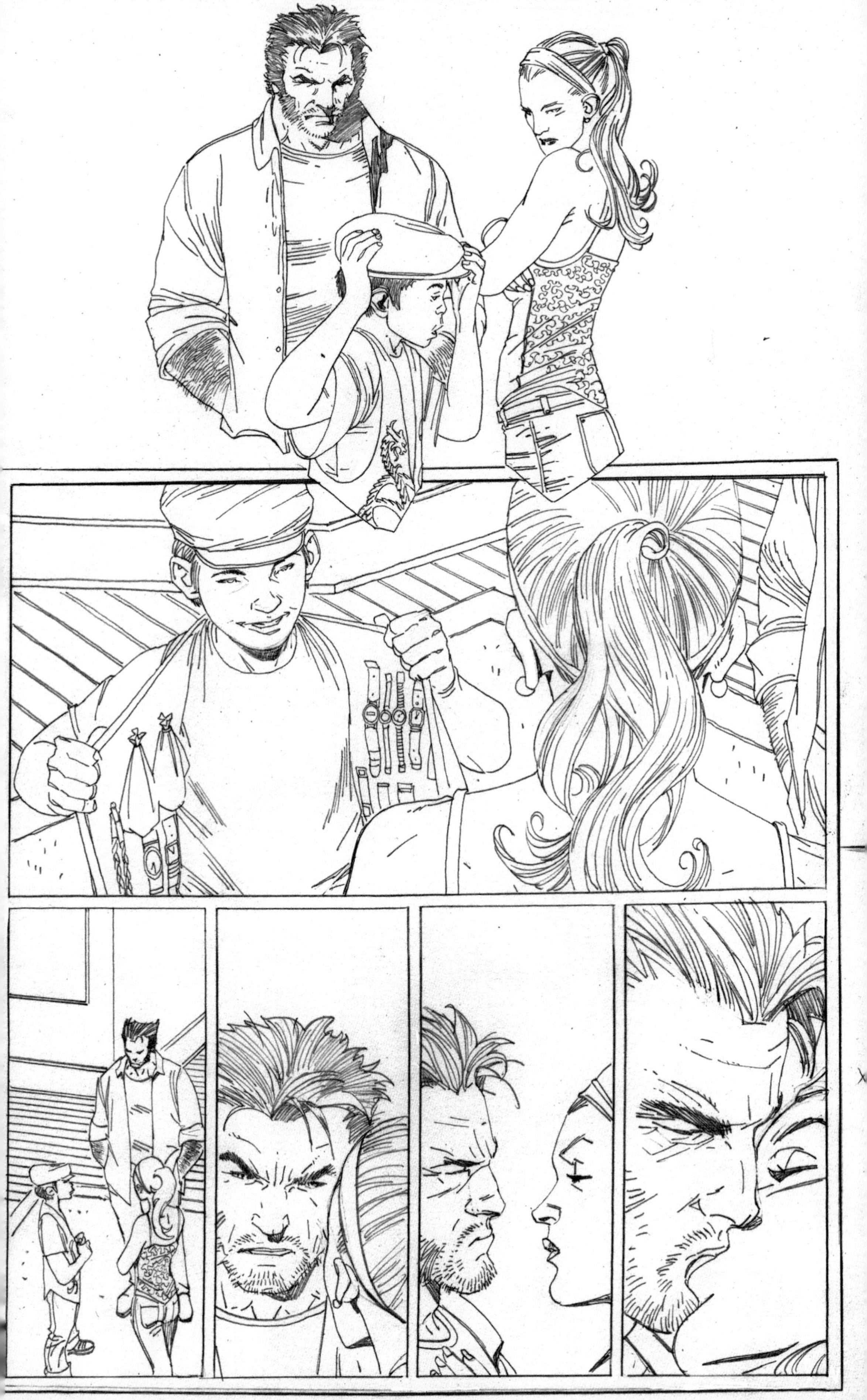

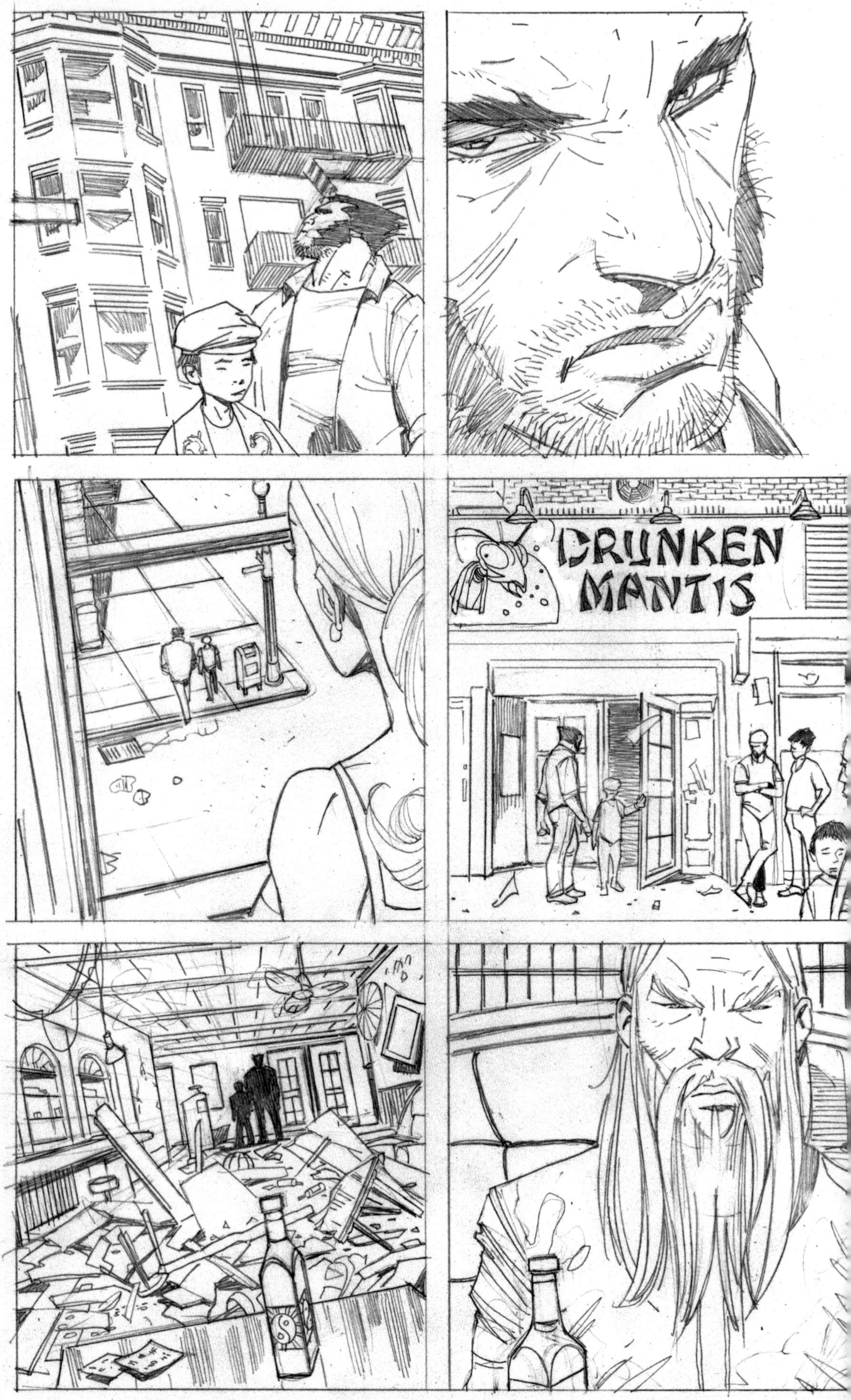
DRUNKEN
MANTIS

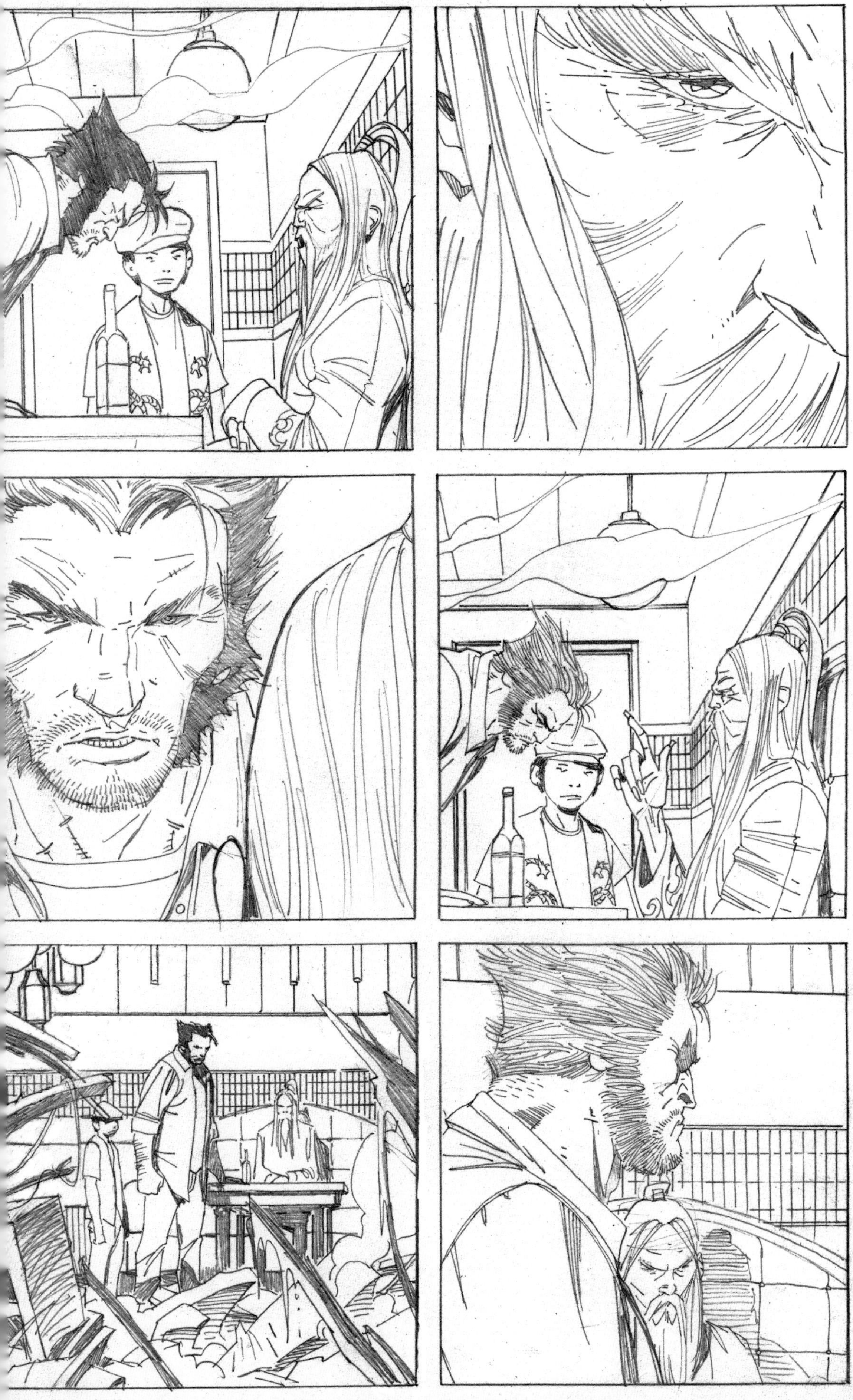

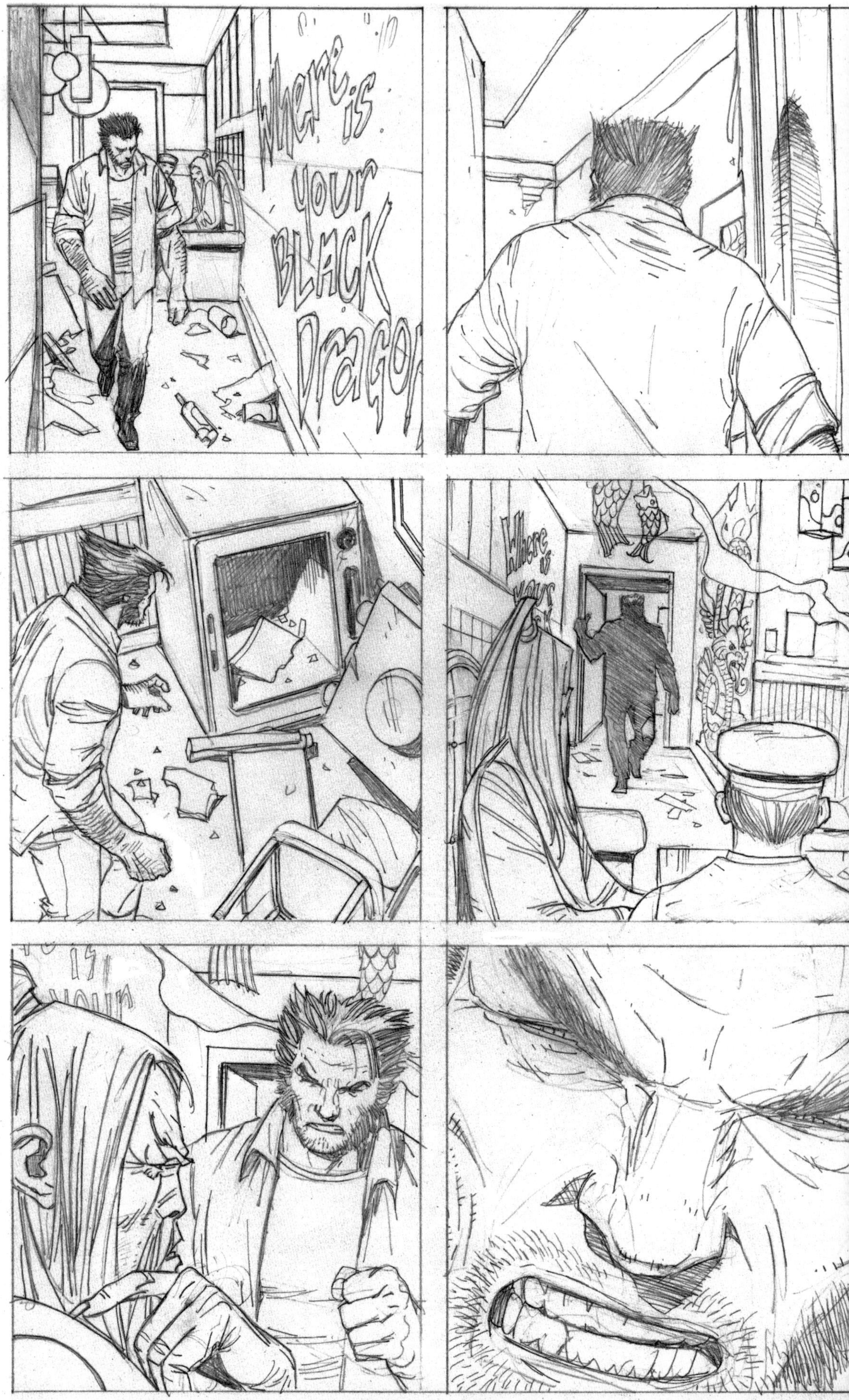
Where is your BLACK Drago
Where is your

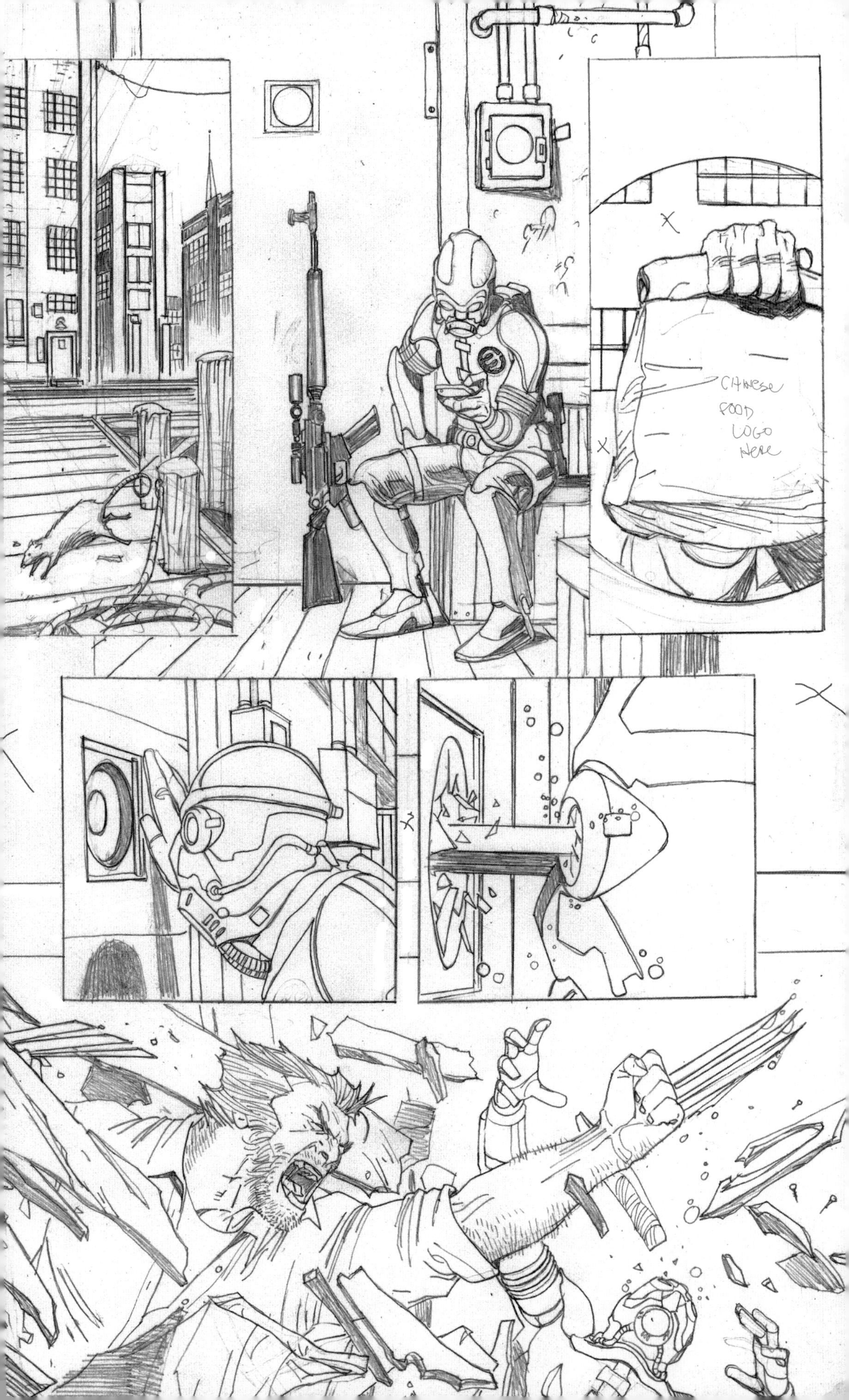
CHINESE FOOD LOGO HERE

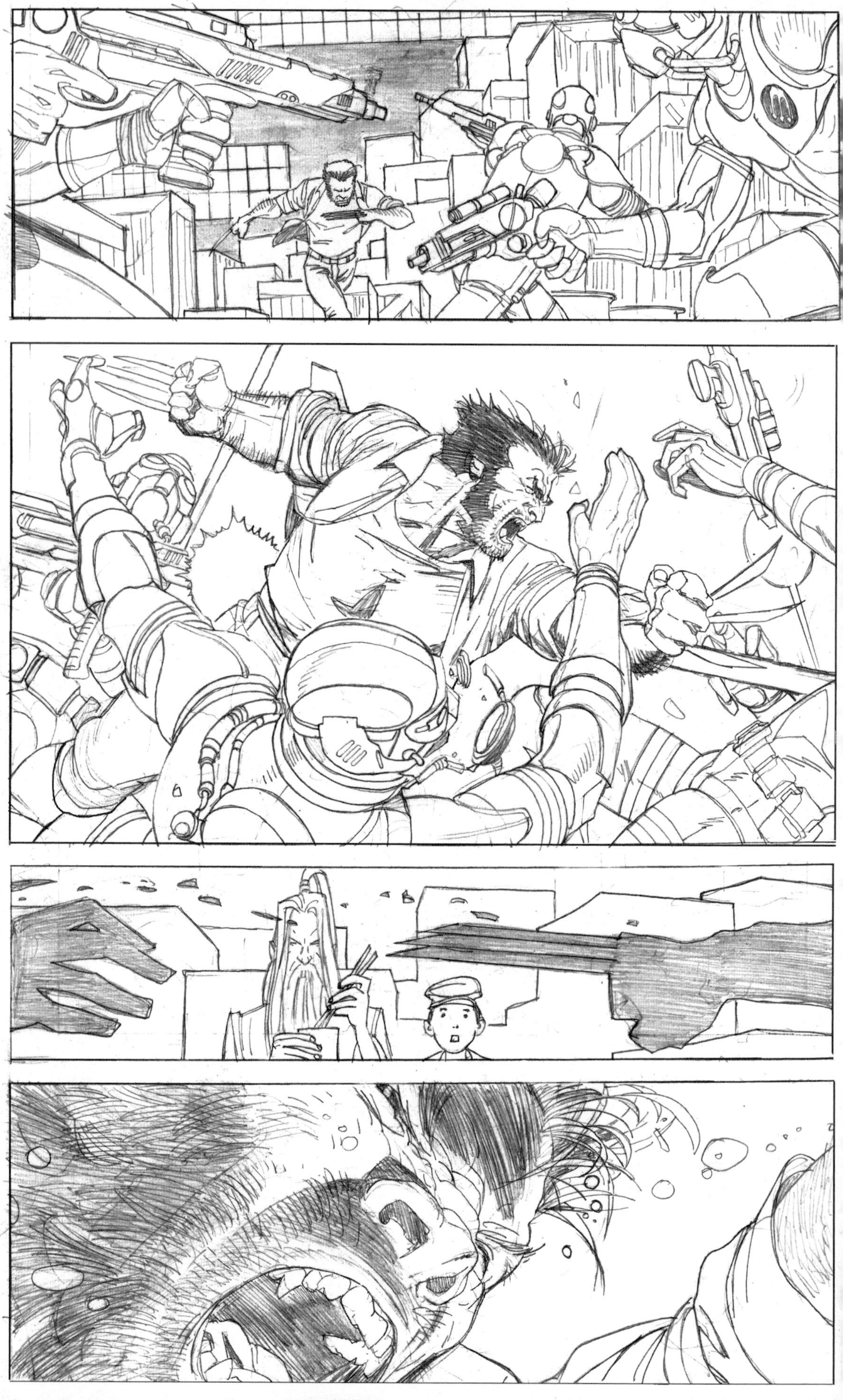

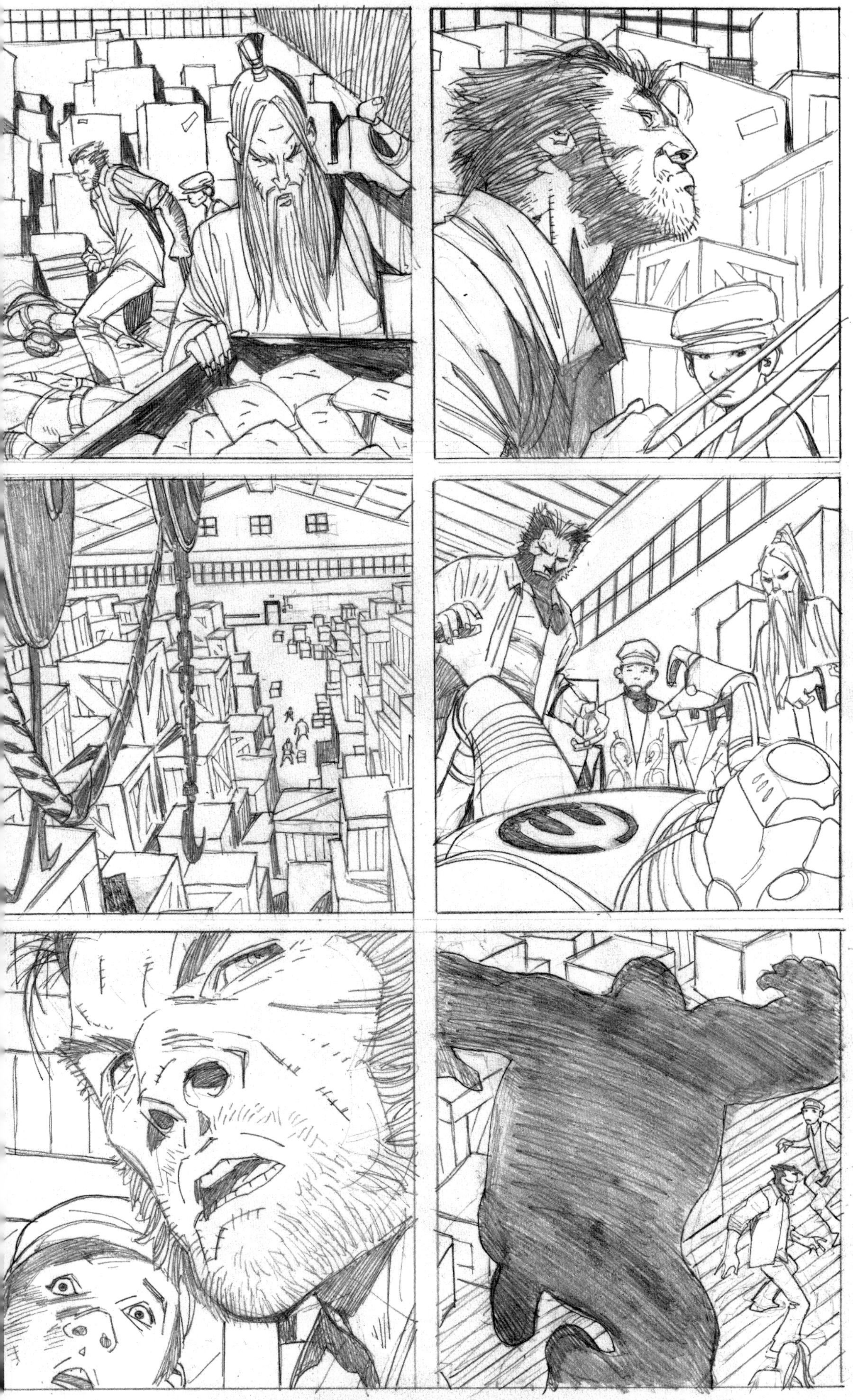

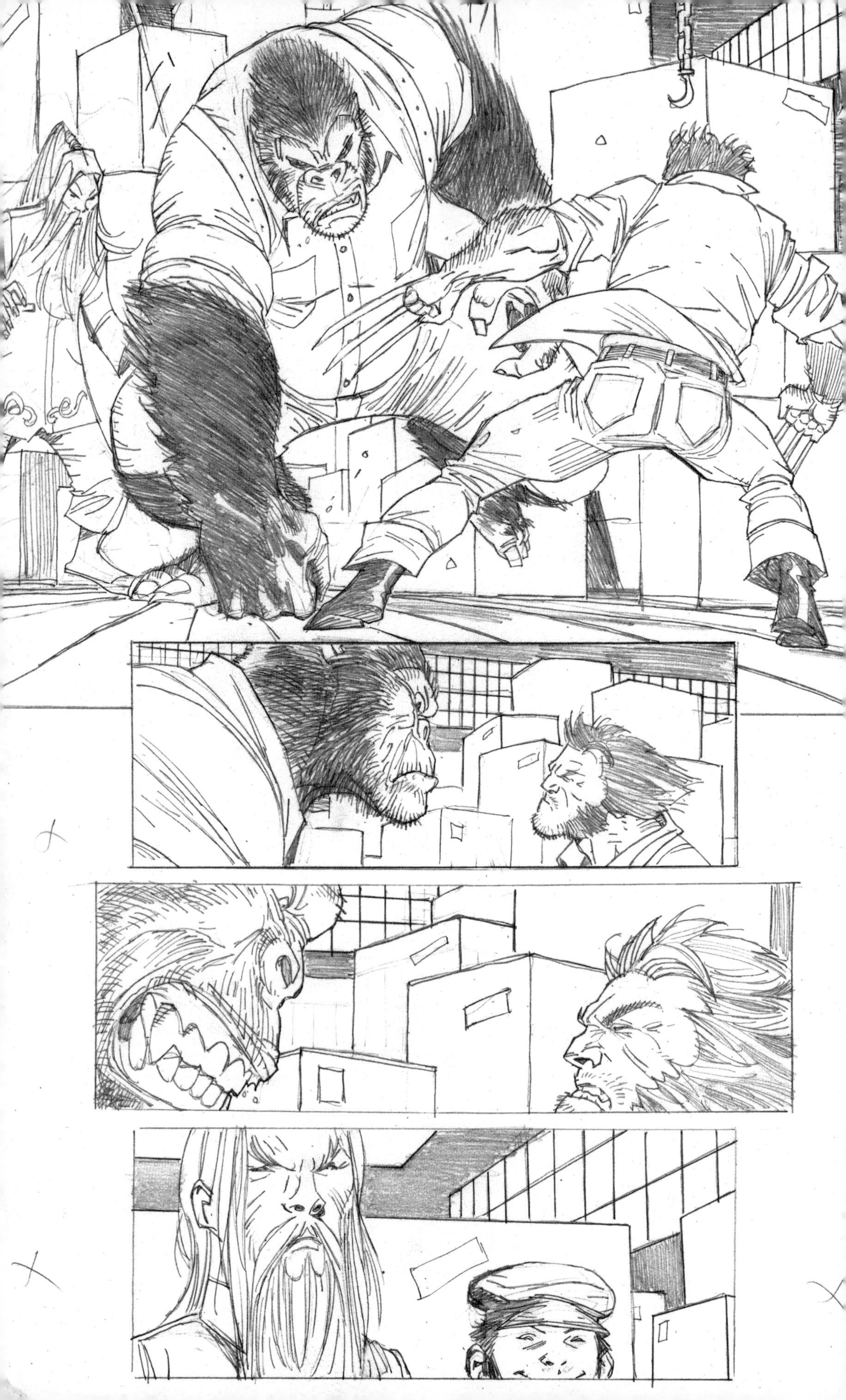

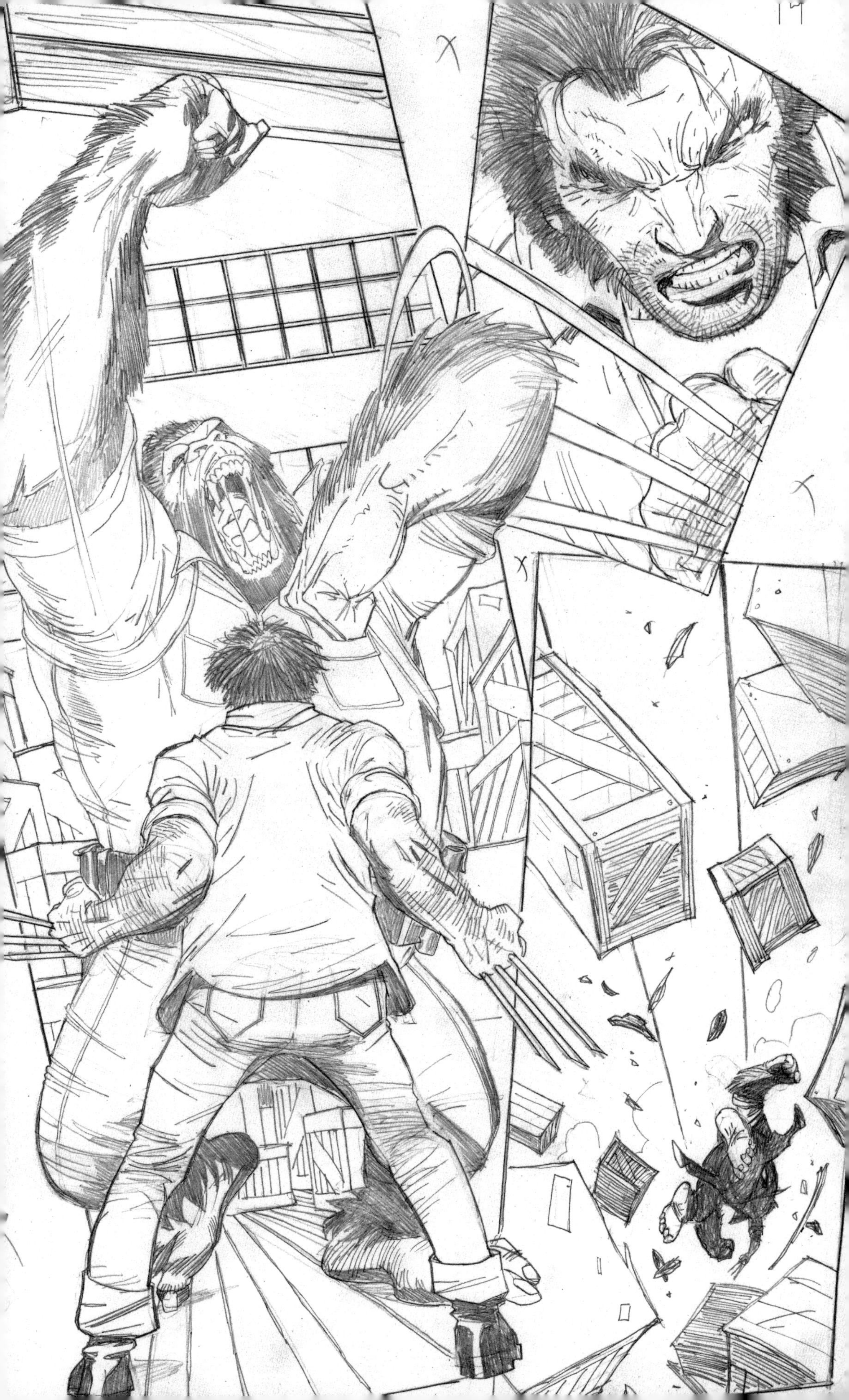

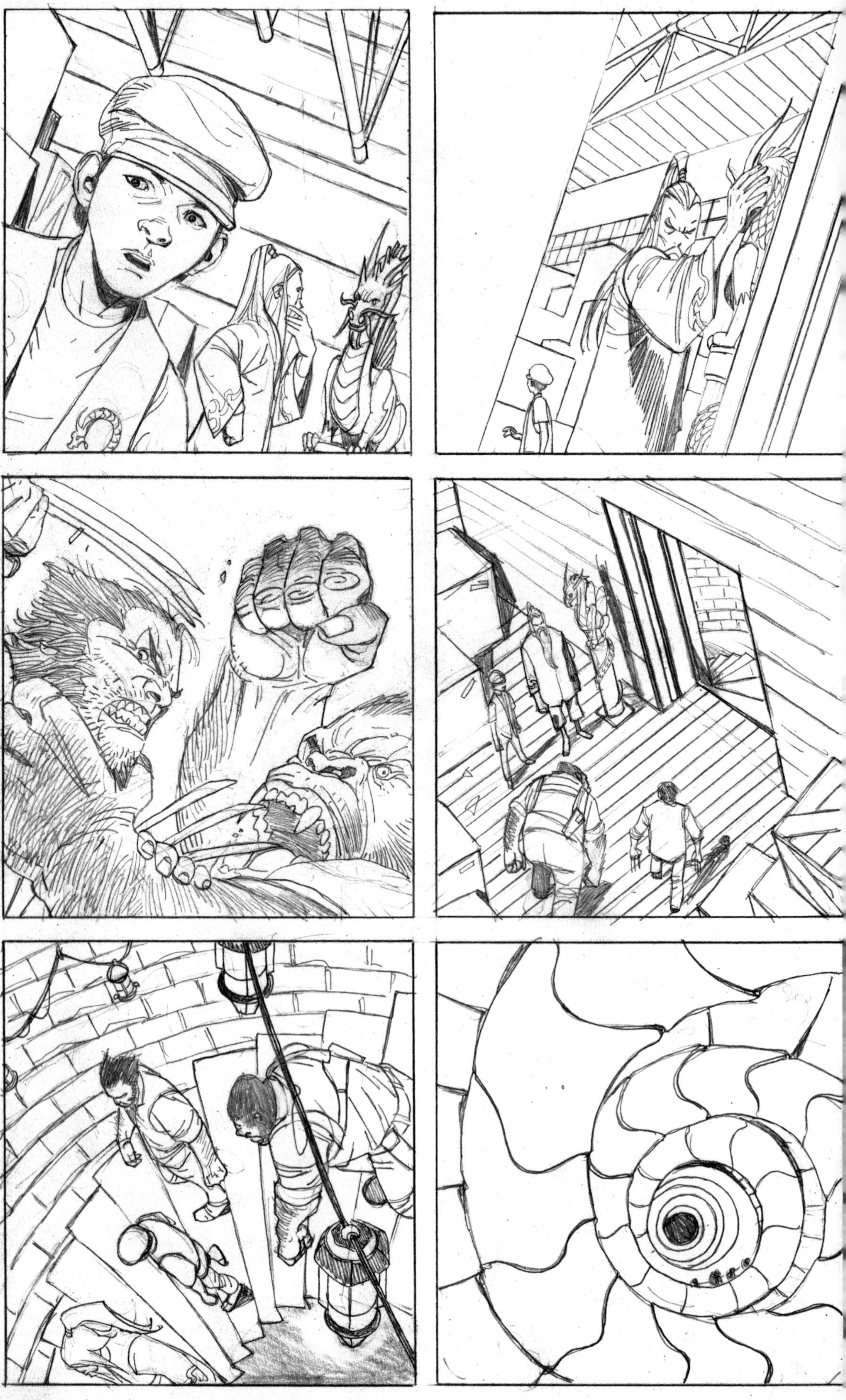

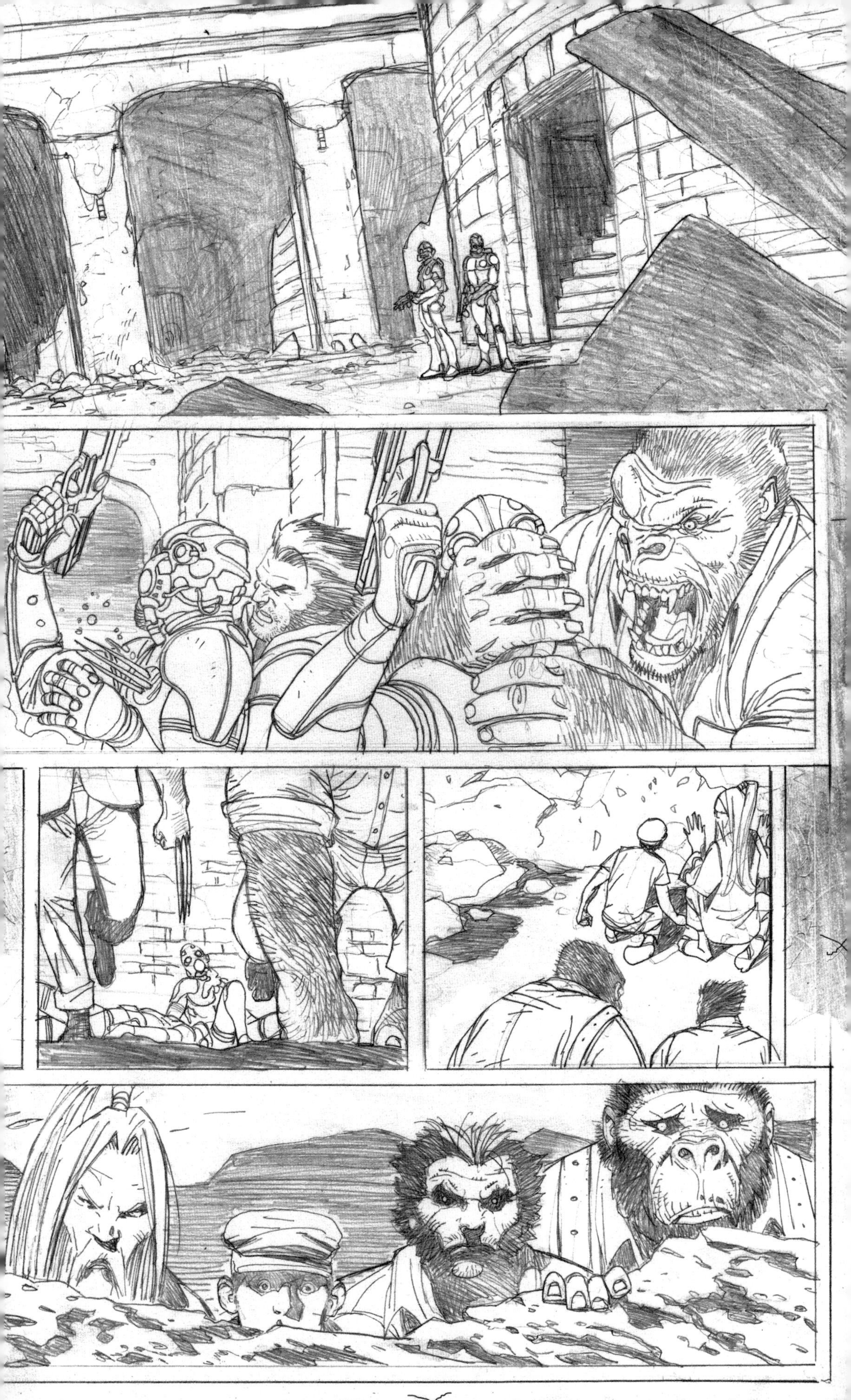

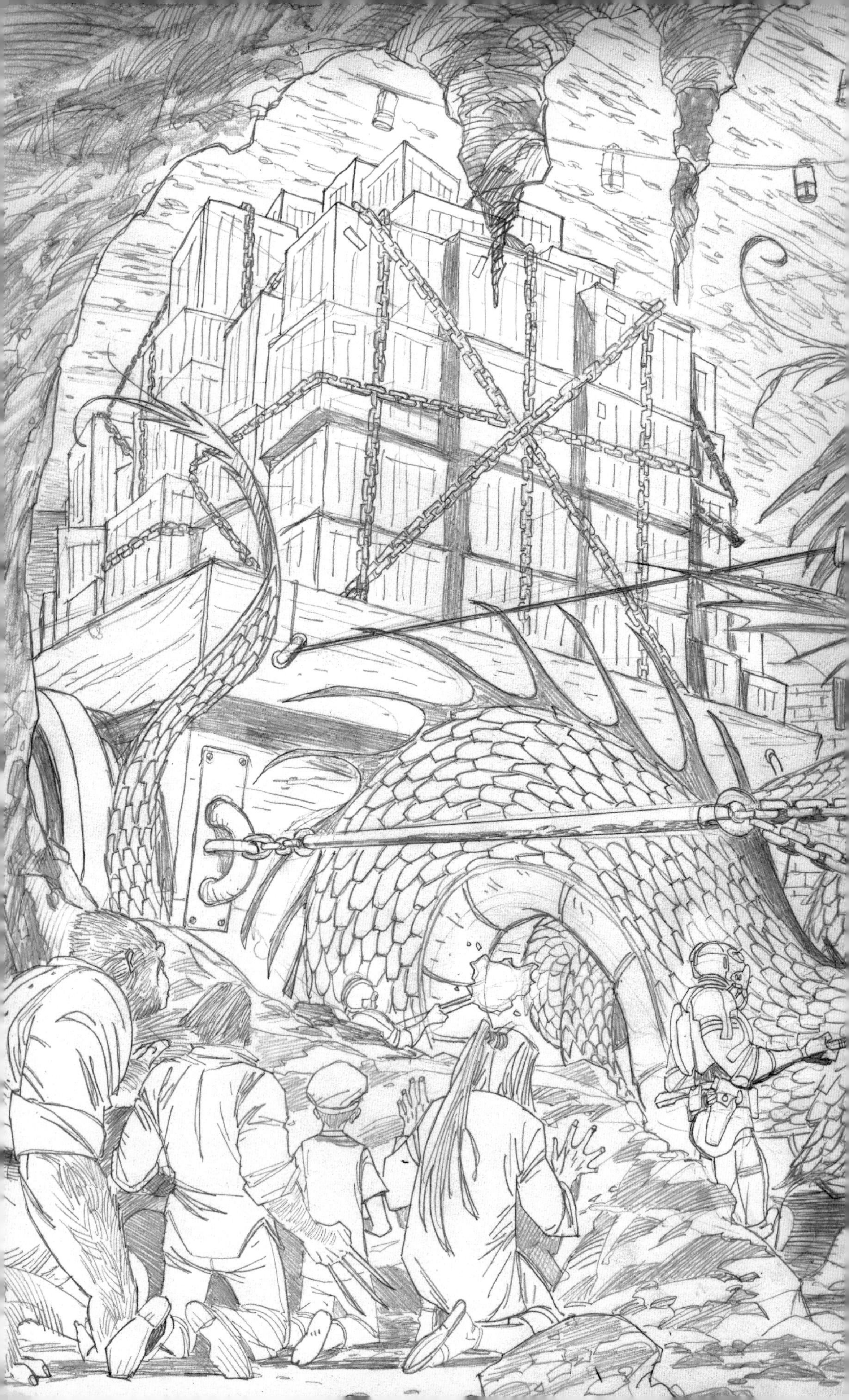

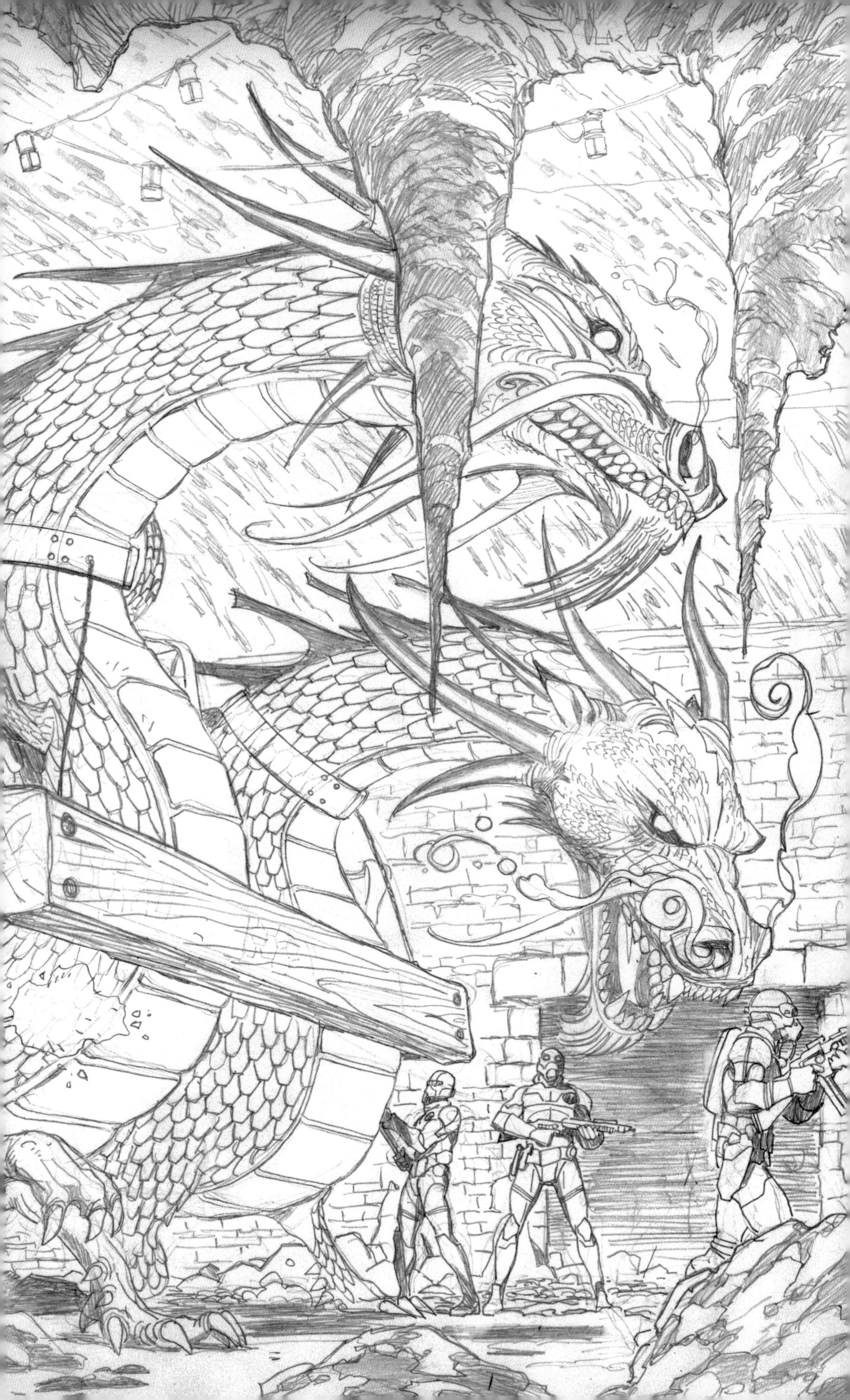

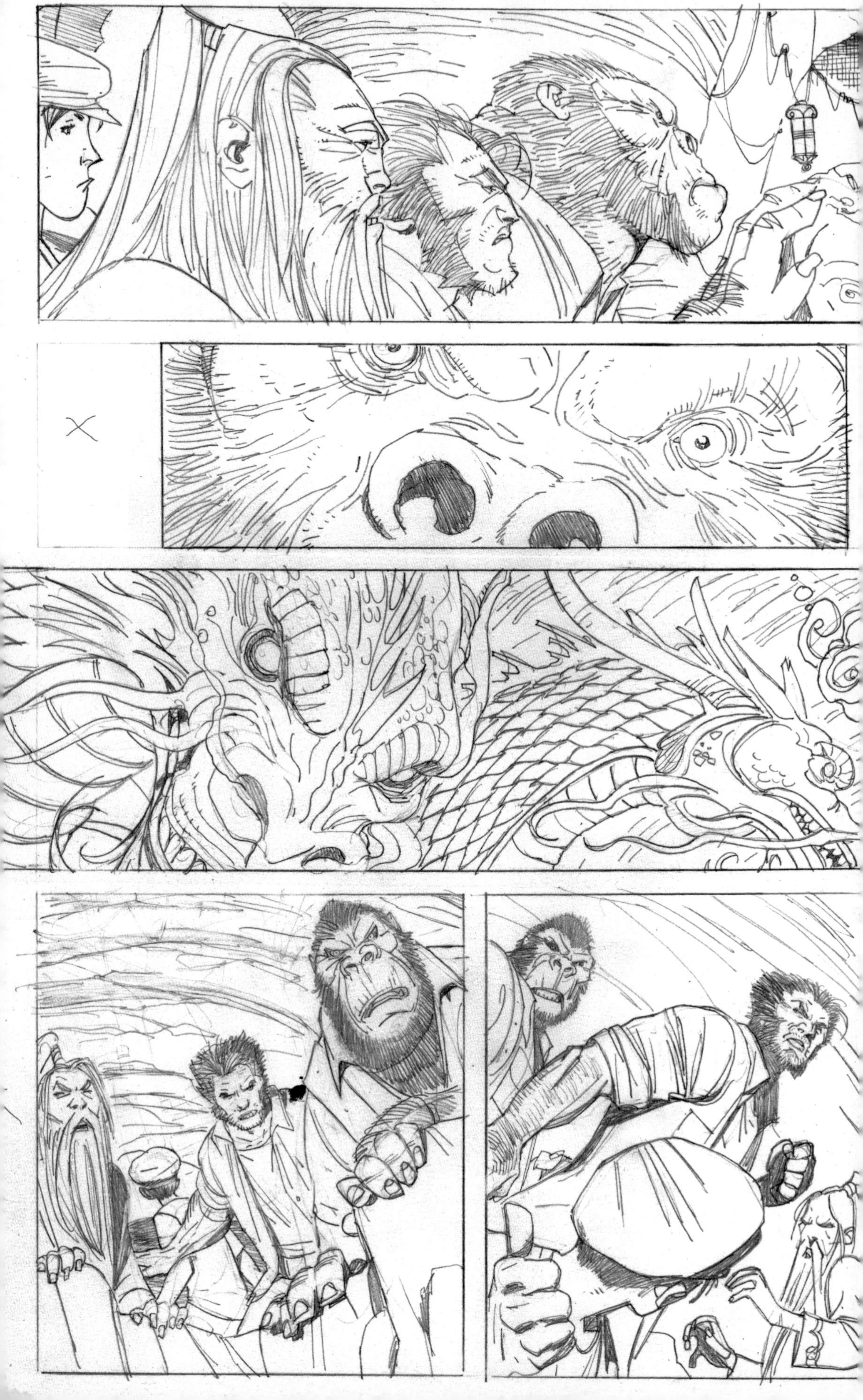

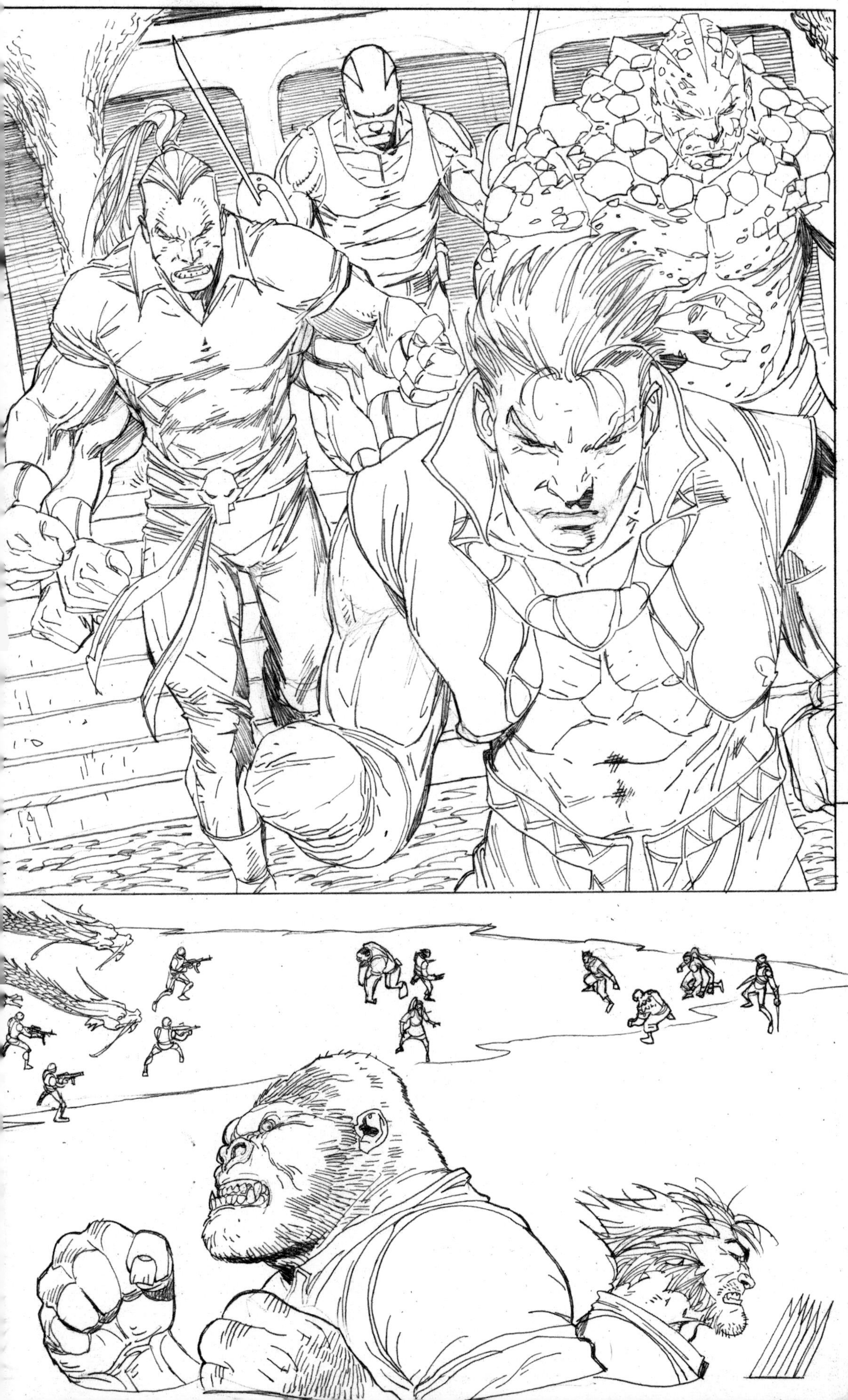

➤ Wolverine: Weapon X Vol. 1: Adamantium Men HC/TP

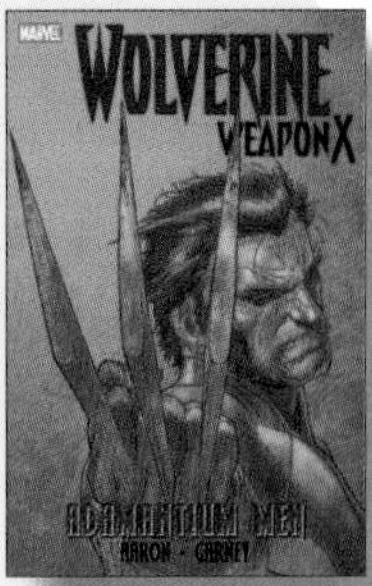
WOLVERINE
WEAPON X
ADAMANTIUM MEN
AARON · GARNEY

Collects *Wolverine: Weapon X* #1-5 and material from *Wolverine (2003)* #73-74

By Jason Aaron and Ron Garney

Someone is building Adamantium-laced super-soldiers like Wolverine!

HC: SEP090511 • 978-0-7851-4017-7
TP: FEB100624 • 978-0-7851-4111-2

➤ Wolverine: Weapon X Vol. 2: Insane in the Brain HC/TP

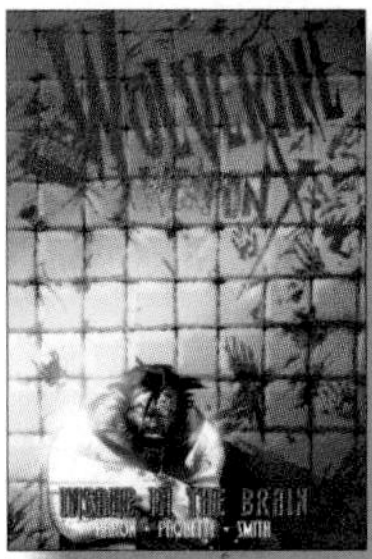
WOLVERINE
WEAPON X
INSANE IN THE BRAIN

Collects *Wolverine: Weapon X* #6-10

By Jason Aaron and Yanick Paquette

Welcome to Dunwich Sanatorium, Wolverine!

HC: JAN100657 • 978-0-7851-4018-4
TP: APR100684 • 978-0-7851-4112-9

➤ Wolverine: Weapon X Vol. 3: Tomorrow Dies Today HC/TP

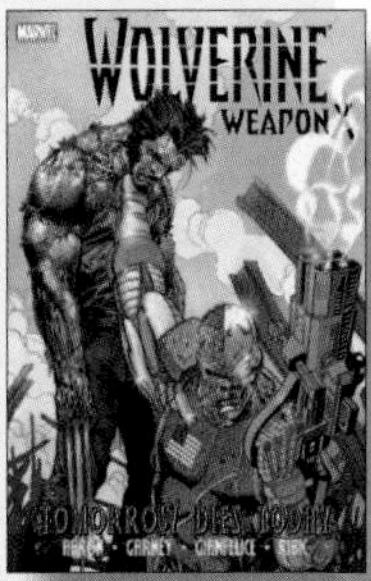
WOLVERINE
WEAPON X
TOMORROW DIES TODAY

Collects *Wolverine: Weapon X* #11-16 and *Dark Reign: The List – Wolverine* one-shot

By Jason Aaron, Ron Garney and Esad Ribic

Killer cyborgs come from the future to kill the heroes of today!

HC: AUG100685 • 978-0-7851-4650-6
TP: JAN110850 • 978-0-7851-4651-3

➤ Wolverine: Wolverine Goes to Hell HC

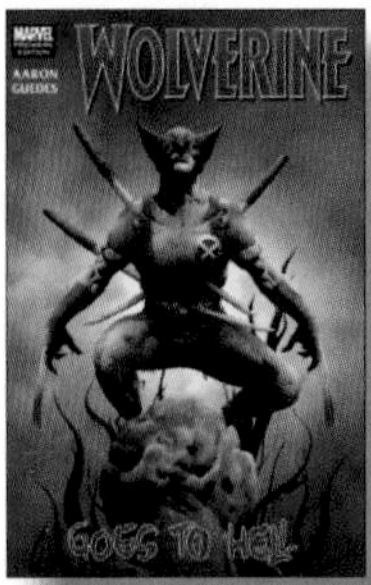
WOLVERINE
GOES TO HELL

Collects *Wolverine (2010)* #1-5 and more!

By Jason Aaron and Renato Guedes

Someone's out to destroy Logan's soul – permanently!

DEC100668 • 978-0-7851-4784-8

➤ Wolverine Noir HC/TP

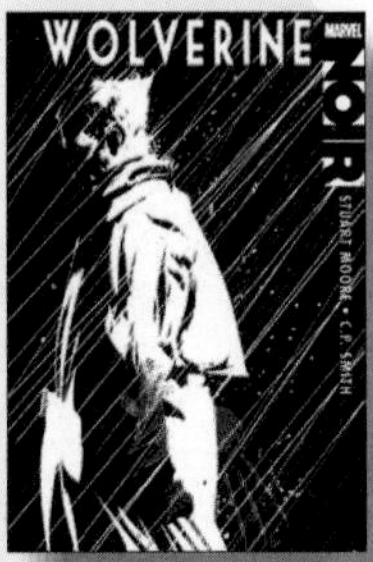
WOLVERINE
NOIR
STUART MOORE · C.P. SMITH

Collects *Wolverine Noir* #1-4

By Stuart Moore and C.P. Smith

Depression-era P.I. Logan takes on a new client: Mariko!

HC: AUG090561 • 978-0-7851-3945-4
TP: JUL100692 • 978-0-7851-3172-4

➤ Wolverine/Black Cat: Claws HC/TP

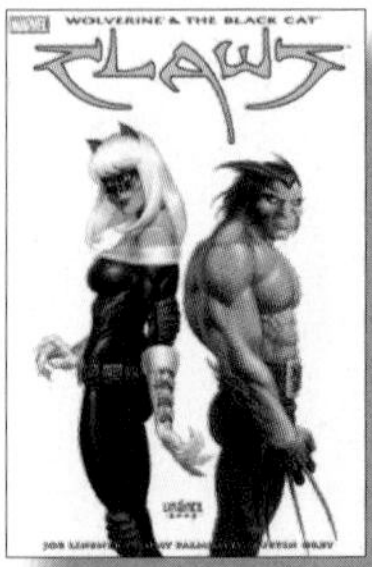
WOLVERINE & THE BLACK CAT
CLAWS

Collects *Claws #1-3*

By Jimmy Palmiotti, Justin Gray and Joseph Michael Linsner

Action-oriented, humorous romp with luscious Linsner art!

HC: NOV062356 • 978-0-7851-1850-
TP: NOV090566 • 978-0-7851-4285-

➤ Wolverine: Flies to a Spider TP

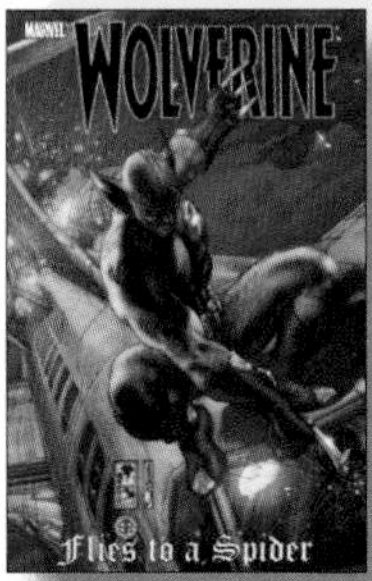
WOLVERINE
Flies to a Spider

Collects Wolverine one-shots *Switchback, Flies to a Spider, Revolver, The Anniversary* and *Cho Shop*

By Mike Benson, Victor Gischler, Jerome Opena and more

Collection chock full of Wolverine solo tales!

JUN090649 • 978-0-7851-3569-2

➤ Wolverine: The End TP

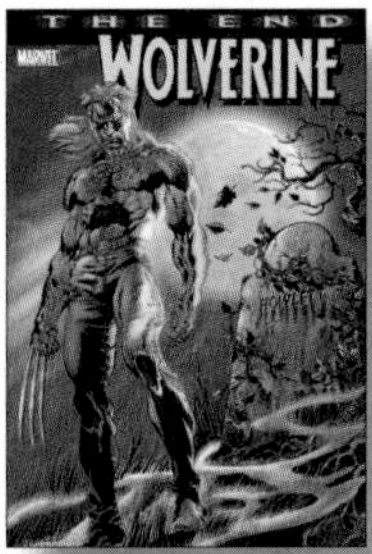
THE END
WOLVERINE

Collects *Wolverine Noir* #1-4

By Paul Jenkins and Claudio Castellini

A look at the final days of Wolverin by Paul Jenkins!

OCT041803 • 978-0-7851-1349-2

➤ Wolverine: Weapon X Files TP

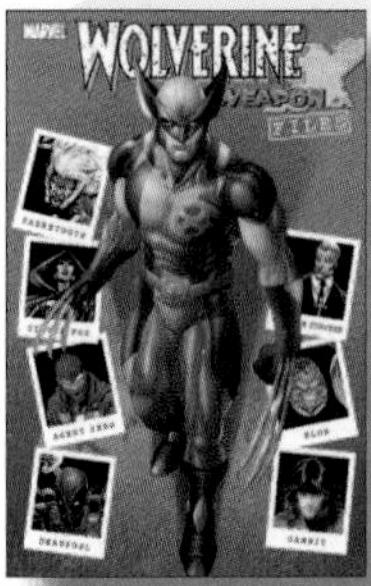
WOLVERINE
WEAPON X
FILES

Collects *Wolverine: Weapon X File* and *Wolverine Encyclopedia* #1-3

By Jeff Christiansen and more

Handbook chock full of Wolverine facts you need to know!

JUL090617 • 978-0-7851-4240-9

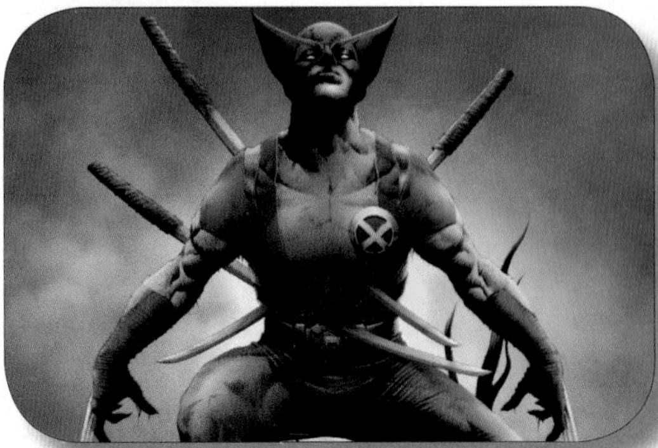